CLOUD COMPUTING

FUNDAMENTALS, INDUSTRY APPROACH and TRENDS

CLOUD COMPUTING

FUNDAMENTALS, INDUSTRY APPROACH and TRENDS

RISHABH SHARMA
Chief Technology Officer (CTO)
JOB Forward, Singapore

WILEY

CLOUD COMPUTING

FUNDAMENTALS, INDUSTRY APPROACH and TRENDS

Other Wiley Editorial Offices:

John Wiley & Sons, Inc. 111 River Street, Hoboken, NJ 07030, USA

Wiley-VCH Verlag GmbH, Pappellaee 3, D-69469 Weinheim, Germany

John Wiley & Sons Australia Ltd, 42 McDougall Street, Milton, Queensland 4064, Australia

John Wiley & Sons (Asia) Pte Ltd, 1 Fusionopolis Walk #07-01 Solaris, South Tower, Singapore 138628

John Wiley & Sons Canada Ltd, 22 Worcester Road, Etobicoke, Ontario, Canada, M9W 1L1

First Edition: 2015

Reprint: 2025

ISBN: 978-81-265-5306-8

www.wiley.com

Printed at: Nisha Enterprises

Preface

The current era of IT is based on cloud computing where all small and large organizations leverage the services of cloud computing directly or indirectly. Nowadays, cloud computing is just not a niche skill but a mandatory one which should be known by every IT professional.

Cloud Computing – Fundamentals, Industry Approach and Trends is the first and unique book which accomplishes all necessities of students, IT professionals or anyone who is willing to know about cloud computing.

The first edition of the book provides the basic fundamentals as well as detailed concepts and current industry scenarios of cloud computing. The prime focus is to present cloud computing in a simple and well-structured manner to make the learning easier and more convenient for the students so that they acquire a strong fundamental base of the subject.

The course contents of the subject cloud computing cover complete syllabi of all major universities of India and are applicable to all CS/IT engineering students.

What the Book Covers

The book is divided into 10 chapters which provide detailed fundamental concepts and clear understanding of the subject in all aspects.

Chapter 1 (Overview of Distributed Computing) explains concept of computing, how computing also serves as a utility, the role of the Internet, the fundamental notion of all trends in computing, and the evolution of cloud computing and its various value drivers. The chapter gives clarity that how cloud computing is similar to and different from other computing systems such as cluster, parallel and grid.

Chapter 2 (Introduction to Cloud Computing) gives clear vision of cloud computing which includes the central idea behind cloud computing, all the properties and key characteristics of cloud computing, conceptual understanding of all the cloud services models and deployment, various cloud supporting services and how they differentiate various deployment models on the basis of their characteristics. The chapter sheds light on cloud computing challenges and some advance services also.

Chapter 3 (Different Cloud Providers and Comparison of Services) provides practical understanding of various cloud service providers, type of their service offerings, detailed architecture, comparisons of different cloud service providers, service approach of giant cloud providers like Amazon, Google and Microsoft and how customers are benefiting from them. The chapter also sheds light on identification of business requirement for choosing any cloud service provider which is a primary thing for any business.

Chapter 4 (Virtualization Techniques) gives details of virtualization technology. Virtualization is a key concept used in cloud computing. It has been around for many years in some form or the other. The chapter covers the concept of virtualization and different types of virtualization techniques, virtualization products for improving system efficiency and some developing open source standard solutions for cloud interoperability.

Chapter 5 (Cloud Databases and File Systems in Cloud) provides understanding of advance database system which is used in clouds such as new relation databases approach, evolution of NoSQL databases which supports cloud environment, file system concept, technical understanding of Google file system (GFS), Hadoop distributed file system (HDFS), MapReduce programming model and different operations using MapReduce programming.

Chapter 6 (Cloud Security and Existing Security Solutions) provides a detailed analysis of cloud security concerns, various categories of cloud risks, cloud computing security architecture, virtual machine (VM) security challenges, currently available vulnerability assessment tools for cloud and open source solutions of cloud security. The chapter provides a realistic picture of current cloud security scenario.

Chapter 7 (Cloud Middleware and Best Practices) describes the need of middleware in cloud services offering, quality of service issues of cloud services, industry approach of data migration and streaming in cloud, and how to achieve resource and cost optimization by applying some best practices of cloud computing. The chapter also sheds light on different performances and quality of service (QoS) monitoring tools for cloud environment.

Chapter 8 (Private Cloud Computing Platforms and Cloud Testing) explores practical and detailed understanding of deploying private cloud computing platforms like OpenStack, Eucalyptus, OpenNebula, Nimbus, Tplaform, Apache Virtual Computing Lab (VCL), CloudStack and Enomaly Elastic Computing Platform. The chapter also sheds light on different testing methodologies of cloud computing and testing strategy for application while moving on cloud.

Chapter 9 (Advance Cloud Application and Supporting Services) gives detail about online sharing and collaborative services on the cloud, overview of various third-party services that use cloud platforms such as webmail services, instant messaging, web conference tools and creating groups on social networks or collaborating via blogs and wikis. The chapter also sheds some light on cloud analytics, software plus services, cloud CDN, mobile cloud computing, inter cloud issues, sky computing and cloud governance.

Chapter 10 (Cloud Computing Consumer Case Studies) is specially meant for students, researchers and industry professionals. It provides different cloud service adoption case studies for a clear understanding that how various customers are getting benefited by various types of cloud providers and their specific services.

The book also provides a number of multiple choice questions and review questions which help in understanding and analysing the concepts learned. After studying this book, students will become competent and more skilful in the domain of cloud computing.

Reader's views, comments and suggestions regarding the book are welcome. Kindly contact me at er.rishabh.sharma@gmail.com for the same.

Acknowledgements

I would like to give special gratitude to my spiritual guru for his guidance and blessings. I am very grateful to my family for its support and encouragement during this project. I would like to give my sincere gratitude to Wiley India for providing me the opportunity to present this book and for their valuable support and guidance during this endeavour.

Rishabh Sharma

email: er.rishabh.sharma@gmail.com

About The Author

About The Author

Rishabh Sharma is currently working as a CTO (Chief Technology Officer) in JOB Forward, Singapore (http://job-fw.sg/). JOB Forward is the first social recruiting platform in Singapore. Prior to this, he has worked for Wipro Technologies, Bangalore as a Solution Delivery Analyst and involved in the research projects of cloud computing, proof of concepts (PoC), infrastructure automation, big data solutions and various giant customer's projects related to cloud infrastructure and application migration.

He has completed his master's thesis in cloud computing and have in-depth knowledge of distributed systems and cloud computing research issues of the industry. He has authored three books: *Advance Computing Technology* for Gujarat Technical University (GTU), and *Software Quality Engineering* and *Mobile Computing* for Uttar Pradesh Technical University (UPTU). His forthcoming book is *Learning Chef*, which is a hands-on guide for infrastructure automation. He has also authored many research papers in International Journal and IEEE on a variety of issues related to cloud computing. He is also an open source enthusiast and writes for the magazine *Open Source for You* (OSFY).

Contents

Preface v
About the Author ix

1 Overview of Distributed Computing 1
1.1 What Is Computing? 1
1.2 Traditional Utilities 2
1.2.1 Utility Computing: Computing as a Utility 2
1.3 Creation of the Internet 3
1.3.1 Variety of Computing Paradigms 3
1.3.2 The Fundamental Notion 4
1.4 Computing Paradigm Trends 6
1.4.1 Cluster Computing 7
1.4.2 Parallel Computing 8
1.4.3 Grid Computing 13
1.5 Computing Paradigm Evolution 15
1.6 Next Big Thing: The "Cloud" 16
1.7 Cloud Computing: A New Paradigm 17
1.7.1 Cloud Computing in Mathematics 17
1.7.2 Cloud Computing in IT 18
1.7.3 Cloud Value Drivers and Effects 18
1.7.4 Typical IT Budget Models 19
1.8 Differences and Similarities Among Different Types of Computing 20
1.8.1 Grid Computing Versus Cloud Computing 20
1.8.2 Cluster Computing Versus Cloud Computing 21
1.8.3 Utility Computing Versus Cloud Computing 21
1.8.4 Parallel Computing Versus Cloud Computing 22
1.8.5 Comparison Between Cluster, Grid and Cloud 22
Summary 23
Multiple Choice Questions 24
Review Questions 25
Answers to Multiple Choice Questions 26

2 Introduction to Cloud Computing 27
2.1 Cloud Computing: Definitions 27
2.2 Central Ideas Behind Cloud Computing 28
2.2.1 Utility Computing 29

2.2.2 *Service-Oriented Architecture* 30
2.2.3 *Service-Level Agreement* 30
2.3 Properties and Characteristics of Cloud Computing 30
2.3.1 *Scalability and Elasticity* 31
2.3.2 *Availability and Reliability* 33
2.3.3 *System Resilience* 34
2.3.4 *System Security* 35
2.3.5 *Manageability and Interoperability* 35
2.3.6 *Control Automation* 36
2.3.7 *System Monitoring* 36
2.3.8 *Automatic Billing System* 37
2.3.9 *Accessibility and Portability* 37
2.3.10 *Performance and Optimization* 38
2.4 Benefits of Cloud Computing 39
2.4.1 *For the Market and Enterprises* 40
2.4.2 *For End Users and Individuals* 44
2.5 Cloud Service and Deployment Models 47
2.5.1 *Service Models* 47
2.5.2 *Cloud Providers* 48
2.5.3 *Cloud Service Models* 48
2.6 Organizational Scenario of Cloud: Cloud Deployment Model 55
2.6.1 *Public Cloud* 56
2.6.2 *PrivateCloud* 56
2.6.3 *Community Cloud* 57
2.6.4 *Hybrid Cloud* 57
2.7 Cloud Architecture 58
2.8 Cloud Vocabulary 59
2.8.1 *Machine Image* 59
2.8.2 *Cloud Instances* 59
2.8.3 *Regions and Availability Zones* 59
2.8.4 *Virtual Private Cloud* 59
2.8.5 *Cloud Burst* 60
2.9 Challenges with Cloud Computing 60
2.10 Cloud-Supporting Services 60
2.10.1 *Cloud Storage Service* 61
2.10.2 *Cloud Database Service* 61
2.10.3 *Cloud Load-Balancing Services* 61
2.10.4 *Cloud Backup and Disaster-Recovery Services* 61
2.11 Management and Administration of Cloud Services 62
2.11.1 *Business Continuity Management* 62
2.11.2 *System Reliability* 62
2.11.3 *Fault Tolerance* 62
2.11.4 *Response Time* 63
Summary 63
Multiple Choice Questions 63
Review Questions 65
Answers to Multiple Choice Questions 66

3 Different Cloud Providers and Comparison of Services **67**
3.1 Infrastructure Service Providers 67
3.1.1 Amazon Web Services 67
3.1.2 Rackspace Cloud 68
3.1.3 Google Compute Engine 69
3.1.4 Microsoft Azure Services 70
3.1.5 GoGrid 70
3.2 Key Benefits of Cloud Infrastructure Services 71
3.3 Comparison Between Infrastructure Service Providers 72
3.4 Identification of Business Requirement for Choosing any Cloud Infrastructure Provider 72
3.5 Cloud Infrastructure Setup Procedure 73
3.6 Platform Service Providers 74
3.6.1 Google App Engine 74
3.6.2 Microsoft Azure 75
3.6.3 Cloud Foundry 76
3.6.4 Salesforce.com 77
3.6.5 Engine Yard 78
3.7 Key Benefits of Cloud Platform Services 79
3.8 Comparison of Platform Service Providers 79
3.9 Identification of Business Requirement for Choosing any Cloud Platform Provider 80
3.10 Cloud Platform Setup Procedure 81
3.11 Cloud Application Development 81
3.12 Software Service Providers 82
3.12.1 Free Cloud Panda Antivirus Online 82
3.12.2 iCloud.com 82
3.12.3 Mint.com 82
3.12.4 eyeOS 83
3.12.5 Cloudo 84
3.12.6 Advanced SaaS Products 84
3.13 Benefits of SaaS 86
3.14 Comparison Between Software Service Providers 86
Summary 87
Multiple Choice Questions 87
Review Questions 88
Answers to Multiple Choice Questions 88

4 Virtualization Techniques **89**
4.1 Virtualization Technology 89
4.1.1 What Is a Virtual Machine? 90
4.1.2 Guest Operating System 90
4.1.3 Virtual Machine Monitor 90
4.1.4 Hypervisor 90
4.1.5 Hosted Virtualization 90
4.2 Overview of x86 Virtualization 90
4.2.1 Before Virtualization 90
4.2.2 After Virtualization 91

4.3 Types of Virtualization 92
4.3.1 *CPU Virtualization* 92
4.3.2 *Memory Virtualization* 96
4.3.3 *Device and I/O Virtualization* 97
4.3.4 *OS-Level Virtualization* 97
4.3.5 *Network Virtualization* 98
4.3.6 *Server Virtualization* 98
4.3.7 *Client (or Desktop) Virtualization* 98
4.3.8 *Application Virtualization* 99
4.4 Virtualization Products 101
4.4.1 *Category of Virtualization Products* 101
4.4.2 *VMware Server* 102
4.4.3 *Benefits of VMware Server* 102
4.4.4 *How does VMware Server Work?* 102
4.4.5 *How Can Anyone Use VMware Server?* 103
4.4.6 *Type 3 Virtualization* 103
4.5 Concept of VLAN (Virtual LAN) and Benefits 104
4.6 Concept of SAN (Virtual SAN) and Benefits 104
4.7 VM Migration 105
4.8 VM Consolidation and Management 106
4.9 Cloud Interoperability Standards 106
4.9.1 *Need of Interoperability: To Avoid Vendor Lock-In* 107
4.9.2 *Open Virtualization Format* 107
4.9.3 *Existing Interoperability Solutions: AppZero, IBM Cloud and Others* 108
4.9.4 *Virtual Application Appliance* 110
Summary 110
Multiple Choice Questions 110
Review Questions 112
Answers to Multiple Choice Questions 112

5 Cloud Databases and File Systems in Cloud **113**
5.1 Cloud Database 113
5.1.1 *Operation Model for Cloud Database* 113
5.1.2 *Types of Cloud Database* 114
5.2 Cloud File System 117
5.2.1 *Distributed File System Basics* 117
5.2.2 *Concept of GFS* 118
5.2.3 *Concept of HDFS* 119
5.2.4 *Comparison of Features* 121
5.3 Cloud Programming Model 122
5.3.1 *Understanding MapReduce Programming* 122
5.3.2 *Operation Using MapReduce Programming* 124
Summary 124
Multiple Choice Questions 125
Review Questions 126
Answers to Multiple Choice Questions 126

6 **Cloud Security and Existing Security Solutions** **127**
6.1 Cloud Security Fundamentals 127
6.2 Cloud Risk 127
6.3 Cloud Risk Division 128
6.3.1 Policy and Organizational Risks 128
6.3.2 Technical Risks 129
6.3.3 Legal Risks 130
6.3.4 Other Risks 131
6.4 Cloud Computing Security Architecture 131
6.5 VM Security Challenges 132
6.6 Vulnerability Assessment Tool for Cloud 135
6.6.1 Netskope 135
6.6.2 CipherCloud 136
6.6.3 Skyhigh Networks 137
6.6.4 Okta 137
6.6.5 Qualys 138
6.6.6 Vaultive 139
6.7 Open Source Security Solution Products in Cloud 140
Summary 141
Multiple Choice Questions 141
Review Questions 143
Answers to Multiple Choice Questions 144

7 **Cloud Middleware and Best Practices** **145**
7.1 Concept and Need of Cloud Middleware 145
7.1.1 Concept of Middleware 145
7.1.2 Cloud Middleware 145
7.1.3 Cloud Middleware Functionalities 146
7.2 QoS Issues in Cloud 147
7.3 Data Migration and Streaming in Cloud 149
7.3.1 Analysis of Cloud Provider 149
7.3.2 Cloud Migration Process 150
7.3.3 Streaming in Cloud 150
7.3.4 Working of Cloud Streaming 151
7.3.5 Key Features of Cloud Streaming 151
7.4 Performance Monitoring Tools in Cloud 151
7.5 Best Practices of Cloud Computing 153
7.5.1 Best Practices for Infrastructure Setup 153
7.5.2 Best Practices for Data and Service Migration 155
7.5.3 Best Practices for Cost Optimization 156
7.5.4 Best Practices for Cloud Capacity Management 157
Summary 158
Multiple Choice Questions 158
Review Questions 160
Answers to Multiple Choice Questions 160

8 Private Cloud Computing Platforms and Cloud Testing **161**
8.1 Private Cloud Computing Platforms 161
8.1.1 Eucalyptus 161
8.1.2 OpenNebula 163
8.1.3 Nimbus 164
8.1.4 TPlatform 165
8.1.5 Apache Virtual Computing Lab 166
8.1.6 Enomaly Elastic Computing Platform 166
8.1.7 OpenStack 168
8.1.8 CloudStack 169
8.2 Cloud-Optimized Linux 170
8.3 Testing in Cloud Computing 170
8.3.1 Types of Cloud Testing 171
8.3.2 Application Testing Strategy in a Cloud Computing Environment 172
Summary 173
Multiple Choice Questions 173
Review Questions 174
Answers to Multiple Choice Questions 174

9 Advance Cloud Application and Supporting Services **175**
9.1 Advance Cloud Applications 175
9.1.1 ECG Analysis in the Cloud 175
9.1.2 Protein Structure Prediction on Cloud 176
9.1.3 Gene Expression Data Analysis on Cloud 177
9.1.4 Satellite Image Processing on Cloud 177
9.1.5 Social Networking on Cloud 179
9.2 Different Sharing and Collaborative Services in Cloud 179
9.3 Outside the Cloud Services 180
9.3.1 Centralizing Email Communications 180
9.3.2 Evaluating Webmail Services 181
9.3.3 Evaluating Instant Messaging 181
9.3.4 Evaluating Web Conference Tools 182
9.3.5 Evaluating Online Groupware 184
9.3.6 Creating Groups on Social Networks 184
9.3.7 Collaborating via Blogs and Wikis 185
9.4 Cloud Analytics 186
9.5 Software Plus Services 186
9.5.1 Benefits of Using Software Plus Services 187
9.6 Cloud Content Delivery Network (CDN) Services 187
9.6.1 Multi-CDN 187
9.7 Mobile Cloud Computing 188
9.7.1 Why Mobile Cloud Computing? 189
9.8 InterCloud Issues: A Grid of Clouds 189
9.9 Sky Computing 190
9.10 Cloud Governance 190

Summary 191
Multiple Choice Questions 191
Review Questions 193
Answers to Multiple Choice Questions 194

10 Cloud Computing Consumer Case Studies **195**
10.1 Cloud Infrastructure Adoption Case Study 195
10.1.1 Challenges of the Nutritious Food 195
10.1.2 Solution 196
10.1.3 Cloud Infrastructure Service Approach 196
10.1.4 Final Outcome 197
10.1.5 Success Factors 198
10.1.6 Lessons Learned 198
10.2 Cloud Platform Adoption Case Study 198
10.2.1 Challenges of Gamysoft 199
10.2.2 Solution 199
10.2.3 Cloud Platform Service Approach 199
10.2.4 Final Outcome 199
10.2.5 Success Factors 200
10.2.6 Lessons Learned 200
10.3 Cloud Software Services Adoption Case Study 200
10.3.1 Challenges of Traditional ERPs 201
10.3.2 Solution 201
10.3.3 Cloud Software Service Approach 201
10.3.4 Final Outcome 201
10.3.5 Success Factors 202
10.3.6 Lessons Learned 202
10.4 Cloud Simulation Tools 202
10.5 Future of Cloud Computing 203
Summary 204
Multiple Choice Questions 205
Review Questions 206
Answers to Multiple Choice Questions 206

Bibliography **207**
Index **211**

CHAPTER 1

Overview of Distributed Computing

Learning Objectives

After reading this chapter, you will be able to:

- Understand computing and all its trends.
- Understand how computing is also served as a utility.
- Understand the role of the Internet and the fundamental notion of all trends in computing.
- Understand the evolution of cloud computing and its various value drivers.
- Understand clearly that how cloud computing is similar to and different from other computing systems such as cluster, parallel and grid.

1.1 What Is Computing?

Computing means designing and building hardware and software systems for various different purposes such as structuring, processing and managing different kinds of information, performing scientific calculations using computers or making computer systems behave intelligently. We can define computing as "searching, analyzing and collecting data for some specific purpose."

Computing includes the following:

1. Structuring hardware and software systems (for many applications) according to the configuration or design.
2. Analyzing, collecting and arranging many types of data for further processing.
3. Conducting technical research and data manipulation studies with the help of processors.
4. Making systems operation work more intelligent.
5. Utilizing applications of communication and media (entertainment purpose) as well as helping create all communication media.

1.2 Traditional Utilities

Utility is an economical term that reflects the satisfaction a customer receives from using goods or services. With advances in technology, basic essential utilities (services) have become easily accessible to everyone. Today, we utilize many such services in our daily life, such as electricity, water, telephone, gas and transportation. If we observe, we would find that all these utilities are demand based, which means that consumers use these accordingly whenever they require them. The consumers then pay for only the amount of usage. All these utilities are governed and managed by someone else; we only use and pay. It is the same with computing, too. We can consider computing as a utility service.

According to John McCarthy (a professor of MIT), "Computing may someday be organized as a public utility just like other utilities and this computer utility could become the basis of new opportunity for industry."

Computing is also being transformed into the utility model, which is a combination of various services that are entirely on-demand basis and is served like a traditional utility. This shift has made computing the next utility.

1.2.1 Utility Computing: Computing as a Utility

Utility computing provides the basic-level computing service, which is considered very essential to meet daily needs. Users can access a variety of services based on their requirements without caring about where the services are being hosted or how they are delivered. It is basically offering computing resources as a metered service.

Figure 1.1 shows the on-demand computing utility model, implying that it is same as other traditional utilities.

Figure 1.1 | Computing as a utility.

1.3 Creation of the Internet

The creation of the Internet has been the greatest step in evolution. It facilitates an individual's computer to communicate with any other computer/s located anywhere in the world.

By maintaining and ensuring worldwide connectivity of standalone computers, the Internet has become the greatest stepping stone toward achieving the 21st century's great idea of using computing as a utility service. The working of these standalone computers explore the hidden power of distributed computing, and these computing resources can have different owners.

If data of the last few years is to be taken, it would show that proposals of new compute paradigms existed and that these paradigms have also been adopted to realize the vision of computing as a utility (Fig. 1.2). Applications of these utility computing resources provide a common platform for sellers and buyers, producing million of dollars worth of business for the utility computing industry.

1.3.1 Variety of Computing Paradigms

Since the evolution of the Internet, various computing paradigms have been proposed and adopted to achieve the vision of enabling computer utilities. When these different paradigms adopt some attributes such as ubiquitous accessibility, reliability, scalability, automation, quality of service (QoS) and service-oriented architecture (SOA), then it provides the right platform to produce a million-dollar business.

Figure 1.2 lists examples of such paradigms.

Peer-to-peer (P2P) computing enables each peer node (computer) to share content directly with each another node in a decartelized manner. In P2P computing, there is no concept of clients and servers. Here all peer nodes are same and work concurrently as both clients and servers.

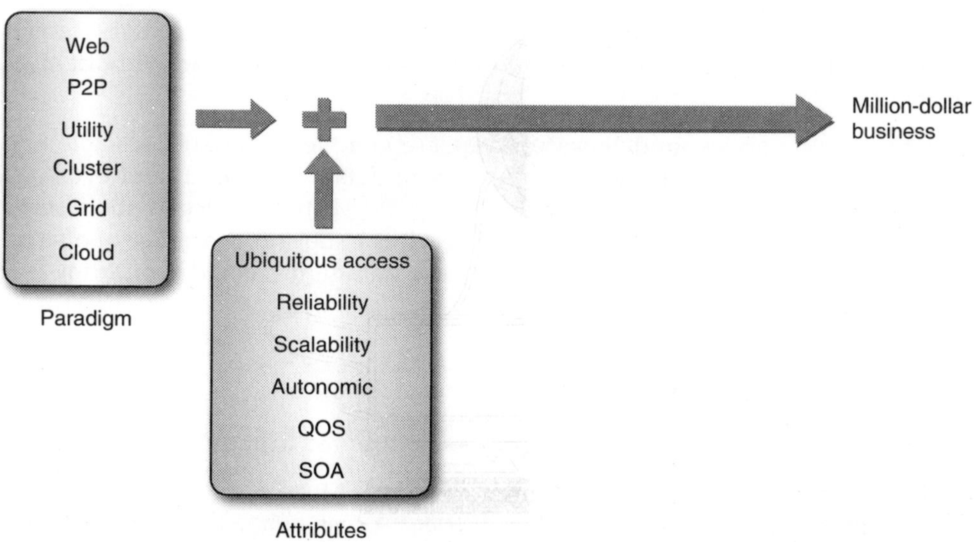

Figure 1.2 | Various paradigms promising to deliver IT as a service.

One node acts as a client and simultaneously works as server. The objective of P2P computing also includes sharing and reduction of cost, resource aggregation and interoperability, improving reliability, scalability, increased autonomy, privacy, dynamism, collaboration and ad-hoc communication.

Grid also works like a utility or infrastructure service, which is used for huge and complex computations. All these computations are done using remote distributed resources, such as servers, desktops, laptops and mobile phones. And these resources could be owned by different organizations.

The special purpose of grid is to solve data-intensive problems, industry-specific computational problems, scientific problems, organizational research issues using different sort of remote resources (most of those resources are geographically distributed). People from different organizations and industries work together as virtual organizations (VOs) and leverage their resources for solving high computational problems. Grid computing is the next great revolution after the Internet.

Services computing mainly focuses on the relation between IT services and business processes so that businesses can be seamlessly automated using IT services. Examples of such services computing technologies include SOA and Web services.

Computing provides various benefits in this economic-based market. One such example is offering incentives to resource providers for further contributing their computing resources to the consumer. A central coordinator is not needed when computing is there because it allows both the users and the providers to make independent decisions to maximize the utilization of every resource to increase their profits. Web services also work in the same way.

Today, the recent paradigm shift has been toward cloud computing where everything is a service and these services are often rendered on an on-demand basis and deliver high availability and scalability. In the cloud computing paradigm, traditional data centers are converted into virtualized data centers and all the services are offered over a virtualization layer. Now, consumers can access their application and data on an on-demand basis. Whole infrastructure, storage service, database services and applications can be built over cloud without any upfront investment cost.

Here everything is a service, and these services are completely elastic, scalable and on an on-demand basis like any other utility. We will study in detail about each and every feature of cloud computing in Chapter 2. Cloud providers integrate all the services with a service-level agreement (SLA), which takes care of the quality of services issue and guarantee of offered service between consumers and providers. Among all discussed paradigms, cloud computing is the most promising and successful.

1.3.2 The Fundamental Notion

The fundamental notion behind all the paradigms is "Distributed Computing."

A computer program that runs in a distributed system is called a *distributed program*, and the procedure of writing such programs is called *distributed computing*. Distributed computing is essentially usage of distributed systems to solve many computational problems. In distributed computing, the main problem is split into many sub-tasks, each of which is then solved by one or more computers.

A distributed system has the following characteristics:

1. All components are autonomous.
2. Scaling can be done at any time by adding additional resources.
3. Availability can be maintained with the help of commodity hardware and network.
4. Scheduling, resource management and security policies are implemented by each system.
5. There are multiple points of control and multiple points of failure.

Distributing system has existed for several decades. We are quite familiar with distributed file system and network file system concepts, these file systems are an integral part of the distributed system because these systems are used for improving reliability and availability in a distributed network. Modern operating system gives users the flexibility to access a file system of any remote machine the same way a local file system is accessed, although there is some communication delay while accessing remote file system. But there are remote procedure calls (RPC) that enables the system to communicate fast to each other with the help of the inter-process communication. RPC was invented by Bruce Nelson in 1970, and it was used in a network file system for the first time. Most programming languages provide the RPC feature, just like the JAVA RMI invocation method is quite similar to UNIX RPC. Apart from this, middleware support is essential in the distributed system, and middleware must support following properties:

1. **Access transparency:** Information saved on local and remote locations can be retrieved easily using identical operations.
2. **Location transparency:** Information objects are accessed without any awareness related to the location of those accessed objects.
3. **Concurrency transparency:** Different types of processes run concurrently with the help of information related to shared objects, and these processes never interfer with each other.
4. **Replication transparency:** For increasing the reliability of the application, several instances of the accessed objects are used without any awareness of users.
5. **Failure transparency:** Various fault-tolerance mechanisms are used to conceal faults and to maintain continuity of the system
6. **Migration transparency:** The accessed information objects are moved from one location to different locations without disturbing the current operations.
7. **Performance transparency:** According to QoS and load balancing requirements, a system can be re-configured at any time without affecting performance.
8. **Scaling transparency:** According to the requirement or business demand, the entire system and application can be scaled up quickly without affecting the running applications.

A distributed system is the main stay of all computing trends – all computing trends are originally related to the concept of distributed computing. All trends such as cluster, grid and cloud are different by their application and design model, but the basic approach is the same; therefore, distributed computing is the key notion behind all the latest computing paradigms. The following paragraphs describe all the aspects in detail.

1.3.2.1 Main Paradigms of Distributed Computing

There are following three main paradigms of distributed computing:

1. Cluster computing
2. Grid computing
3. Cloud computing

The reason behind the evolution of different computing paradigms is the demand for more computing power. On the basis of existing resources, varieties of computing paradigms have been proposed by researchers over last two decades.

1.3.2.2 Demand for Computing Power

To solve data-intensive applications such as image processing, natural language processing, sharing GPS/Internet data, sensor data applications, gaming applications, social networking, computer modeling, simulation and analysis, we need more computing power. Now the question is: How to run applications faster?

1.3.2.2.1 How to Run Applications Faster?

We can understand this notion from our general life. Let us think of how we can improve performance of any work. In our practical life, whenever we think about increasing the efficiency or improving the performance of any individual, there are following three simple ways to improve performance:

1. Hard work
2. Smart work
3. Take help from others

Now, we need to think of how to apply these ways to computer systems. In computer terminology, same procedures can be applied in a computer system, too. In computer terminology, we can simulate these three objectives as follows:

1. Using faster hardware, for example, high processors, high memory (referred to as super computing).
2. Using optimal techniques and algorithm to solve computational tasks (referred to as parallel computing).
3. Using several similar computers to solve a particular task (referred to as cluster, grid computing).

1.4 Computing Paradigm Trends

In this section, different trends of computing paradigm are discussed.

1. **History:** To provide more computing power, different paradigms and techniques evolved and many are still in progress. In the 1980s, computer performance was best improved by creating

faster and more efficient processors. Then in the early 1990s, the increasing trend was to move away from expensive and specialized proprietary parallel supercomputers toward networks of workstations.

2. **Toward commodity computing:** After parallel supercomputers, specific supercomputing platforms moved to inexpensive, general commodity systems that are built up by loosely coupled components from single or multi-processor PCs or workstations.
3. **Low-cost commodity computing:** It means that connecting two or more computers horizontally can solve many computational problems quickly and provide high-performance computational facilities for large-scale challenging applications.

1.4.1 Cluster Computing

A cluster is a collection of parallel and distributed system, which comprise a combination of organized and unified standalone computer systems that work together as a solo machine with fully integrated collections of computing resources.

1.4.1.1 The Cluster

Clusters have the following characteristics:

1. A node refers to one or more multi-processor systems that contain memory, OS and I/O facilities.
2. Two or more than two nodes (computers) are joint together, as in general term.
3. They are physically separated and connected through a LAN when in a single cabinet.
4. Network connections are being used by joint connected systems.
5. Resources are shared by the means of machines as in commonly used home directory. In very large clusters, NFS can create halt or difficulty. For this reason, binary data and information data must be pushed to scratch on every node.
6. Clusters provide a cost-effective way to gain features and benefits.

1.4.1.2 Minimum Requirements for a Server Cluster

Following are the minimum requirements for building the cluster:

1. Two servers connected by a network.
2. A method for each server to access the other's disk data and network services.
3. If you are building a cluster using the Windows operating system, then the Microsoft cluster service (MSCS) can be used. Special software helps provide cluster monitoring services such as failure detection and backup recovery.

Figure 1.3 explains an example of a cluster.

1.4.1.3 Advantages of Cluster Computing

Following are the advantages of cluster computing:

1. Scalability and availability to a smaller range (according to your set up); availability to help reduce downtime, and scalability to help flexible growth and investment protection.

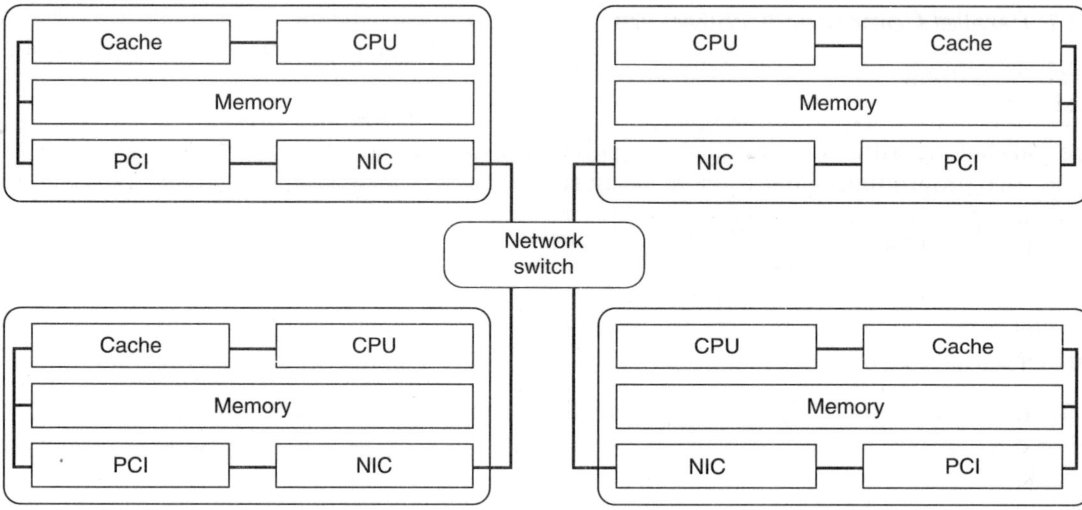

Figure 1.3 | Example of a cluster.

2. Simple and easy administration with low cost of ownership.
3. Provision of fault-tolerance capacity and support for rolling upgrades.

1.4.1.4 Applications of Cluster Computing

Cluster computing is basically used for the following purposes:

1. Sharing of data
2. Sharing of files and messages
3. Business application
4. Critical database management systems
5. Research projects (cluster lab set-up is done in various organizations for R&D)

1.4.2 Parallel Computing

Parallel computing helps solve problems by splitting larger problems into smaller sections and parallelly solves them. In all spheres such as science and enterprise computing, parallelism has always played a very important role in solving data-intensive problems. It has played a key role in several parts such as algorithms, programming languages and environments, computer architecture, networks, monitoring, operations in many fields, complex technologies and also solid-state science.

Parallel software and hardware systems provide solutions to problems. They demand more resources as compared with a single system, and parallel processing saves a lot of processing time.

1.4.2.1 Parallel Computer Architecture

Parallel computing requires specialized hardware and system software and a communication fabric is necessary to link the systems.

The parallel algorithms simultaneously solve all the problems at once, but the challenge is to develop such programming models which can support in the development of parallel applications. There is a list of companies that aim at supporting parallel computing and this includes names such as Tandem, Convex, Floating Point Systems, Kendall Square Research, Thinking Machines, MasPar, Sequent, Encore and Inmos.

Parallel computer architecture starts with the recognition that parallelism at different levels can be further divided as follows:

1. **Bit-level parallelism:** The amount of bits that are processed during one clock cycle is increasing day by day. This is also known as *word size*. We now have 64-bit processors. If we look back, word size has increased gradually from 4 bit to 8 bit to 16 to 32 and now 64 bit. Greater number of bits means means bigger address space for instructions. This reduces the time taken for large-size operands.
2. **Instruction-level parallelism:** To increase execution time, the pipelining technique is used, in which multi-stage processing is commonly used and where, *n*-stage pipelining with a complete set of instructions is completed in every cycle. Reduced instruction set computing (RISC) and complex instruction set computing (CISC) are the two popular techniques for this. RISC uses 5 stages and CISC uses a huge number of stages for pipelining. CISC is mainly used nowadays. Intel P4 works on the CISC architecture and uses the 35-stage pipelining.
3. **Data parallelism:** In data parallelism, the program loops can be processed in parallel.
4. **Task parallelism:** In task level parallelism, one problem can be split into several tasks and then those tasks can be run simultaneously. It is also called *same program multiple data*. As the name suggests, individual processors run the same program but on different segments of the input data. According to a number of concurrent operations or one instruction, a classification model was proposed by Michael Flynn in 1966. Task-level parallelism can be further divided into four parts: SISD (single instruction, single data), SIMD (single instruction, multiple data), MISD (multiple instructions, single data) and MIMD (multiple instructions, multiple data) (Fig. 1.4).
   - *Single instruction, single data (SISD) stream:* A computer executes one operation at a time, that is, it does not support any parallelism in instructions as well as data streams. The control

	Single instruction	Multiple instruction
Single data	SISD	MISD
Multiple data	SIMD	MIMD

Figure 1.4 | Types of parallelism.

unit (CU) fetches one instruction stream from memory after that CU produces signals for executing signals, for example, old mainframes and uniprocessors (Fig. 1.5).

- *Single instruction, multiple data (SIMD) stream:* A computer processes multiple data streams for a single instruction for handling data operations. And this process occurs on the basis of parallelism, for example, an array processor or GPU (Fig. 1.6).
- *Multiple instruction, single data (MISD) stream:* A computer processes multiple instructions on single data stream for performing operations. A space shuttle is controlled by the means of this operation. Heterogeneous systems are based on MISD, for example, the shuttle flight controlling system (Fig. 1.7).

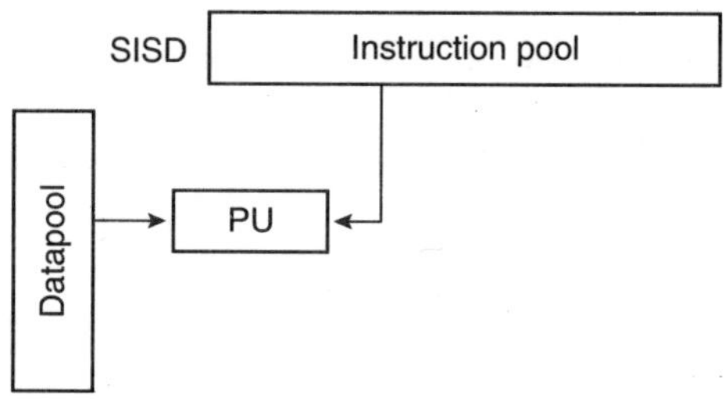

Figure 1.5 | SISD.

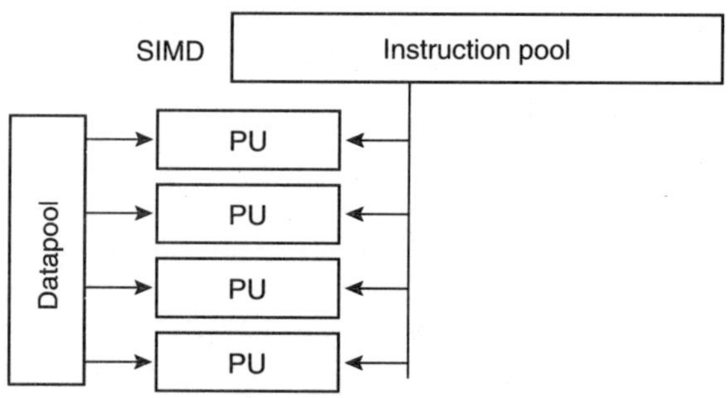

Figure 1.6 | SIMD.

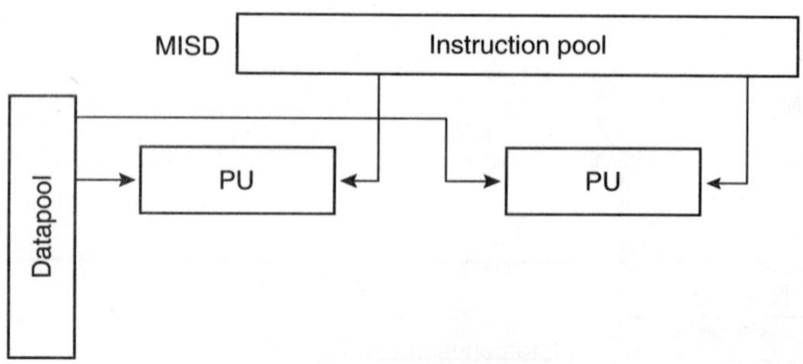

Figure 1.7 | MISD.

- *Multiple instruction, multiple data (MIMD) stream:* The computer processes multiple instructions on multiple data stream. This processing is simultaneous controlling of all the instructions so that all the multi-core processors work on the principle of MIMD, for example, multi-core processors (Fig. 1.8).

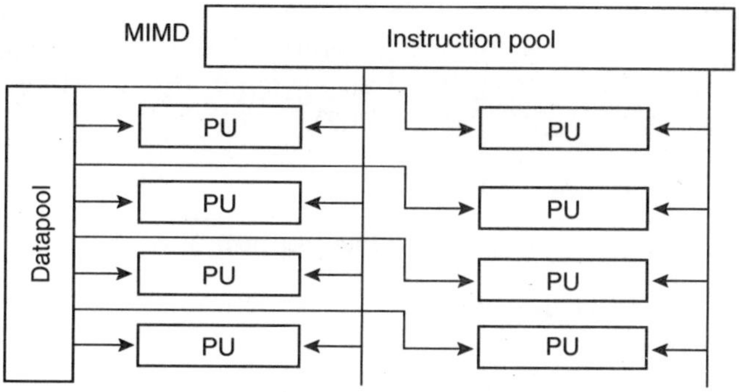

Figure 1.8 | MIMD.

5. **Hardware-level parallelism:** We can achieve hardware-level parallelism in the following ways:
   - *Shared memory model:* Memory can be simultaneously accessed by multiple processes with intent to provide communication among them or avoid redundant copies (Fig. 1.9).

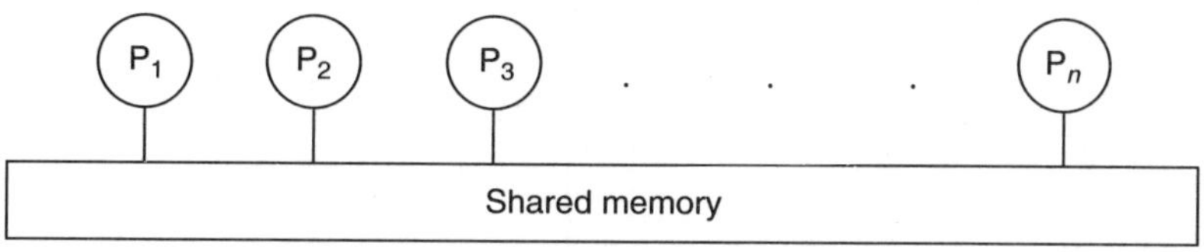

Figure 1.9 | Shared memory model.

   - *Distributed memory model:* In a multi-processor system, every processor contains its own memory, which means any kind of computational job can be done using local data as well remote data from different interconnected processors (Fig. 1.10).

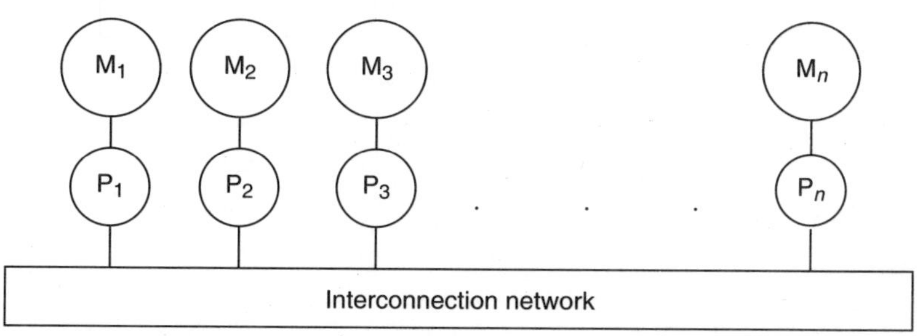

Figure 1.10 | Distributed memory model.

1.4.2.2 Message Passing Interface

To ensure that all computers communicate with each other, a message passing interface (MPI) is used, which is developed on the distributed memory programming mode. By using this model, synchronization is achieved among all communicating systems (Fig. 1.11).

1.4.2.3 Single Program with Multiple Data (SPMD)

The functioning of SPMD is similar to SIMD (single instruction, multiple data). However, the same programme is simultaneously executed by two different processors, as shown in Fig. 1.12.

1.4.2.4 Applications of Parallel Computing

Following are the different applications of parallel computing:

1. **Manufacturing:** Used in various processes such as the crash test analysis, the stress analysis, the vibrational analysis and in aerodynamics.
2. **Petroleum:** Used in petrochemical sciences, involving various processes such as seismic processing, geophysical modeling and reservoir modeling.
3. **Life sciences:** Used in life sciences, drug design, bioinformatics, DNA mapping and disease research.

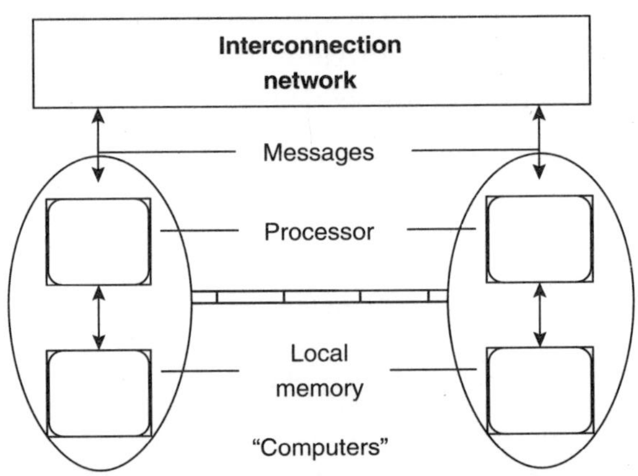

Figure 1.11 | Message passing interface.

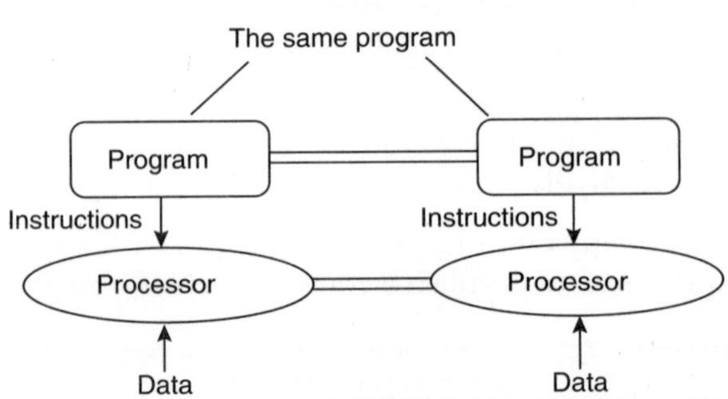

Figure 1.12 | SPMD.

4. **Finance:** Used in finance phases such as portfolio management and risk analysis.
5. **Electronic design automation:** Used in processes such as simulation and complex auto routes.

1.4.2.5 Advantages of Parallel Computing

Following are the major advantages of parallel computing:

1. **Cost efficiency:** Saves time and/or money because of the ability to multi-thread on a large scale and therefore simultaneously process several streams of data.
2. **Power consumption:** This is because the electrical power used by a processor generally increases by the square of its switching speed, and power-sensitive applications can reduce power use by compensating for reduced switching speed with additional computing units; for example, quartering the switching speed (using 1/4 power) and doubling the processing elements (for a fully parallelizable problem) results in half the power use for about the same computing ability.
3. **High performance:** This is because it provides concurrency.
4. **Improve utilization:** This is because of the use of non-local resources.

Although parallel computing solved many problems, it is not enough for large-scale problems.

1.4.2.6 Demand for More Computing Power

The large-scale, computational data intensive scientific applications require more resource in various applications such as:

1. Scientific application
2. Computer animation
3. Computer games
4. Image processing
5. Data mining

1.4.3 Grid Computing

To serve most computational data-intensive scientific applications, grid computing has been proved as a successful paradigm after parallelism and clustering. Let us see the details of grid computing (Fig. 1.13).

Grid computing is basically a collection of interconnected computer systems where the systems utilize the same resources collectively.

It usually consists of one main computer that is used to distribute information and tasks to a group of networked computers to accomplish a common goal. These goals are as follows:

1. To coordinate resource sharing and problem solving in a dynamic, multi-institutional VO.
2. To provide the generic approach for a general resource-sharing framework that address the VO requirement.

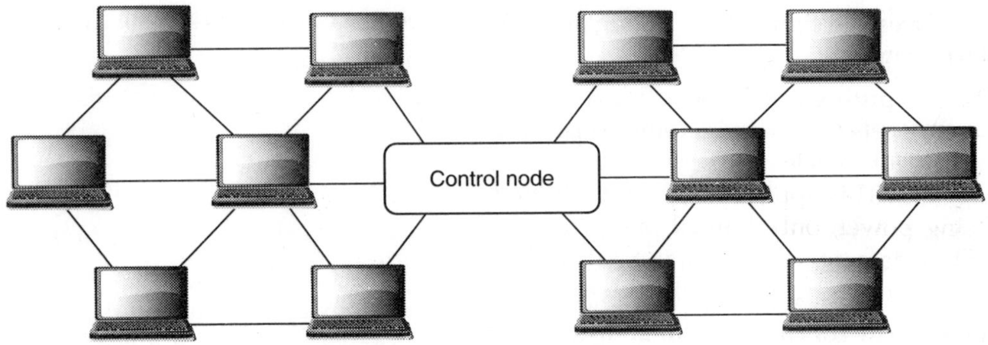

Figure 1.13 | Grid architecture.

3. To support the creation and use of computation- and data-enriched environments.
4. To use open standards and interfaces.

1.4.3.1 The Grid

Grid is a name given to denote a proposed distributed computing. This name originated in the mid-1990s as a reference to the electric power grid.

1.4.3.2 Resource Collaboration in Grid

Collaboration of resources in grid computing is done with the help of VOs. People from different organizations and industries work together as a VO and leverage their resources for solving high-computational problems. VO refers to a set of individuals, organizational people or an institution who had adopted the following rules of sharing:

1. What is being shared?
2. Whom to share permission with?
3. Which conditions are favorable under which this sharing occurs?
4. By sharing resources, an actual organization can participate in one or more VOs.

1.4.3.3 Grid Environment

In a grid environment, there is resource collaboration to solve one common problem. Resources in the grid are distributed, and often, heterogeneous means of resources can be computer systems, supercomputers, data storage systems or any specific computing devices that are managed by different organizational domains.

1.4.3.4 Examples of Grid Computing

Following are some famous project applications of grid computing:

1. **SETI@HOME:** SETI is the acronym for Search for Extra-Terrestrial Intelligence. It is one of the most popular examples of grid computing. The application works to provide proof of

extra-terrestrial signals by reaching out to any existing radio or any kind of signal to exchange information.

2. **LHC computing grid:** LHC is Large Hadron Collider. This is a very famous grid application that supports CERN (originally Conseil Européen pour la Recherche Nucléaire or European Council for Nuclear Research now changed to the European Organization for Nuclear Research). This application is quite different to SETI. Here every system cannot use its processing power, only limited organizations have the access to it. Collider almost produces 27 Tb of data per day, and these data only be accessed by authenticated limited systems. This kind of processing is very difficult even for supercomputers.
3. **NFCR centre for computational drug discovery:** Better known as the "Screensaver Lifesaver," the computational grid at the Oxford University Centre for Computational Drug Discovery is built on the same principles as the BOINC (Berkeley Open Infrastructure for Network Computing) infrastructure but for research purposes and for making computational drug discoveries. The project focuses on finding the methods to cure cancer by using computation methods by studying or screening small molecular structures, and this is done with the help of donations of computing cycles by volunteers while their screensavers are running.

1.4.3.5 Other Grid Applications

Other grid applications are weather forecasting, protein folding and earthquake simulation. Grids have been used in entertainment and animations projects also. Volume of data that is generated and grows every day is analyzed as its application.

1.4.3.6 Advantages of Grid Computing

Following are the major advantages of grid computing:

1. There is no need to spend on buying large SMP servers, which may be divided and further worked into smaller servers.
2. There is efficient and appropriate use of the idle resources. Many jobs can be oriented to get into work during idle hours. They can be given to idle server and idle desktops.
3. There is no doubt of failure as it is modular.
4. It can manage policies.
5. There is scalability and upgrading. Because of scalability more compute resources are fulfilled by just plugging them by installing the grid client on servers and desktops.
6. There is an advantage with running multiple tasks as in parallel processing by which performance speed is increased.

1.5 Computing Paradigm Evolution

As discussed at the beginning of this text, computing has been evolving since the time of desktops or multi-processor. Figure 1.14 depicts the various changes in the evolution of different computing paradigms.

Till now, we have understood all the fundamentals of parallel computing, cluster computing and grid computing. So, what is next?

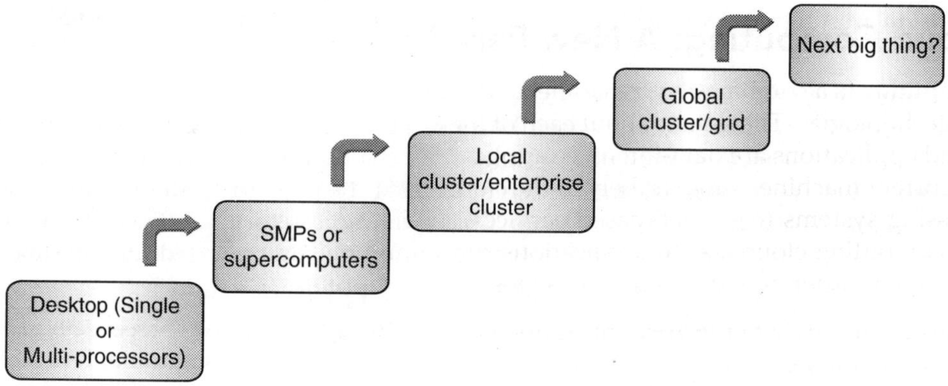

Figure 1.14 | Evolution of computing paradigm.

1.6 Next Big Thing: The "Cloud"

Cloud is a term that reflects the *Internet*, which means something available on the Internet and people use it. Although this is not new, the technology used by cloud providers is a combination of many things. Some services that were not available before now comes under the cloud definition, such as platform services and infrastructure services. Following are the unique features of cloud computing (Fig. 1.15):

1. Integration of virtualization techniques, and some older concepts such as grid, cluster and utility computing are the backbone of cloud computing.
2. Availability of a set of abstracted resources. You need not worry about what is below that abstraction.
3. Anything that involves "delivering hosted services over the Internet."
4. A metaphor for the Internet. A simplified way to represent the complicated operations in the network.
5. An abstraction of complexities, for example, servers, applications, data and heterogeneous platforms.

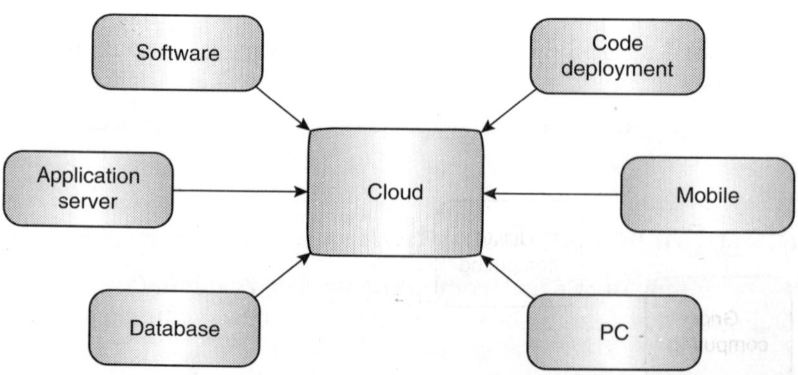

Figure 1.15 | Cloud computing view.

1.7 Cloud Computing: A New Paradigm

Cloud computing is a combination of parallel and distributing computing. It is also a combination of various technologies. The details about each of these technologies will be discussed in Chapter 2. Often, cloud applications are data-intensive applications, where computation is done on the cloud. Many concurrent machines run parallely in the cloud environment. An example would be transaction processing systems (e.g., Web-based services), which represent a large class of applications hosted by computing clouds; such applications run multiple instances of the service and require reliable and an in-order delivery of the messages.

After the advancement of the grid computing paradigm in 1990, various service delivery models evolved such as utility computing and the SaaS (Software as a Service) model.

As we already have an idea of utility computing, SaaS is the next model after utility. Although software as a service comes under the umbrella of cloud computing, it was the first service model that initiated various other services of cloud offering. We will study about each service in detail in Chapter 2.

Before the evolution of core cloud, services such as infrastructure and platform services such as SaaS existed in the market. We were familiar with Google Docs even before 2009 (the year cloud services started). After that market demand and innovation helped develop other services. Cloud infrastructure and platform services are based on SaaS and the utility model. Figure 1.16 shows the different trends of the computing service model.

1.7.1 Cloud Computing in Mathematics

To make comprehension simple, let us talk in mathematical terms.

1. **1 (One)**
   - One single integrated environment
   - A collection pool of resources and services

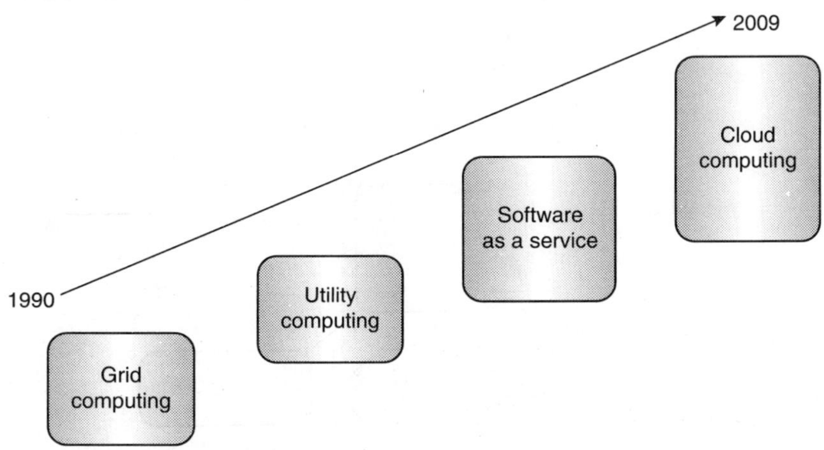

Figure 1.16 | Innovative service model for application.

2. **0 (Null)**
   - Null capital investment in upfront infrastructure
   - Auto-management or sustainance of resource or service (active, inactive, fail in status)
3. **∞ (Infinity)**
   - Infinite possibility
   - Availability, accessibility, scalability, manageability and performance

1.7.2 Cloud Computing in IT

An acquisition and delivery model of IT resources helps in the improvement of business performance and controls the costs of IT-delivering resources to the organization. Following are the two different perspectives of cloud computing in IT:

1. **A user perspective:** Users do not need to worry about how and who is taking care of all the offered services. Users just use all the services over the Internet using the Web browser. There is full layer of abstraction and invisibility from the user point of view.
2. **An organization perspective:** Cloud delivers services for consumer and business needs in a simple way, providing on-demand scalability and distinguished QoS to increase rapid innovation and decision making in the business rather than focusing on the infrastructure need and complexity.

1.7.3 Cloud Value Drivers and Effects

Following are the key benefits of the cloud that are the main value drivers of cloud computing (Fig. 1.17):

1. **Lower IT operating and capital costs:** The leading value driver of cloud computing is lower IT operating and capital costs. We get lower IT cost because many techniques such as

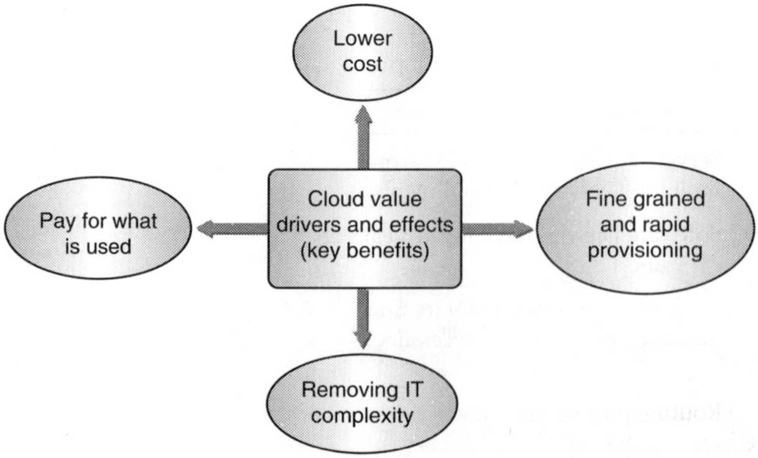

Figure 1.17 | Cloud value key benefits.

virtualization, workload migration, server consolidation and optimization are used. It helps improve maximum capital utilization with less energy and management costs.

2. **Fine grained and rapid provisioning:** Cloud computing enables fast grained access of all the services while using infrastructure services. We can easily set the exact level of disk volume, instance size, storage capacity and many more. Provisioning of all the services in cloud is very fast and we can quickly spin up or down any service.
3. **Removing IT complexity:** Cloud computing removes IT infrastructure complexity from providers as well as from users. Using cloud services, small-, medium- or large-sized organizations can build their infrastructure in few minutes and end users can access all services with the help of simple Web interface. End user gets fast and richer interface for accessing all the services.
4. **Pay for what is used:** Cloud pricing is based on the pay-per-use model. This model allows you to pay for what is used. It avoids the upfront cost for infrastructure and the financial risk because huge capital investment is not required in building and operating infrastructure.

1.7.4 Typical IT Budget Models

A typical IT budget model uses the overall cost investment in the following ways:

1. **Infrastructure (≈60%):** Most of the initial capital investment of IT budget is involved in purchasing space and servers, installing the network, and providing security and overall administration.
2. **Applications (≈35%):** After infrastructure, most of the capital expenditure is spent on purchasing original OS, licence development software and tools.
3. **Others (≈5%):** Some part of the budget is involved in administration and management tasks.

Using the cloud pricing model, the typical IT budgets can be reduced. If any start-up organization or industry plans to start any business that needs high global access, on-demand scalability and fault-tolerance capability, then they do not need to put any upfront cost in building IT infrastructure, installing licensed software, management and procurement of entire data center operations. All these efforts and cost can be reduced drastically using various cloud services. Table 1.1 shows the difference between traditional IT and cloud services.

Table 1.1 Comparison between traditional IT process and cloud

Key Elements	Traditional IT	Cloud
Servers	Servers are purchased on lease or through multiple-year capital installments	Cloud provides a pay-on-demand option on the basis of requirement
Software	Software licenses have multi-year expiration	In cloud SaaS model, customer has to pay on a monthly basis
Infrastructure	Large infrastructure capacity and management costs are necessary	The costs are demand based and follow the pay-as-you-go model. No extra infrastructure management cost is required
Rapid provisioning and on-demand scaling	Routine provisioning takes 2–3 weeks	Provisioning is completed in minutes to hours

1.8 Differences and Similarities Among Different Types of Computing

In this section, we are going to learn about differences and similarties of cloud computing among different types of other computing.

1.8.1 Grid Computing Versus Cloud Computing

Cloud computing eliminates the upfront cost of investing capital in purchasing and managing hardware and software. We can use all the applications, software and hardware on a rental basis over the Internet. Although in grid computing, resources of different computers that are geographically distributed work simultaneously for solving one specific problem, grid systems are basically designed for the collaboration of sharing resources.

1.8.1.1 Similarities

Following are the key similarities between grid and cloud computing:

1. Cloud computing and grid computing both are scalable. Scalability is realized by the means of "load balancing of application" going on differently on many operating systems and those operating systems are connected through internet services and application.
2. Both grid and cloud have multitasking as well as multi-tenancy. It means that the application instances can be accessed by different customers as well as on the same time, they can perform different tasks.
3. Cloud and grid computing both have the facility to provide SLA guaranteed for time accessibility of, say, 99%. If the service gets over before the uptime service, then the client will have the pleasure of having a service credit for receiving data after time.

1.8.1.2 Differences

Following are the key differences between grid and cloud computing:

1. Grid systems are configured for co-action of joint resources that belong to different admin domains. But this is not the case with clouds. Clouds unmask the resources of one domain worldwide externally.
2. Grid systems assist the execution of end-users practical applications as activities of computation. An action is accepted by a grid endpoint and then locally handled by a batch system, whereas clouds are mainly used for remote deployment of services.
3. In a cloud, companies can increase their capacities in less than an instant without investing in new infrastructure, without training new personnel, without renewing license new software, whereas this is not the case in a grid.

1.8.2 Cluster Computing Versus Cloud Computing

1.8.2.1 Similarities

Following are the main similarities between cluster and cloud computing:

1. Cluster computing and cloud computing both have resource pooling capabilities.
2. Cloud computing has broad network access, and cluster computing can also have broad network access.

1.8.2.2 Differences

Following are the key differences between cluster and cloud computing:

1. Cluster computing is a united bundle of computers that work together. It can be considered as a case of working together as a single computer. These clusters are made up of many standalone equipped machines. They all are connected by a network. In cloud computing, virtualization is provided within a system, such as OS virtualization and para virtualization. Because of the virtualization in one system, we get different operating systems and through different operating systems, the user gets heterogeneous services simultaneously.
2. Cluster set-up is not on demand basis, whereas cloud computing is on demand basis.
3. Cluster computing cannot provide instant scalability, whereas cloud computing can easily provide it.

1.8.3 Utility Computing Versus Cloud Computing

1.8.3.1 Similarities

Following are the main similarities between utility and cloud computing:

1. Utility computing involves the renting of computing resources such as hardware, software and network bandwidth on an as-required, on-demand basis. In other words, what were earlier considered products are treated as services in utility computing, such as electricity service, telephone service, railway service or transportation service. We do not buy rail or bus, but we pay to use it; we do not produce electricity for our home use, but we pay for whatever we use. This is the concept of utility computing.
2. Cloud computing inherits this concept of utility computing in the pay-per-use model.

1.8.3.2 Differences

The main difference between utility and cloud computing is that utility computing is not based on virtualization, whereas cloud computing is mainly based on virtualization of resources.

1.8.4 Parallel Computing Versus Cloud Computing

When more than two processors work simultaneously to solve one problem, the technique is called *parallel computing*. It is the responsibility of the programmer to split the problems into pieces and relate each piece with the other.

Take, for example, chess. A parallel program can guess the possible first moves it can make and every first turn can be explored by a separate processor.

As we have learned earlier, parallelism can be achieved through different ways, for example, bit-level parallelism, instruction-level parallelism, data parallelism, task parallelism and hardware parallelism. (Here the concept of shared memory and distributed shared memory are used, for example, Uniform Memory Access (UMA), Non-Uniform Memory Access (NUMA).

In cloud computing, however, instead of parallelism, virtualization is used, which adds a new layer in the existing system known as the *virtualization layer*. Through virtualization, different services of cloud become accessed.

1.8.5 Comparison Between Cluster, Grid and Cloud

To clarify the fundamental differences between the three main paradigms of distributed computing, Table 1.2 compares the cluster, grid and cloud computing methods.

Table 1.2 Comparing cluster, grid and cloud

System Characteristics	Cluster	Grid	Cloud
Population	Commodity computers	High-end computers	Commodity computers, high-end virtual servers and network attached block storage
Size/Scalability	In 100s	In 1000s	From 100s to 1000s or more
Node Operating System (OS)	Standard OS (Windows, Linux)	Any typical OS (most often Unix/Linux)	A hypervisor (VM) where multiple OSs run
Ownership	Single	Multiple	Single
Interconnection Network Speed	With low latency and high bandwidth	Internet with high latency and low bandwidth	With low latency and high bandwidth
Security/ Privacy/ Authentication	Traditional login password – depends on user privilege	Public/Private key pair-based authentication. Limited support for privacy	High security, authentication and privacy; every user provided with a virtual machine. Access control list (ACL) used
Service Negotiation	Limited	SLA based	Limited
User Management	Central management system within an organization	Distributed and also VO-based system management	Centralized/Managed by third party, for example, public, private or hybrid clouds

(Continued)

Table 1.2 Continued

System Characteristics	Cluster	Grid	Cloud
Resource Management	Centralized	Distributed	Centralized/Distributed
Allocation/Scheduling	Centralized	Decentralized	Centralized and decentralized
Standards and Interoperability issues	Cluster follows virtual interface architecture	Grid follows own standards, for example, open grid forum standards	Web services, mostly REST-based interface; interoperability of cloud providers under research
Single System Image	Possible	Nothing like image	Elective choice from different type of images, for example, AMI (Amazon machine image)
Capacity	Assured but very constant	Very high, but varies	On-demand provisioning
Failure Management	Limited (often failed)	Limited (often failed)	Strong support for fail over and content replication; possible to transport VMs from one node to another
Pricing of Service	Restricted	Controlled by public good or private assigned	Pay-per-use service model; discount allowed for vast-service users
Internetworking	Cluster of cluster (grouping) within an industry or organization	Controlled and limited adoption but discovered by the means of scientific efforts in research and collaboration, for example, SETI@HOME	High potential, third-party solution provider can gather all services from one or many cloud providers
Application Drivers	Science, business, enterprise computing	Scientific and high throughput in collaboration	High traffic Web applications, large and mid-size business applications, data-intensive computing applications

Summary

We have understood the concepts of computing, various types of computing paradigms, and how utility is served as computing. We have also learned about the fundamental notion of cloud computing and main paradigms of distributed computing.

This chapter gave us details and comparative understanding of cluster, grid, cloud computing, with their respective advantages, applications and examples.

The chapter showed the evolution of cloud computing paradigm and different perspective of cloud computing in IT and how cloud computing tremendously reduced typical IT budget expenditures.

The chapter also provided crystal clear differences and similarities of cloud computing among different types of other computing with detailed comparative analysis. In the next chapter, we are going to learn about detailed and practical understanding of cloud computing.

Multiple Choice Questions

1. Cloud is a term which actually reflects ____________.
   (a) Service
   (b) Internet
   (c) Virtualization
   (d) Integrations

2. In computer analogy, we can run application faster using faster hardware and ____________.
   (a) Optimized algorithm
   (b) Work harder
   (c) Cluster computing
   (d) None of these

3. Computing can be defined as ____________ for any particular purpose.
   (a) Designing solution
   (b) Creating algorithm
   (c) Gathering information
   (d) All of the above

4. Utility is an economical term that reflects ____________ received from using goods or services.
   (a) Customer's need
   (b) Customer's satisfaction
   (c) Market demand
   (d) Market price

5. A cluster consists of a collection of interconnected standalone computers working together as a ____________.
   (a) Single integrated computing resource
   (b) Multiple computing resources
   (c) Could be multiple or single
   (d) Depend resource

6. The minimum requirements for a server cluster are ____________.
   (a) One server connected by a network
   (b) Two servers connected by a network
   (c) Three servers connected by a network
   (d) There is not any minimum condition

7. Parallel computing allows us to solve large problems by splitting them into smaller ones and solving them ________.
   (a) Serially
   (b) Collectively
   (c) Serially and parallel
   (d) Concurrently

8. Parallelism at different levels can be exploited; these levels are bit-level parallelism, instruction-level parallelism, data parallelism and ________.
   (a) Network parallelism
   (b) Task parallelism
   (c) System parallelism
   (d) Processing parallelism

9. Grid computing is basically a collection of interconnected computer systems where the systems utilize the same resources ________.
   (a) Repeatedly
   (b) Continuously
   (c) Collectively
   (d) Virtually

10. All computing trends are originally related to the ________.
    (a) Parallel computing
    (b) Distributed computing
    (c) Super computing
    (d) Data processing

11. For starting cloud computing services, ________ initial capital investment is required.
    (a) Little
    (b) Huge
    (c) Zero
    (d) None of the above

Review Questions

1. Explain the different trends of computing in detail.
2. Explain how distributed computing is the key notion of cloud computing.
3. What are the similarities and differences between the grid and cloud computing service models?
4. What are the key points of difference between cloud computing and parallel computing?
5. What are the basic requirements for building a cluster? Explain the installation process of a cluster with an example.
6. Explain parallel computing architecture and the basic model of parallel computing.

7. What is the role of virtual organization in grid computing and how does grid computing solve the increasing demand for computing power?
8. Explain in detail cloud computing drivers and the key benefits of cloud computing.
9. Differentiate cluster, grid and cloud on the basis of their applications and advantages.
10. What are the key advantages a user gets in cloud computing compared to those with grid and cluster?

Answers to Multiple Choice Questions

1. (b), 2. (a), 3. (d), 4. (b), 5. (a), 6. (b), 7. (d), 8. (b),
9. (c), 10. (b), 11. (c)

CHAPTER 2 Introduction to Cloud Computing

Learning Objectives

After reading this chapter, you will be able to:

- Acquire a clear vision of cloud computing.
- Understand the central idea behind cloud computing.
- Understand all the properties and key characteristics of cloud computing and how they are delivered to customers.
- Acquire a proper understanding of all the service models and deployment models used in cloud computing.
- Differentiate various deployment models on the basis of their characteristics.
- Understand cloud architecture, cloud computing challenges, cloud vocabulary, cloud supporting services and cloud management.

2.1 Cloud Computing: Definitions

Cloud computing is a paradigm of computing and a new way of thinking about IT industry. It is not any specific technology, and due to its evolving nature its definition is also evolving. Here we are going to study some standard definitions of cloud computing which are widely accepted:

1. A scientific definition is proposed by the GRIDS Lab at the University of Melbourne as follows:

   A cloud is a type of parallel and distributed system consisting of a collection of interconnected and virtualized computers that are dynamically provisioned and presented as one or more unified computing resources based on service-level agreements established through negotiation between the service provider and consumers.

2. The NIST (National Institute of Standards and Technology) definition is as follows:

   Cloud computing is a model for enabling convenient, on-demand network access to a shared pool of configurable computing resources (e.g., networks, servers, storage, applications and services) that can be rapidly provisioned and released with minimal management effort or service provider interaction. This cloud model is composed of five essential characteristics, three service models and four deployment models.

3. The Berkeley RAD Lab (University of California, Berkeley) defines cloud computing as follows:

   Cloud computing refers to both the applications delivered as services over the Internet and the hardware and systems software in the datacenters that provide those services. The services themselves have long been referred to as Software as a Service (SaaS). The datacenter hardware and software is what we will call a cloud. When a cloud is made available in a pay-as-you-go manner to the general public, we call it a public cloud; the service being sold is utility computing. We use the term private cloud to refer to internal datacenters of a business or other organization, not made available to the general public. Thus, cloud computing is the sum of SaaS and utility computing, but does not include private clouds.

4. Lizhe Wang and colleagues proposed the following definition for cloud computing based on their research:

   A computing cloud is a set of network enabled services, providing scalable, QoS guaranteed, normally personalized, inexpensive computing platforms on demand, which could be accessed in a simple and pervasive way.

2.2 Central Ideas Behind Cloud Computing

From the definitions provided earlier and from the basic concepts provided in Chapter 1, it can be concluded that the central ideas behind cloud computing are as follows (Fig. 2.1):

1. Utility computing
2. SOA – Service-oriented architecture
3. SLA – Service-level agreement

This combination of utility computing, SOA and SLA provides scalability, elasticity, availability, reliability, manageability, interoperability, performance optimization and accessibility portability. These functionalities serve users in numerous ways.

1. **Users' perspective:** Users are more interested in the "service" they get rather than how they get it. Their only concern is the quality of service, because they do not own any physical infrastructure; they want to pay for only as much as they have used.

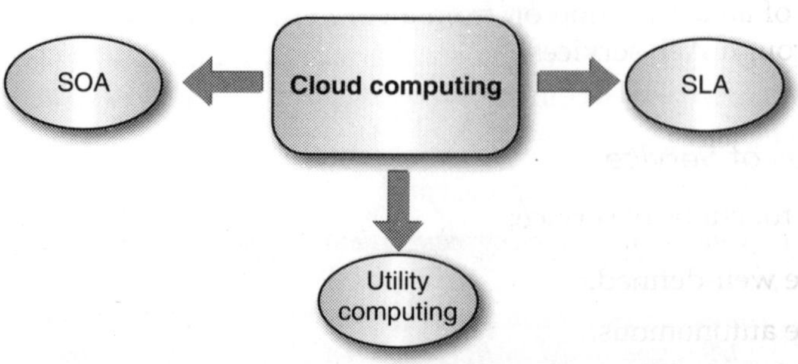

Figure 2.1 | Central ideas behind cloud computing.

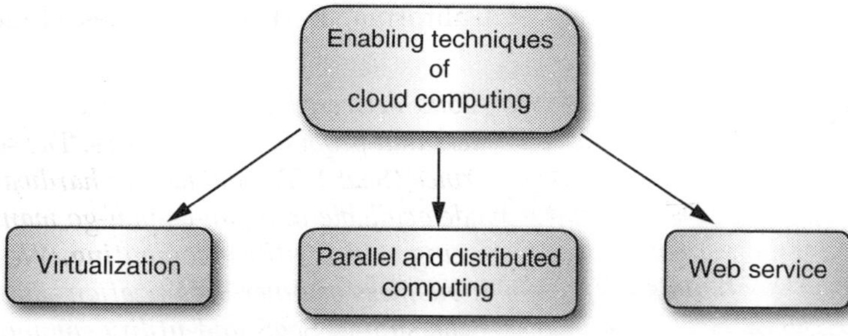

Figure 2.2 | Enabling techniques of cloud computing.

2. **Providers' perspective:** Cloud providers use the following three main enabling techniques to help users benefit from cloud computing (Fig. 2.2):
   - Virtualization
   - Parallelized and distributed computing
   - Web service

As *virtualization* is one of the most important enabling techniques of cloud computing, we will discuss it in Chapter 4. We will also discuss distributed database and web services in detail later in this book. However, for now let us discuss at length the central ideas behind cloud computing for a deeper understanding about the concept.

2.2.1 Utility Computing

Utility computing provides a service provisioning model. As discussed in Chapter 1, the service provider makes the infrastructure and computing resources available to its customers. The customers then use it as per their requirement and make a monthly usage payment for computing, storage and network resources just as they would do for any other utility service. Let us understand some details about service.

2.2.1.1 Service

Service is the endpoint of an association or, from a computer science perspective, service is what we connect together through Web services.

2.2.1.2 Functionalities of Service

Following are the main functions of service:

1. A service should be well-defined.
2. A service should be autonomous.
3. A service should be independent and not depend on the circumstance or state of other services.

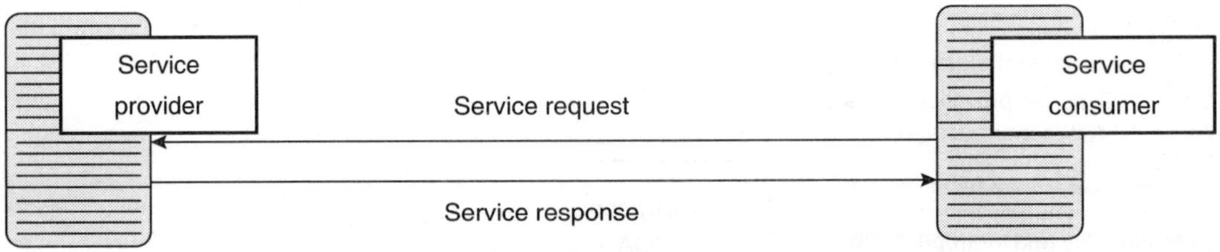

Figure 2.3 | Service-oriented architecture.

2.2.2 Service-Oriented Architecture

SOA is a grouping or combination of various services that communicate with each other (Fig. 2.3). It provides loosely coupled services that can be used for multiple business requirements. It enables full flexibility in designing services, which helps during system integration.

SOA is usually implemented by a Web service model.

2.2.3 Service-Level Agreement

SLA is a mutual agreement between consumers and service provider that defines detailed service offerings, delivery time, quality of service (QoS) and scope or constraints of the offered services.

2.2.3.1 Common Content in the Contract

Metrics related to performance assurance depends on the following components:

1. Uptime and downtime ratio
2. System throughput
3. Response time

2.3 Properties and Characteristics of Cloud Computing

Following are the key properties and characteristics of cloud computing (Fig. 2.4):

1. High scalability and elasticity
2. High availability and reliability
3. High manageability and interoperability
4. High accessibility and portability
5. High performance and optimization

These key properties can be achieved only when utility, SOA and SLA combine together and give us cloud computing.

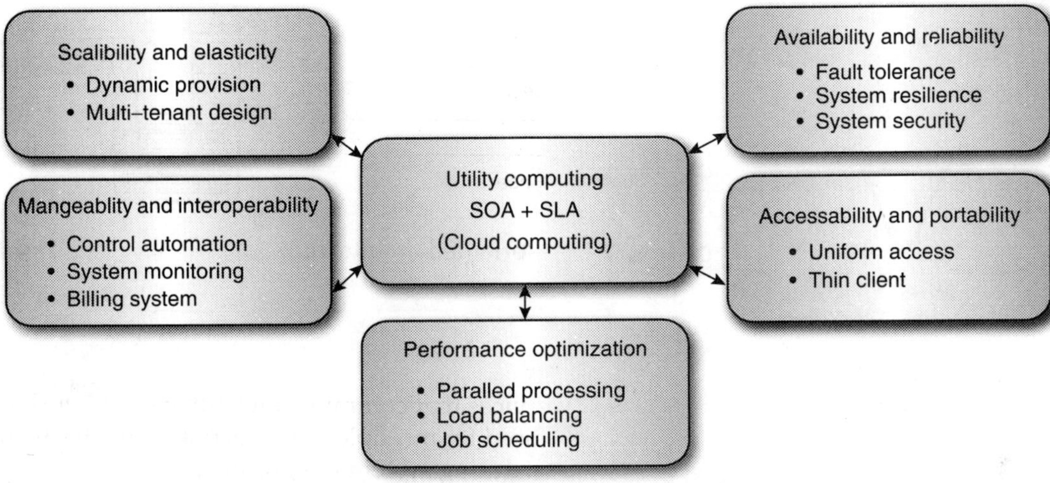

Figure 2.4 | Properties and characteristics of cloud computing.

2.3.1 Scalability and Elasticity

As scalability and elasticity are the key properties of the system, let us discuss them in detail.

1. **Scalability:** Scalability of a system, process or network is its ability to quickly handle any unexpected rise in the volume of work within a gap or discontinuity in service delivery. In a nutshell, scalability is "increasing" the capacity to meet the "increasing" workload. Scalability can be divided into two basic categories:
   - *Horizontal scaling:* When scaling is done by adding more machines into your pool of resources.
   - *Vertical scaling:* When scaling is done by adding more power (CPU, RAM) to your existing machine.
2. **Elasticity:** In cloud environment, elasticity represents responsiveness of demand and supply to price changes. If demand moves by more than the price change, it is described as relatively elastic; if it moves by less than the price change, it is relatively inelastic.

2.3.1.1 Method for Achieving Scalability and Elasticity

To achieve scalability and elasticity, the two methods are commonly used:

1. Dynamic provisioning
2. Multi-tenant design

Let us understand each method in detail.

2.3.1.1.1 Dynamic Provisioning

As the name suggests, dynamic provisioning means those instances when a virtual server is provisioned on the basis of the customer's requirement through a cloud administration console, client application or through the network and system administrator. In the traditional computing model, two following common problems occur:

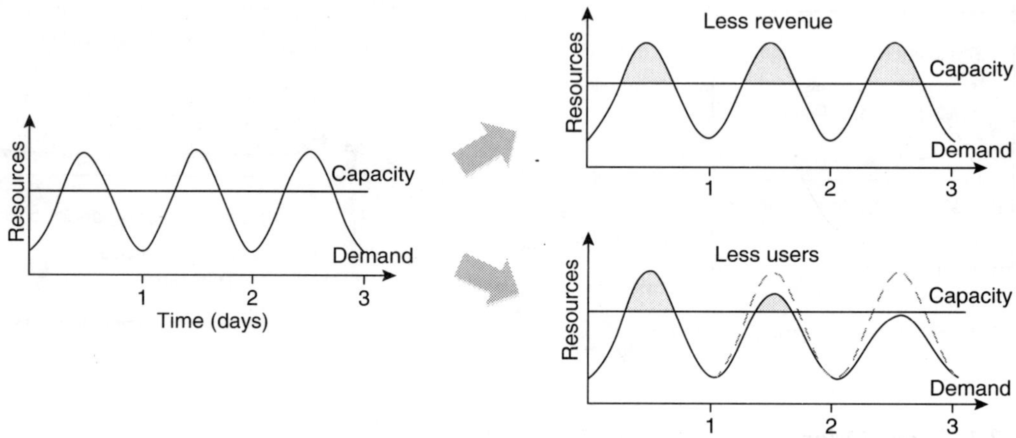

Figure 2.5 | Underestimated system utilization, which results in under-provision.

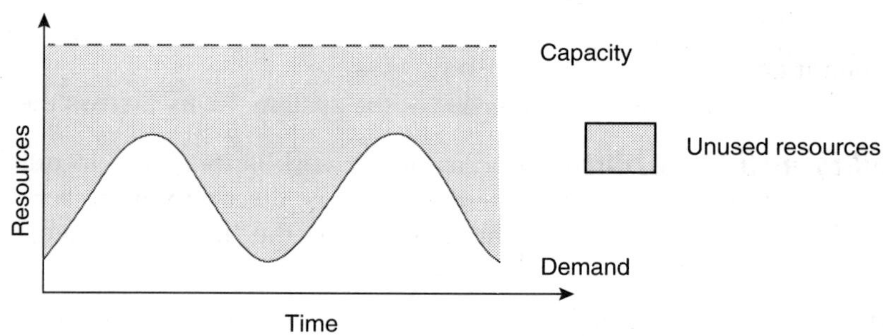

Figure 2.6 | Overestimated system utilization, which results in low utilization.

1. Underestimated system utilization, which results in under-provision (Fig. 2.5).
2. Overestimated system utilization, which results in low utilization (Fig. 2.6).

2.3.1.1.1.1 Solution of System Utilization Problems

Following are some possible solutions for system utilization problems:

1. **Dynamically provisioned resources:** Cloud resources must be provisioned dynamically because the system encounters periodic demand variations among different industries as well as burst demand for certain extraordinary events as described in Fig. 2.7.

2.3.1.1.2 Multi-Tenant Design

Multi-tenant design architecture is a kind of software architecture that can handle multiple client organizations or where a software that runs on one server has the ability to serve multiple client requests simultaneously.

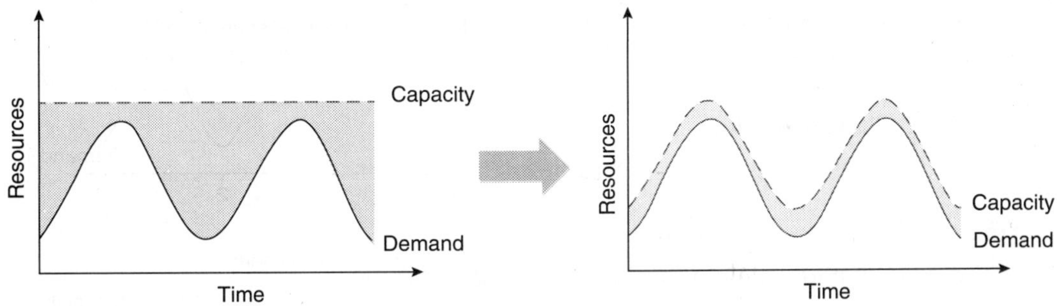

Figure 2.7 | Dynamically provisioned resources.

2.3.1.1.2.1 Client-Oriented Requirements

Following are the key requirements of the multi-tenant design:

1. **Customization:** Multi-tenant applications are generally mandatory to deliver good quality customization to support every organization's objectives and goal.
2. **QoS:** Multi-tenant applications must offer high levels of security and robustness.

2.3.2 Availability and Reliability

Availability and reliability are significant properties of cloud computing. Let us study them in detail.

1. **Availability:** The degree to availability is the ratio of time a system or component is functional to the total time it is required or probable to function. This can be conveyed as a direct proportion (e.g., 9/10 or 0.9) or as a percentage (e.g., 90%). A cloud system generally needs high availability. For example, a "Five Nines" system would statistically provide 99.999% availability.
2. **Reliability:** Reliability means the capability of a system hardware or software to perform constantly without fail according to defined specifications.

2.3.2.1 Method of Achieving Availability and Reliability

Following are the methods for achieving reliability and availability:

1. Fault-tolerant system
2. System resilience
3. Reliable system security

2.3.2.1.1 Fault-Tolerant System

Fault-tolerance is that special property of a system which empowers it to continue operating properly even in the event of the failure of some of its components.

If its operating quality reduces at all, this reduction is proportional to the severity of the failure, as related to a naively designed system where a minor failure can cause total breakdown.

2.3.2.1.1.1 Basic Characteristics

Following are some key characteristics of a fault-tolerant system:

1. Not even a single chance of failure.
2. Detection of fault and isolation for the component that failed.
3. Control of fault for preventing dissemination of failure.
4. Accessibility of reversion modes.

We can achieve above characteristics of fault tolerant system by applying following principles:

1. **Prevention of single point of failure:** If a failure occurs in a system, then system must be in working state continuously without any interruption during the repairing process of that failure.
2. **Fault detection and isolation (FDI):** FDI is a kind of control engineering that continuously monitors and controls the system state. Therefore, when a fault occurs, it identifies the type of fault and its location immediately.
3. **Isolate failing component:** At the time of failure, a system must be intelligent enough to disconnect the failure component with other working components.
4. **Fault containment:** Many failed processes could be the reason of system failure caused by the spread of failure to the rest of the part. Fault containment does an action for limiting the force of the faults for some extent. A system should be able to maintain some check points, which can be used in managing the state changes.

2.3.3 System Resilience

Resilience is a system's capability for providing and maintaining an adequate level of services despite faults and challenges with existing operations. Resiliency preserves the system's capability to return to its original state after meeting trouble. If a risk event hits a system offline, an extremely resilient system will return to work and function as planned as soon as possible.

2.3.3.1 Some Risk Events

Following are some risk events:

1. If power is lost at a plant for two days, then how would our system recover?
2. If a key service is lost because a database becomes corrupt, can the business recover?

2.3.3.2 Disaster Recovery

Disaster recovery is a procedure and a set of policies regarding preparing for recovery or maintenance of technology infrastructure critical to an organization after a human-induced or natural disaster.

2.3.3.3 Some Common Strategies

Following are some common strategies for disaster recovery:

1. **Backup:** Replication of data and frequent data backups to off-site locations or the entire system.
2. **Preparing:** Enabling local mirroring systems, hard disk protection system and uninterruptible power supply (UPS).

2.3.4 System Security

System security is the most important concern in information security. It enables various security policies, encryption techniques and control for protecting application, data and entire infrastructure.

2.3.4.1 Important Security and Privacy Issues

Following are some main security issues related to cloud computing:

1. **Data protection:** To provide protected data, cloud providers must ensure that one customer's data is properly segregated from that of another.
2. **Application security:** Cloud providers must guarantee that applications available as a service via the cloud are secure.
3. **Identity management:** Every enterprise must have its individual identity management system to control access to information and computing resources.
4. **Privacy:** Providers must guarantee that all critical data are masked and that only authorized users have access to data in its entirety.

2.3.5 Manageability and Interoperability

Manageability and interoperability are the two most attractive features of cloud computing and are described as follows:

1. **Manageability:** Manageability means managing entire cloud systems. System management in cloud computing is much more dependent on overall network and offered services management; for example, management of telecommunication services.
2. **Interoperability:** Interoperability is that characteristic of a system or product which provides an easy-to-understand interface or platform to enable work with any other services and platforms with unlimited access.

2.3.5.1 Method of Achieving Manageability and Interoperability

Following are the three main methods for achieving manageability and interoperability:

1. System control automation
2. System state monitoring
3. Automatic billing

2.3.6 Control Automation

Control automation is *autonomic computing*. Its final purpose is to develop computer systems capable of self-management, to overcome the rapidly growing complexity of computing systems administration and to diminish the barrier that complexity poses to any additional development.

2.3.6.1 Architectural Framework

It is combined with autonomic components (AC), which cooperate with each other. AC can be presented in terms of two main control loops (local and global) with sensors (for self-monitoring), effectors (for self-adjustment) and knowledge for developing policies based on self and environment alertness.

2.3.6.2 Functional Areas

Following are the functional areas of control automation:

1. **Self-configuration:** Automatic configuration of components.
2. **Self-healing:** Enablement mechanism for automatic detection of any system faults and correction of those faults.
3. **Self-optimization:** Enablement mechanism for monitoring and controlling of system resources for ensuring optimal resource utilization with specified requirements.
4. **Self-protection:** Active identification of all kinds of threats and enablement of self-protection from random attacks.

2.3.7 System Monitoring

A system monitoring is a process within a distributed system for collecting and storing state data in cloud computing. There are certain things that need to be always monitored, such as the following:

1. Status of physical machine and virtual machine
2. Detail resource utilization metrics
3. Network and bandwidth performance
4. System logs
5. Billing details

2.3.8 Automatic Billing System

A cloud environment usually follows the pay-per-use model (users pay according to their usage). A cloud provider must first decide the price for the list of service usage. After that it has to record the supply or service usage of each user, and then charge them by these records.

2.3.8.1 Methods of Knowing User's Usage

Following are the methods for enabling automatic billing:

1. Get that information by means of a monitoring system.
2. Repeatedly calculate the total amount of money a user should pay and automatically request money from user's banking account.

2.3.9 Accessibility and Portability

Accessibility and portability are very important characteristics of cloud computing. Let us study these in detail.

1. **Accessibility:** Accessibility is the word used to define the degree to which a device, product or service is accessible to as many people as possible.
2. **Service portability:** Service portability is the capacity to access services with the help of devices, anywhere, constantly with mobility provision and dynamic variation to resource variations.

2.3.9.1 Methods for Achieving Accessibility and Portability

Methods for achieving accessibility and portability are discussed in the following subsections.

2.3.9.1.1 Consistent Access

Cloud providers offer a set of cloud services just as we access general media, which means users can access cloud services from any operating system or any platform directly across the globe. Currently, Web browser technique is the most extensive platform in any intelligent electronic devices. Cloud services incorporate this and deliver their services with a Web-based interface through the Internet.

2.3.9.1.2 Thin Client

Thin client is a program that depends completely on another computer for achieving all traditional roles. It does not contain any internal memory so thin clients utilize different browsers such as Internet Explorer, Google Chrome or Mozilla Firefox for access to Internet Cloud. Currently, a thin client program is used more than other clients because it is low priced, provides security, consumes less power, has less noise, is easily reparable and replaceable, etc.

2.3.9.1.2.1 Features of Thin Client

Following are some of the key features of a thin client:

1. **Variety of end devices:** The end user can access the cloud service via various electronic devices, such as mobile phones, iPads, tablets and smartphones.
2. **Cheap client hardware:** The clients can be made out of much cheaper hardware, whereas cloud providers are capable of handling numerous client sessions at once.
3. **Client simplicity:** Client local system does not require complete operational functionalities.

2.3.10 Performance and Optimization

For a cloud to provide great computing power, application performance must be guaranteed. Cloud providers make use of powerful infrastructure or other highlighting resources to develop a high-performance and highly optimized environment, and then bring the entire bunch of services to cloud users.

2.3.10.1 Methods for Achieving Performance and Optimization

Following are the methods of achieving performance and optimization:

1. Parallel processing
2. Load balancing
3. Job scheduler

2.3.10.1.1 Parallel Processing

Parallel processing is an advanced method of computation where multiple calculations are carried out simultaneously. In parallel processing, a big computation problem is first split into small ones and then further divided into even smaller problems.

2.3.10.1.2 Parallelism at Different Levels

Following are the types of parallelism across different levels, as was discussed in Chapter 1:

1. Bit-level parallelism
2. Instruction-level parallelism
3. Data-level parallelism
4. Task-level parallelism

Following are two methods of achieving parallelism:

1. **Hardware approaches:** Following are the hardware approaches:
    - Multi-core computer
    - Symmetric multi-processor

- General purpose graphic processing unit
- Vector processor
- Distributed computing

2. **Software approaches:** Following are some software approaches:
    - Parallel programming language
    - Automatic parallelization

2.3.10.1.3 Load Balancing

Load balancing is a procedure to allocate workload equally across two or more computers, network links, hard drives, CPUs or additional resources to receive best resource utilization, decrease response time, maximize throughput and prevent overload.

Load balancing is necessary to improve resource utilization, system performance and energy efficiency.

2.3.10.1.4 Job Scheduler

A job scheduler is a kind of software application that is responsible for unattended background executions, usually known for historical details such as batch processing.

Dynamic increasing tasks, computation exhaustive tasks and complex processing tasks could be scheduled in the cloud.

2.3.10.1.5 Methods for Achieving Scheduling

Following are the methods for achieving scheduling in a cloud:

1. Use pre-defined workflow.
2. System automatic configuration.

2.4 Benefits of Cloud Computing

Cloud computing brings many benefits both for market and enterprises as well as individual users.

1. **For the market and enterprises:** Following are the key benefits of cloud computing from the market and enterprises perspective:
    - Reduction of initial upfront investment.
    - Reduction of capital expenditure.
    - Improvement in industrial specialization.
    - Improvement in resource utilization.

2. **For end users and individuals:** Following are the key benefits of cloud computing from the perspective of end users and individuals:
    - Reduction of local computing power.
    - Reduction of local storage power.
    - Availability of a variety of thin client devices in daily life.

2.4.1 For the Market and Enterprises

Let us understand in detail about each and every benefit of cloud computing in terms of the market and enterprises.

2.4.1.1 Reduction of Initial Upfront Investment

The general process for enterprises to start a business is to first estimate the quantity of supply and demand, survey and analyze the industry and market, purchase and deploy IT infrastructure, install and test the software system, design and develop enterprise-specific business services and finally declare the business service to clients.

2.4.1.1.1 Limitations

Following are some limitations while setting up infrastructure from scratch:

1. Infrastructure deployment is time-consuming.
2. The survey, analysis and estimation may not be 100% correct.
3. Enterprises should consider the threat of wrong investment.

2.4.1.1.2 Initiate Business with Cloud Computing Services

With the help of a cloud provider, survey and analysis of the industry and market could be done easily. Select one cloud provider for enterprise design, deployment of business service on a cloud environment and then broadcast the business service to clients.

2.4.1.1.3 Benefits

Following are the benefits from cloud computing:

1. Enterprises can develop and deploy business service in less time.
2. Enterprises do not need to own the infrastructure.
3. Enterprises can decrease the chance of business loss due to wrong investment.

2.4.1.1.4 What Does Cloud Computing Achieve?

From Table 2.1, we can identify the differences between traditional IT and cloud computing in terms of investment benefits.

Table 2.1 Differences between traditional IT and cloud computing with respect to business

Matrices	Traditional IT	Cloud Computing
Initial Investment	The enterprise takes the risk.	A cloud reduces the risk.
Infrastructure	The enterprise maintains the infrastructure.	A cloud provider maintains the infrastructure.
Time Period	Deployment duration is lengthy.	Business readiness is quick.

2.4.1.2 Reduction of Capital Expenditure

The section describes traditional capital expenditure of enterprises, the limitations of traditional capital expenditure methods and how cloud computing services can overcome those limitations.

2.4.1.2.1 Traditional Capital Expenditure of Enterprises

In the traditional approach, each enterprise established its own IT department and the IT department was able to handle the following jobs:

1. Administrate and manage hardware as well as software.
2. Purchase new infrastructure and remove the outdated one.
3. Apply regular data backup and check point process.
4. Always standby for any unpredicted IT problems.

2.4.1.2.1.1 Limitations

Following are some limitations with traditional IT:

1. Enterprises must take the risk of software or hardware malfunction.
2. Substituting and updating infrastructure is time-consuming and unsafe.
3. Enterprises pay for IT investment, which is not its business focus.

2.4.1.2.2 Capital Expenditure with Cloud Computing Service

With the help of cloud computing, enterprises can almost terminate its IT department and the cloud provider can take up the role of the IT department. Cloud computing can do the following:

1. Dynamically upgrade and ensure patch management of software and hardware.
2. Dynamically deploy and deliver infrastructure for enterprises.
3. Recover from a self-breakdown or any system disaster.
4. Automatically backup data and perform consistency checks.

2.4.1.2.2.1 Benefits

Following are some key benefits of cloud computing:

1. Enterprises can move its effort to its business focus.
2. Enterprises can pay a cloud provider for only as many as services as they use.
3. Enterprises can reconfigure their IT services in a short time.

2.4.1.2.3 What Does Cloud Computing Achieve?

Table 2.2 depicts the differences between traditional IT and cloud computing in terms of capital expenditures.

Table 2.2 Differences between traditional IT and cloud computing with respect to capital expenditures

Matrices	Traditional IT	Cloud Computing
Business Focus	The enterprise needs to own its IT department.	A cloud provider takes care of everything.
Payment	The enterprise pays for all assets and human resource.	The enterprise pays as per the service used.
Time Duration	Establishment time is lengthy.	Business readiness is quick.

2.4.1.3 Improvement in Industrial Specialization

In traditional industry and market, each enterprise has to have its own IT department with the IT resource being managed by the organization itself. The administration of IT complexity is the responsibility of the enterprise itself.

2.4.1.3.1 Limitations

Following are the limitations with traditional industry:

1. IT department is not the business focus area of enterprises.
2. Most enterprises are not capable of preserving their IT resources.
3. Enterprises find it difficult to optimize their IT resource usage.

2.4.1.3.2 Collaboration with Cloud Providers

With the help of cloud computing, cloud providers centrally preserve IT infrastructure for clients and employ experts for administration and management. They emphasise on providing consistent IT services, and enterprises only rent the service they need.

2.4.1.3.3 Benefits

Following are the benefits of cloud computing:

1. Enterprises can be assured of more industrial specialization.
2. Enterprises' business focus will improve.
3. The performance of IT services will be optimized.
4. IT resource waste will be compact.

2.4.1.3.4 What Does Cloud Computing Achieve?

Table 2.3 shows the differences between traditional IT and cloud computing in terms of collaboration.

Table 2.3 Differences between traditional IT and cloud computing with respect to industrial specialization

Matrices	Traditional IT	Cloud Computing
Collaboration	The enterprise needs to take care of everything.	The enterprise minds its own business.
Management and Control	The enterprise works with inadequate manageability.	A cloud provider provides professional control.
Industry Relationship	It is a standalone enterprise.	It is a win–win partnership.

2.4.1.4 Improvement in Resource Utilization

In traditional industry, the enterprise rarely takes care of IT resource utilization. It keeps its IT resource without proper management and this resource is typically overinvested for topmost demand.

2.4.1.4.1 Limitations

Following are the limitations of resource utilization in traditional industry:

1. IT assets across enterprises cannot be shared.
2. Power and space consumption among enterprises are lost.

2.4.1.4.2 Collaboration with Cloud Providers

IT resources are optimized and centrically managed by cloud providers. They manage cooling the system with optimized hardware. The provider also has serious concerns about legal policy and geographic issues.

2.4.1.4.3 Benefits

Following are the benefits of cloud computing:

1. Performance of IT infrastructure and utilization can be enhanced.
2. IT infrastructure can be shared among enterprises.
3. Large-scale integrated optimization can be more practical.

2.4.1.4.4 What Does Cloud Computing Achieve?

Table 2.4 shows the differences between traditional IT and cloud computing in terms of resource utilization.

Table 2.4 Differences between traditional IT and cloud computing with respect to resource utilization

Matrices	Traditional IT	Cloud Computing
IT Resource Utilization	IT resource underutilization is a problem.	Enables sharing to increase the consumption of IT resource.
Power Consumption	Wastage of power and cooling system is a problem.	A cloud system should be worldwide optimized.

2.4.2 For End Users and Individuals

Let us understand in detail about the benefits of cloud computing for end users and individuals.

2.4.2.1 Reduction in Local Computing Power

In traditional local computing power, if you are to purchase a personal computer, you think about a powerful processor if you need intensive computing. You also need large memory capacity to meet application requirement, and you may have to install many applications to fulfill your needs.

2.4.2.1.1 Limitations

Following are some limitations of the traditional storage system:

1. Regular update and upgradation of software and hardware are required.
2. It is difficult to replicate the entire environment.
3. If an operating system is reinstalled, all applications need to be reinstalled, too.

With the help of cloud computing, you can utilize the remote computing power in the cloud and need you only elementary computing power to connect to the Internet. Applications in the cloud are automatically upgraded.

2.4.2.1.2 Benefits

Following are the benefits of cloud computing:

1. A customer can dynamically request for computing power on demand.
2. A customer can access his/her applications everywhere over the Internet.
3. An application does not require reinstallation even if the operating system is reinstalled.

2.4.2.1.3 What Does Cloud Computing Achieve?

Table 2.5 lists the differences between traditional IT and cloud computing in terms of computing power.

Table 2.5 Differences between traditional IT and cloud computing with respect to end-user experience

Matrices	Traditional IT	Cloud Computing
Hardware Necessity	The user wants to buy powerful hardware.	Only necessary hardware is required for connecting to the Internet.
Software Necessity	Application has to be installed in the local computer.	No installation is necessary on the system.
Portability	It is not really portable.	It is natively portable.

2.4.2.2 Reduction in Local Storage Power

In traditional local storage systems, all the programs, official data and customer-related data are stored in local devices, and it is customer's responsibility to take the regular backups to avoid any risk of hard disk crash.

2.4.2.2.1 Limitations

Following are the limitations of traditional storing:

1. Storage space may be over-needed, which results in resource waste.
2. Storage space may not be enough for burst data requirement.
3. Part of the storage space has to be sacrificed for data backup.
4. Data consistency is hard to preserve between computers.

With the help of cloud computing, user programs and data files are stored in the cloud. The cloud service provider guarantees data availability.

2.4.2.2.2 Benefits

Following are the benefits of cloud computing:

1. Users can dynamically distribute storage space on demand.

2. Users can access data everywhere over the Internet.
3. Users do not need to worry about data consistency between computers or devices.
4. Users do not need to worry about data loss due to hardware loss.

2.4.2.2.3 What Does Cloud Computing Achieve?

Table 2.6 shows the differences between traditional and cloud computing in terms of storage power.

Table 2.6 Differences between traditional IT and cloud computing with respect to storage

Matrices	Traditional IT	Cloud Computing
Storage Space	Limited to local disk, may be less consumed.	Dynamically allocated on demand.
Storage Data Consistency	Hard to retain data consistency.	Data consistency continued by cloud.
Availability	Consistent user backup.	Cloud service assurance.

2.4.2.3 Variety of End Devices

In traditional computing, one can connect to the Internet from an individual PC or systems (laptop, tablet, smartphone, etc.). PCs can bring sufficient computing power but a minor device cannot perform data-intensive computation because of its power and hardware limitation.

2.4.2.3.1 Limitations

Following are the limitations with traditional end devices:

1. Computing power is not movable.
2. Small devices can only perform basic work.

Using cloud services, a device connects to the Internet via wireless or a wired network, and these devices access cloud services via the Web service interface. Then these devices send computational work into the cloud and wait for further results.

2.4.2.3.2 Benefits

Following are the benefits of cloud computing:

1. The user can utilize approximately limitless computing power at any place and time.
2. The user can utilize all types of offered services in the cloud with small smart devices.
3. Small smart devices can also be managed through the cloud.

2.4.2.3.3 What Does Cloud Computing Achieve?

Table 2.7 lists the differences between traditional and cloud computing in terms of device collaboration.

Table 2.7 Differences between traditional IT and cloud computing with respect to end devices

Matrices	Traditional IT	Cloud Computing
Small Device Intelligence	Functionalities are restricted because of their power consumption.	Transfer computing-intensive jobs into cloud, and then wait for results.
Computing Power	Can be accessed only through a desk-top computer.	Can be accessed via small smart devices.

2.5 Cloud Service and Deployment Models

Cloud computing has three service models and four deployment models. Let us first discuss the service models.

2.5.1 Service Models

Cloud computing combines various services. It is the same as choosing a service according to your needs. Let us take a real-time scenario from your daily life. You move to a new city and are looking for a place to live. What choices do you have?

1. Constructing a new house.
2. Buying a house.
3. Staying in a hotel.

If you were to choose to construct a house, you can control everything you want your new house to have. But that is hard work.

Instead, if you buy a house, you can customize only certain parts of the house, but you will most likely not be able to change the original architecture.

Now, how about if you choose to stay in a hotel? Staying in a hotel would probably be a better idea if your concern is enjoying life. You need to nothing with the hotel except staying in it.

Let us translate above analogy to cloud computing.

What if you want to have an IT department?

1. **Similar to constructing a new house:** Opt for the *Infrastructure as a Service* (IaaS) solution, which allows to rent some virtualized infrastructure and develop your own IT system from among those resources, which you may control entirely.
2. **Similar to buying a house:** Opt for the *Platform as a Service* (PaaS) solution, which lets you develop your IT system through one cloud platform without at all bothering about lower-level resource management.

3. **Similar to staying in a hotel:** Opt for the *Software as a Service* (SaaS) solution, which lets you use pre-existed IT system solutions that were provided by some cloud application service providers, without ever having to know anything about how these services were accomplished.

2.5.2 Cloud Providers

A cloud provider is any organization that delivers some element of cloud computing – classically IaaS, PaaS or SaaS – to other businesses or individuals. Cloud providers are also referred to as *cloud service providers* or *CSPs*.

When you estimate cloud costs, you have to consider several things:

- Type of cloud service
- Instance running cost
- Memory and CPU utilization
- Database running cost
- Storage cost
- Data transfer cost
- Additional security implementation cost

The cost is usually based on the pay-per-use utility model, but to handle sensitive data. The physical location of the servers could also become an essential factor to consider.

2.5.3 Cloud Service Models

There are three service models of cloud computing (Figs. 2.8 and 2.9):

1. IaaS
2. PaaS
3. SaaS

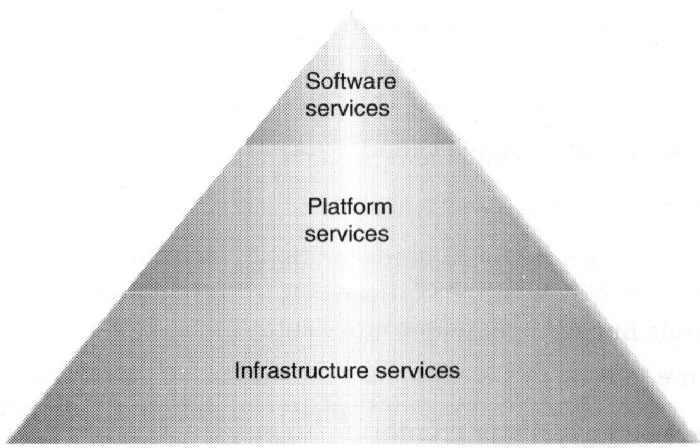

Figure 2.8 | Three main cloud services.

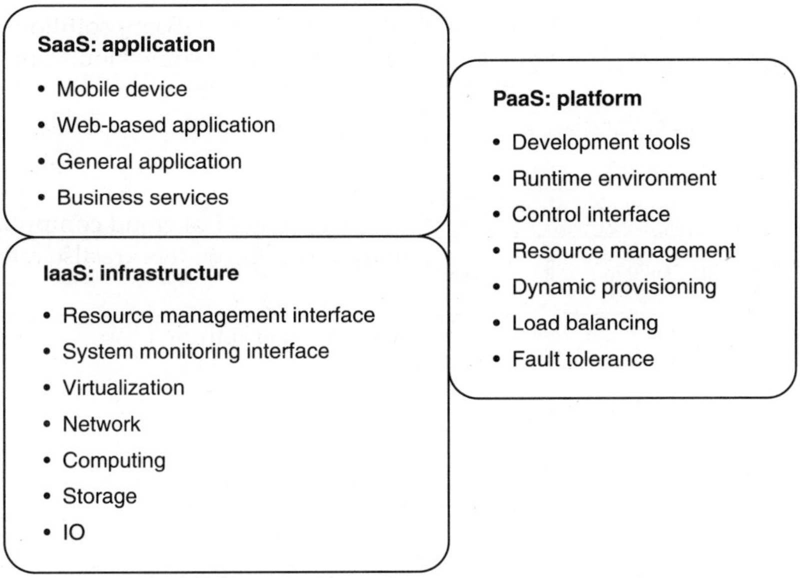

Figure 2.9 | Cloud service models overview.

Let us now understand each service model in detail.

2.5.3.1 Infrastructure as a Service

IaaS means renting hardware. The IaaS service offers raw infrastructure resources that are the base requirement for the establishment of a data center such as network, storage, processing power, memory, bandwidth, operating system installations, and overall network and system administration.

The most revolutionary benefit of IaaS is that customers do not require to manage or to control the system-, storage- and network administration–related tasks. Customers can dynamically make provisions for all their infrastructure resources on demand basis. They can select a particular resource and customize it according to their requirement. Following are some IaaS providers and their services:

- Amazon's EC2 or Elastic Compute Cloud
- Rackspace's Cloud Servers
- Flexiant's FlexiScale
- GoGrid's Cloud Hosting and Storage
- Google's Compute Engine
- Microsoft's Azure

The billing models also contain daily or monthly subscription plans or the "pay-as-you-go" billing in addition to data transfer – "server RAM hours" (GoGrid), and separate cloud storage billing.

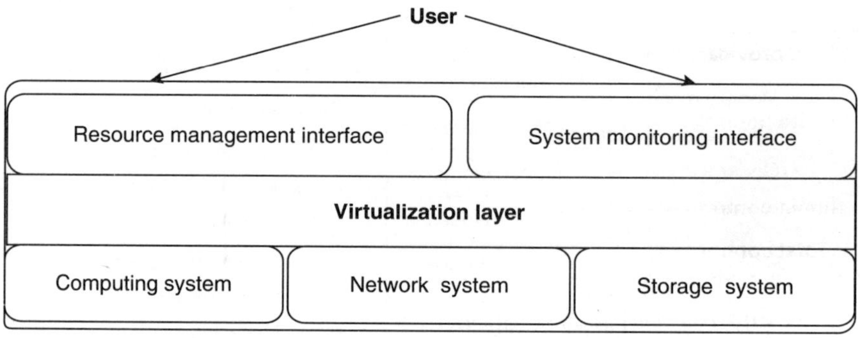

Figure 2.10 | System architecture of IaaS.

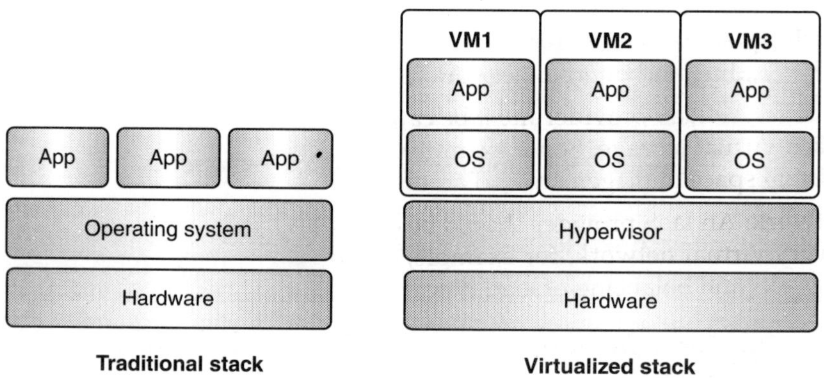

Figure 2.11 | Traditional stack and virtualization stack.

2.5.3.1.1 System Architecture

Virtualization is the main enabling technique in the IaaS system architecture (Fig. 2.10). It is the abstraction of logical resources away from fundamental physical resources. The virtualization technique move the OS onto the hypervisor and with the help of this technique, multiple OS share the physical hardware and offer different services. It increases availability, utilization, security and accessibility (Fig. 2.11).

Elasticity, scalability, reliability and availability are the key features of cloud that become available because of this virtualization effect.

2.5.3.1.2 Main Service of IaaS

The main service of IaaS is *resource management interface*, which is experienced by users in reality; it means managing several types of virtual resources. Figure 2.12 shows the IaaS component stack and scope of controls defined by NIST. The figure clearly shows the components that are controlled by IaaS cloud provider and that are controlled by cloud subscribers.

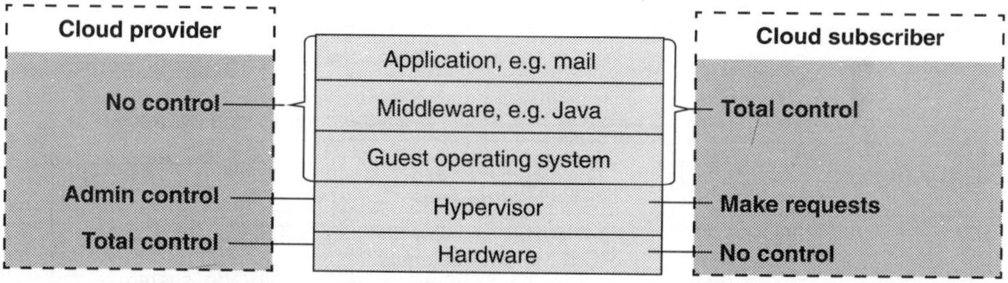

Figure 2.12 | IaaS component stack and scope of control.

2.5.3.1.3 Types of Virtualized Resources

Following are the various types of virtualized resources:

1. **Virtual machine:** An IaaS provider must be capable of controlling system states. Memory utilization, CPU loading and internal network loading are some examples of virtual machines.
2. **Virtual storage:** An IaaS provider must be capable of controlling and monitoring the storage states of each virtual storage. Some examples are duplication of data information, effective usage of virtual space management and access bandwidth.
3. **Virtual network:** An IaaS provider should be capable of controlling and monitoring network states of every virtual network; for example, connectivity between networks, bandwidth of virtual networks and balancing of load of each network.

2.5.3.2 Platform as a Service

PaaS is a computing platform offered through the Web. Web applications can be created and codes deployed without purchasing any license software or hardware. PaaS offerings are specific to Web developers, Web designers and application developers. According to NIST 2009:

The consumer does not manage or control the underlying cloud infrastructure including network, servers, operating systems or storage, but has control over the deployed applications and possibly application hosting environment configurations.

Some PaaS providers and the environments they provide are as follows:

- Microsoft's Azure
- Google's App Engine
- Salesforce.com's Force.com
- VM Ware's Cloud Foundry
- Engine Yard

2.5.3.2.1 System Architecture

Platform services provide an end-to-end application development environment for developers (Fig. 2.13).

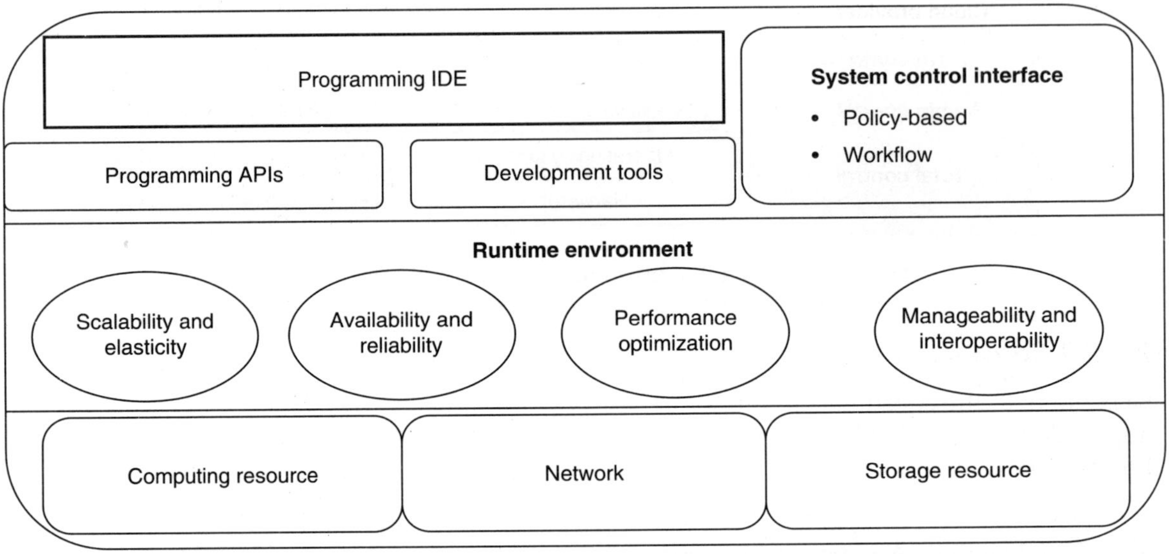

Figure 2.13 | System architecture of PaaS.

In the PaaS system architecture, the main enabling technique is the *Runtime Environment Design*. Runtime environment refers to the gathering of software services accessible. It is usually implemented by a collection of program libraries.

2.5.3.2.2 Main Services of PaaS

Following are the two main features of PaaS experienced by users:

1. **Programming IDE:** Users can use programming integrated development environment (IDE) to develop their offered services in PaaS. This IDE integrates all development functionalities together which are supporting it from runtime environment. The IDE should also offer certain development tools such the debugger, profiler and testing environment.
2. **System control interface:** PaaS also facilitates the system control interface in following two ways:
   - *Police-based control*: Classically defined as a principle or rule to guide decisions and attain rational outcomes, it makes decisions according to some requirements.
   - *Workflow control*: It defines the flow of installation and configuration of resources. Different workflow processes bring quick and efficient construction and management of cloud.

Figure 2.14 shows the PaaS component stack and scope of control as defined by NIST.

PaaS includes development environment, programming languages, compilers, deployment mechanism and testing tools. In some cases, Google's App Engine, the developers may download the development environment and use them locally in the developer's infrastructure or the developer may access tools in the provider's infrastructure over a browser.

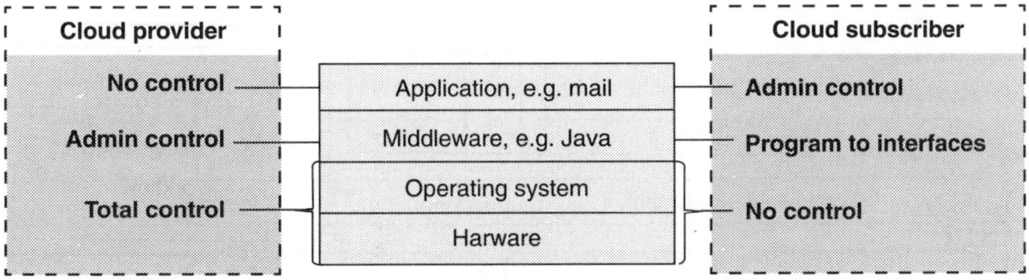

Figure 2.14 | PaaS component stack and scope of control.

2.5.3.3 Software as a Service

SaaS offers to the consumers applications over the Web that run on a cloud infrastructure. These applications are available from several client devices via a thin client interface such as a Web browser, for example, email.

Consumers need not worry about the fundamental cloud infrastructure, servers, storage, operating system, application abilities and procedures of deployment. The SaaS service model delivers the services as applications to the consumer, using standardized interfaces. The services run on top of a cloud infrastructure, which is obscure to the consumer.

In a SaaS offering, the cloud provider is only responsible for the control and management of the underlying infrastructure, the operating system and the applications. Subscribers can only control some user-specific and application-related settings.

Some SaaS providers and their offerings are as follows:

- Google's Google Apps such as Gmail, Google Docs and Google sites
- Apple's iCloud
- Panda Security's Panda Cloud Internet Protection (PCIP), Panda Cloud Office Protection (PCOP) and Panda Cloud Email Protection
- Intuit's Mint.com
- Workday
- eyeOS Web Engine
- Microsoft's Office 365
- Google Drive
- Microsoft One drive
- Dropbox

2.5.3.3.1 System Architecture

In the SaaS system architecture, the main enabling technique is a Web service like Web2.0. Web 2.0 is a loosely defined intersection of Web application features that enables sharing, user's participation and collaboration on the World Wide Web.

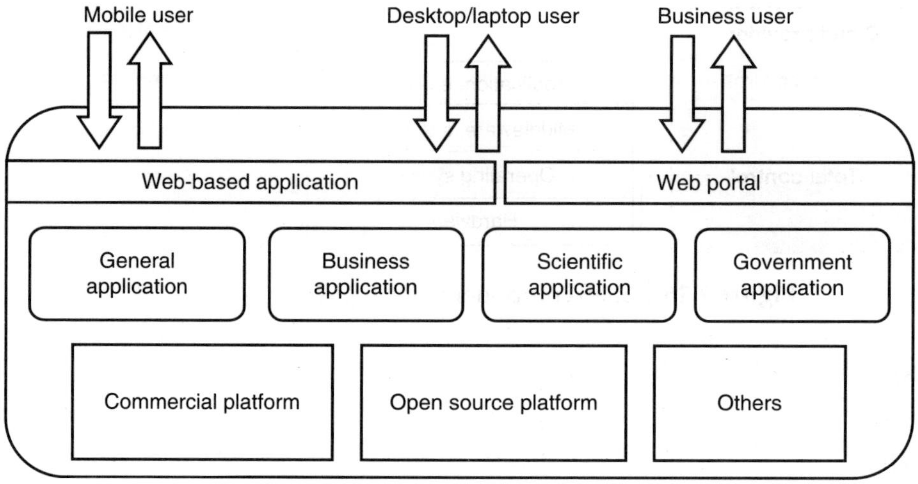

Figure 2.15 | System architecture of SaaS.

It is the new trend in using the Web to its full potential, such as:

- Viewing the Internet as a computing platform.
- Running interactive applications through Web browsers.
- Leveraging interconnectivity and mobility of devices.
- Enjoying enhanced effectiveness with greater human participation.
- Using properties provided by the Internet.

Let us understand system architecture of SaaS by Fig. 2.15.

It provides accessibility and portability through Web-based applications. Traditional applications first convert their access interfaces into a Web-based platform. Applications in different domains are as follows:

1. **General applications:** These applications are developed for our daily needs such as instant messaging, working with multimedia, making presentations and documentation. We can categorize this as a general purpose application.
2. **Business applications:** Applications that are designed for business proposes, such as ERP, CRM and market trading system.
3. **Scientific applications:** These applications are specifically designed for research and scientific purpose such as creating various types of simulation, for example, biomedical simulation and aerospace simulation.
4. **Government applications:** Applications that are designed for government proposes, such as national medical systems and public transportation system services.

Another SaaS offering is the *Web portal*. The Web portal also offers various services such as email, latest news, currency exchange rates and stock prices. Portals provide the enterprises with methods to offer a constant look and features with access control capability. Some examples are:

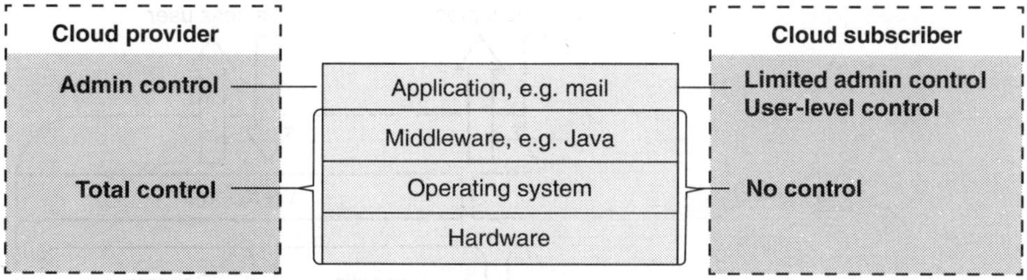

Figure 2.16 | SaaS component stack and scope of control.

- iGoogle
- Yahoo
- MSNBC
- Netvibes

Figure 2.16 illustrates the relative levels of control between the provider and the subscriber.

2.5.3.3.3 Classification Based on the Services Provided

On the basis of the services offered, clouds are classified as follows:

1. IaaS includes offering hardware-associated services using the principles of cloud computing. These could contain storage type of services (database or disk storage) or virtual servers. Some vendors that deliver IaaS are Amazon's S3, Amazon's EC2, Rackspace's Cloud Servers and FlexiScale.
2. PaaS includes offering a development platform on the cloud. Platforms offered by different vendors are characteristically not compatible. Typical PaaS players are Google (App Engine), VM Ware (Cloud Foundry), Microsoft (Azure) and Salesforce.com (force.com).
3. SaaS includes all application- and software-related offerings over the Web. Users can access software applications on a pay-per-use basis. This is a well-established sector. The innovator in this field has been Salesforce.com's offering in the online Customer Relationship Management (CRM) space. Other examples are online email providers such as Google (Gmail, Google Docs) and Microsoft (Hotmail, Office 365).

2.6 Organizational Scenario of Cloud: Cloud Deployment Model

The four primary cloud deployment models are as follows (Fig. 2.17):

1. Public cloud
2. Private cloud
3. Community cloud
4. Hybrid cloud

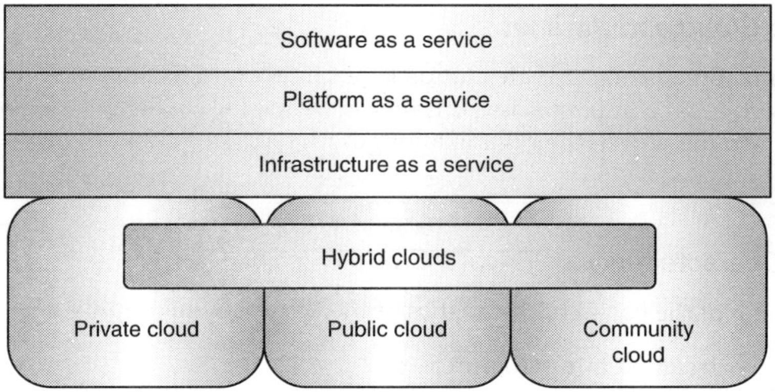

Figure 2.17 | Cloud deployment models.

Each type of cloud deployment model can demonstrate previously discussed characteristics, but difference lies in the access of cloud services. Let us understand each type of deployment model in detail.

2.6.1 Public Cloud

The cloud infrastructure is available to the general public or a large industry group, and the owner is an organization that sells cloud services. Public cloud is available for anyone including huge organization, mid-size or small industries and individuals. Because of its public accessibility, it is also known as external cloud.

2.6.1.1 Basic Characteristics of Public Cloud

Following are some of the basic characteristics of the public cloud deployment model:

- Uniformly designed infrastructure
- Common policies
- Resources occupied as a share
- Multi-tenant scenario – infrastructure rented or leased
- Economies of scale

2.6.2 PrivateCloud

The private cloud infrastructure is operated solely for an organization. A private cloud could be totally managed by the industry or the organization itself or by a third party, such as an outsourcing service, and the third party service could be present on or off premise. On-premises cloud, local cloud and internal cloud are other names for a private cloud. Private clouds generally have limited features when compared to public clouds, but they could be fully customized as per organizational needs.

2.6.2.1 Private Cloud and Intranet

The size of organizations using private clouds is not important. It could be a small company or a huge MNC. In fact, most companies use intranet in their offices. The private cloud model can be delivered using intranet within the organization, though private cloud model is accessible via the Internet as well.

2.6.2.2 Basic Characteristics of Private Cloud

Following are some of the basic characteristics of the private cloud deployment model:

- Non-uniformly designed infrastructure
- Custom and modified policies
- Specific resources
- Internal infrastructure
- End-to-end control

Table 2.8 lists the exact difference between public and private clouds on the basis of cloud infrastructure performance matrices.

Table 2.8 Comparison between public cloud and private cloud

Matrices	Public Cloud	Private Cloud
Policy Model	Provider defined	Customized and personalized
Resource Model	Shared and Multi-tenant	Dedicated
Cost Model	Pay-per-use basis	Pay-per-use basis
Scalability	Unlimited	Limited
Infrastructure Type	Homogeneous	Heterogeneous

2.6.3 Community Cloud

Community cloud shares infrastructure between numerous organizations from an explicit community with common requirements, such as security, mission, compliance, policy and jurisdiction, and is controlled internally by a third party, which could be hosted internally or externally. The costs of the community cloud are spread over less number of users compared to those with the public cloud (but more than those with a private cloud), so only some of the advantages of cloud computing are recognized.

2.6.4 Hybrid Cloud

Hybrid cloud is a combination of two or more cloud deployment models, where at least one private cloud and one public cloud coexist. A hybrid cloud is classically accessible in the following two ways:

1. A vendor has a private cloud and forms a corporation with a public cloud provider.
2. A public cloud provider forms a partnership with a vendor that offers private cloud platforms.

A hybrid cloud is a cloud computing scenario in which an organization offers and manages some resources in house and simultaneously has other external providers. For example, one industry uses the Amazon public cloud and the AWS S3 service for data archival but simultaneously maintains in-house storage related to sensitive customer data.

Preferably, the hybrid method allows a business to take benefit of the more scalability, security and cost effectiveness for critical business application. This kind of hybrid cloud is also known to as *hybrid IT*.

2.7 Cloud Architecture

Cloud computing architecture is a general high-level view to visualize the structure of the system, various cloud resources, middleware, software components, services and relationships among them. Figure 2.18 represents the cloud computing architectural view.

Users can use various services according to their choice and usage; service providers provide those services with the help of various virtualization techniques. The customer cannot see the hidden complexities of the cloud provider such as data centers and VM management. They only see the Web interface through which various services are offered simultaneously and all these services are metered according to usage. These users may be business users, developers or home users who mainly use IaaS, PaaS and SaaS.

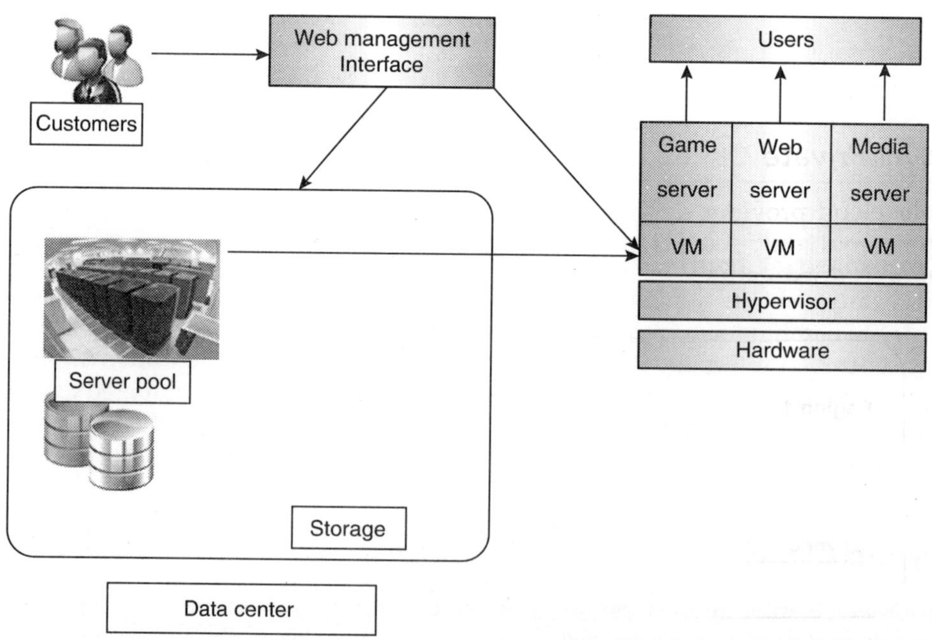

Figure 2.18 | Cloud architecture.

2.8 Cloud Vocabulary

It is necessary to be familiar with some cloud computing–specific terms and jargons. Following are some examples.

2.8.1 Machine Image

Machine image is a virtual application for initiating or creating a virtual machine that runs within the cloud infrastructure. Machine images contain the images of different operating system such as Linux and Window server. After initiating machine image, the virtual machine is immediately ready to use. All types of virtualization techniques will be discussed in Chapter 4.

2.8.2 Cloud Instances

In the cloud computing environment, a cloud instance refers to one virtual machine or virtual server. Cloud infrastructure service providers make a variety of instance offerings. Usually, a machine image is used for initializing cloud instances.

2.8.3 Regions and Availability Zones

Cloud service providers generally build their own infrastructure in multiple locations across the world and all physical locations are divided into regions and availability zones. A region is a geographically distributed area where multiple isolated locations of data center are identified as availability zones.

Figure 2.19 shows the multiple availability zones in one region.

2.8.4 Virtual Private Cloud

When a public cloud provider offers you an isolated portion of a cloud fully dedicated to your organization without multi-tenants, it is known as *virtual private cloud* (VPC). VPC is preferred for acquiring more security features.

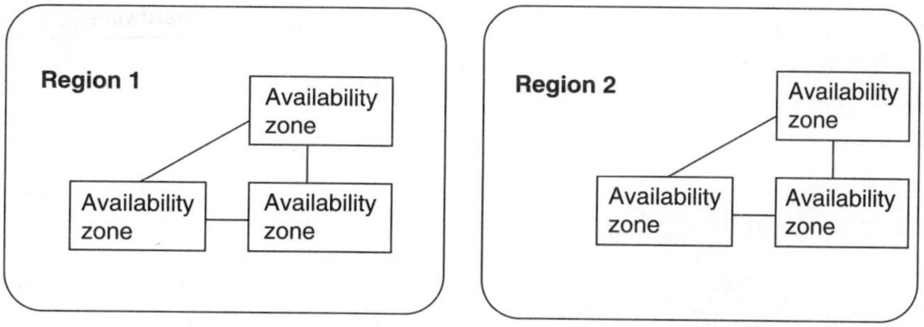

Figure 2.19 | Regions and availability zones.

2.8.5 Cloud Burst

Cloud burst is a specific situation that indicates the failure of the cloud computing environment to handle the spikes of on-demand workloads.

2.9 Challenges with Cloud Computing

Following are some of the major challenges cloud service providers face while offering a variety of infrastructure, platform and software services to consumers.

1. **Security:** Cloud security always has been a prime concern for every organization and individuals. All surveys also indicate that customers are more concerned about security on cloud. Therefore, it is a significant challenge for cloud providers to enable various security features on every layer and provide assurance of data protection to all customers.
2. **Quality of services:** While dealing with external cloud providers, quality of service is a defining success factor outlined in the service-level agreement (SLA) as integral to the partnership. Quality of service must be accomplished by the cloud provider because the SLA sets expectations for both parties and acts as the roadmap for transforming the quality of services in cloud.
3. **Integration of services:** Many applications require some complex integration, where connection of on-premises applications or connection with other cloud providers also becomes necessary. In this case, proper integration is extremely important to offer a quick and simple interface of service offering.
4. **High network response time:** Providing complex and exhaustive computing services over the Internet is quite challenging for cloud providers. Therefore, enabling high bandwidth and network performance in their own data centers at cheaper costs is difficult in the face of current market competition.
5. **The problem of metering:** In cloud services, users pay only for the amount of usage. This business model looks attractive at the beginning, but in the long run, it does not prove any cheaper. For example, living in rented room for a very long time becomes costlier than purchasing a new house.

It is the responsibility of consumers to be aware about the cloud resources usage especially in infrastructure services. Nowadays, cloud infrastructure providers offer a variety of usage plans. Consumers must select the optimum plan and consider some reserved plans if necessary; for example, AWS offers a reserved instance if you intend to host the service for a long duration and your Website traffic does not have much fluctuation.

2.10 Cloud-Supporting Services

Apart from the three prominent services (IaaS, PaaS and SaaS), there are various services offered by cloud providers for enhancing collaboration and effective utilization of resources. Here we will learn about those offered services.

2.10.1 Cloud Storage Service

Cloud storage services are the most important offerings in the IaaS model. Following are two types of storage services of cloud computing:

1. **Object storage:** Object storage is basically an object-based store, which means different discrete units of objects. Cloud providers offer object storage capability for enabling online storage capability. Object storage is a medium to store unlimited amount of data from any location using a simple Web interface and stored objects are highly scalable, available, secure and quickly accessible. It is the same as the pen drive we use for storing different objects.
2. **Block storage:** Block storage provides persistent virtual block mode storage for cloud virtual servers, so we can use it just like a hard drive on a physical server. Block storage services are mostly fit for use as the primary storage for a file system, database or any other application that requires regular granular updates and access to raw, unformatted block-level storage. The high-level view of block storage service is similar to the hard disk we use in our computer system, where the operating system can be installed and the file can be saved.

2.10.2 Cloud Database Service

Most of the giant cloud providers offer both types of relational and non-relational database services nowadays. Cloud Database Service is a kind of Web service that makes it easy to set up, operate and scale a relational or non-relational database in the cloud.

Cloud database services provide resizable capacity while taking care of cheaper cost and less database management efforts so that we can focus on developing applications rather than on database administration–related tasks. A cloud relational database service allows automatic software backups of databases and regular patch ups. We can also enable backup retention period and recovery point in time. We will learn more about cloud database in the subsequent chapters.

Along with storage services, there are other services as well that are equally important for hosting and delivery of any Web-based application on a cloud. Let us get some idea about those services offerings.

2.10.3 Cloud Load-Balancing Services

Many cloud computing providers offer load-balancing services that are quite attractive when it comes to handling unexpected traffic of hosted applications or Websites and uneven load. This service provides great fault tolerance capacity in hosted applications. Generally, all major cloud infrastructure and platform providers offer load-balancing and auto-scaling services.

2.10.4 Cloud Backup and Disaster-Recovery Services

Cloud providers offer various backup and disaster-recovery services. A disaster-recovery plan can be built if some good architectural approach is being followed when designing cloud infrastructure for an organization.

Cloud providers also offer data archival and backup facility in both online and offline modes. They generally take the replica of the data in multiple regions and availability zones.

Usually, all giant cloud providers have global data centers across the globe, so if any data center experiences outage, some other data center is immediately capable of handling the data and entire load of the data center with the problem. They build their infrastructure in such a way that it is highly reliable, consistent, always available and completely fault tolerant.

2.11 Management and Administration of Cloud Services

When handling cloud computing services, a company has to ask itself many questions about the efficiency of various services. The supervisors must know if the performance is at the expected level, and they must be able to tell if data deleted is actually gone. You have to do a lot of market research when evaluating the providers. Here is a list of issues to consider:

1. What vendors are available to solve your problem?
2. How effective are the providers in managing their individual environment?
3. How do these vendors handle an outage?
4. Do they offer frequent services always?
5. What is their experience in negotiation with customer issues?

2.11.1 Business Continuity Management

Cloud service providers offer fast content distributions and high-speed data migration services from one region or availability zone to another region or availability zone. Therefore, businesses across the globe are never interrupted and continuity is always maintained.

2.11.2 System Reliability

Examining the reliability and feasibility of a cloud provider is one of the most complex areas faced when managing the cloud. It is mainly essential for the IT industry to allow administration systems that let them monitor every dimension of the service they are receiving.

Although the cloud service provider can build and provide a very constant service that is less expensive than a customer can implement internally, there could be a big difference between the promises made in sales text by the provider and the actual service rendered.

2.11.3 Fault Tolerance

As we have understood, a cloud provider enables various fault tolerance features to provide high availability of services, but it is also the shared responsibility of consumers and providers to develop fault tolerant applications. If we use the IaaS feature, then it is the responsibility of the system or solution architect to design a fault tolerant application that can leverage maximum and optimal utilization of cloud resources.

2.11.4 Response Time

Generally, customers are more concerned about the response time than the overall performance because the response time creates the first impact of a service offering. The workload in cloud computing is quite dynamic in nature and changes according to the service request of users. It is, therefore, the responsibility of the cloud provider to continuously monitor the response time of the virtual servers and other resources to ensure quality of service and then, if required, always enable high response time across the globe.

Summary

This chapter has given us a detailed understanding of cloud computing concepts and the benefits and challenges associated with cloud.

The chapter has provided various definitions of cloud computing and has outlined in detail the central idea of cloud computing with explanations of each technique. It has listed the exact differences between various traditional computing and cloud computing features. The chapter has also introduced several commonly used cloud vocabulary, and has provided a high-level view of cloud architecture.

The chapter has showed both the aspects of cloud computing – the cloud provider's view and the cloud subscriber's view – and the individual benefits of cloud computing. The next chapter discusses each of the cloud services in detail and about various giant cloud providing companies and their offerings.

Multiple Choice Questions

1. Infrastructure as a service is like _______.
   (a) Constructing a new house
   (b) Buying an empty house
   (c) Staying in a hotel
   (d) Staying on lease

2. Identify the type of cloud services in which runtime environment is offered.
   (a) IaaS
   (b) SaaS
   (c) PaaS
   (d) Is not a type of cloud service

3. Identify the kind of cloud service of which on-line storage like Google Drive is an example.
   (a) PaaS
   (b) SaaS
   (c) IaaS
   (d) Both IaaS and SaaS

4. What does/do Microsoft Azure offer?
   (a) PaaS
   (b) PaaS and IaaS
   (c) IaaS and SaaS
   (d) IaaS

5. Virtual private cloud (VPC) is _______.
   (a) Secure cloud
   (b) Isolated portion of cloud
   (c) Private cloud
   (d) Hybrid cloud

6. Availability zones exist _______.
   (a) Within a region
   (b) Outside a region
   (c) Both inside and outside
   (d) None of these

7. Which one of the following storage services is similar to pen drive storage?
   (a) Block storage
   (b) Object storage
   (c) Instance storage
   (d) Content delivery

8. Cloud computing is combination of utility computing, SLA and _______.
   (a) Virtualization
   (b) SOA
   (c) Web service
   (d) Distributed computing

9. Enabling technique of cloud computing according to provider's perspective is web service, virtualization and _______.
   (a) SOA
   (b) SLA
   (c) Parallelized and distributed computing
   (d) Utility computing

10. Nature of resource provisioning in cloud is _______.
    (a) Static
    (b) Sometimes dynamic
    (c) Strictly dynamic
    (d) Industry-dependent

11. Thin client program depends completely upon _______.
    (a) Same computer
    (b) Another computer

(c) Internal memory
(d) External memory

12. An organization which delivers some elements of cloud computing is called _______.
    (a) Cloud seller
    (b) Cloud provider
    (c) Cloud enabler
    (d) Cloud manager

13. Google compute engine is an example of _______.
    (a) SaaS
    (b) PaaS
    (c) IaaS
    (d) Both PaaS and IaaS

14. Scalability in private cloud is _______.
    (a) Unlimited
    (b) Limited
    (c) Depends on workload
    (d) Unpredictable

15. Hybrid cloud consists of at least _______.
    (a) One private cloud
    (b) One public cloud
    (c) One private and one public cloud
    (d) Two private clouds

16. What does horizontal scaling mean?
    (a) Addition of more machines
    (b) Addition of more computing power
    (c) Addition of cloud computing resources
    (d) Dynamic provisioning

Review Questions

1. Explain the high-level architectural view of cloud computing with a proper diagram.
2. Describe private cloud computing and differentiate between public and private cloud on the basis of cloud infrastructure parameters.
3. What do you understand by cloud storage system? What are the storage options available with cloud storage?
4. Explain the availability and reliability in terms of cloud computing and how these properties are achieved in cloud computing.
5. What are the four cloud deployment models? Explain each with examples.

6. What do you understand by Platform as a Service (PaaS)? Explain with the system architecture of PaaS.
7. What are the benefits of cloud computing for end users and individuals? Explain in detail.
8. What are the key challenges that cloud computing providers face?

Answers to Multiple Choice Questions

1. (a),	2. (c),	3. (b),	4. (b),	5. (b),	6. (a),	7. (b),	8. (b),
9. (c),	10. (c),	11. (b),	12. (b),	13. (c),	14. (b),	15. (c),	16. (a)

CHAPTER 3 Different Cloud Providers and Comparison of Services

Learning Objectives

After reading this chapter, you will be able to:

- Understand various cloud service providers and different types of their service offerings.
- Assess all existing cloud services and show how customers benefit from them.
- Learn about each service such as infrastructure, platform, software services and list the key benefits of each of these.
- Compare various cloud service providers.
- Understand the detailed architecture and service approach of cloud providing giants such as Amazon, Google and Microsoft.

3.1 Infrastructure Service Providers

This section discusses the most popular and successful cloud infrastructure service providers and their offerings. It focuses on public cloud infrastructure service providers, but private cloud providers are also briefly reviewed later in this chapter. This section also sheds light on competition in the existing cloud providers' market.

Some of the giant and well-reputed infrastructure providers in the current market scenario are discussed in the following subsections.

3.1.1 Amazon Web Services

Amazon Web Services (AWS) is one of the largest and most popular cloud Infrastructure as a Service (IaaS) providers. As we have learned from the preceding chapters, IaaS users are not bothered about the technicalities of software and applications. IaaS allows the underlying hardware and operating system resources to do anything a user wants.

AWS offers a CPU, memory, storage, networking and security as a packaged service. With AWS public cloud IaaS, you can choose from a range of operating systems including all major distribution of the Linux and Windows operating systems. You can define a size for your hardware (number of CPUs and CPU power) according to your requirement and unlimited storage.

3.1.1.1 Salient Features of AWS

AWS can help one architect scalable and on-demand IT infrastructure systems because it has the following key features:

1. **Reliability:** All cloud services run within Amazon's own tested datacenters that are highly available and fault tolerant and those which Amazon uses to run its own business.
2. **Instant security:** Amazon provides high security and authentication mechanism to all AWS users. Users can also build an extra security layer and more granular-level access to their AWS account according to their hosted application and specific requirements. AWS allows various third-party tools for providing specific security solutions on the top of the AWS infrastructure.
3. **Cost benefits:** There are no fixed or maintenance costs. Users pay for services as they go, and scale their resources and budget as needed.
4. **Ease of development:** AWS provides various APIs, easy console access and also command-line interface for accessing cloud services. Users can easily learn them and apply these quickly.
5. **Elasticity:** Users can scale up or scale down their computing resources on an on-demand basis. They can go from one to any number of servers quickly to serve their application needs.
6. **Cohesiveness:** The core building blocks (storage, computing and networking, database, and deployment and management) of AWS work together. All these building blocks serve all the needs of the variety of hosted applications.
7. **Community support:** AWS provides exemplary community support for any kind of user query related to the AWS setup and for the troubleshooting of any issue. It also provides different types of forums and blogs where customers can share their experiences and receive technical advice from experts.

3.1.2 Rackspace Cloud

Rackspace is one of the most attractive public cloud providers. It offers various cloud services in which cloud infrastructure services are prominent. Rackspace enables very high-quality storage area network (SAN) and all up-to-date hardware in its datacenters.

Rackspace also offers databases, load balancing, backup and monitoring, and migration and cloud architectural planning services.

3.1.2.1 Salient Features of Rackspace Cloud

Following are the key features of Rackspace Cloud:

1. **Security and compliance:** Rackspace shares all datacenter security–related audit reports with its consumers. Rackspace already has the PCI DSS, ISO27002, ISO27001, Safe Harbor certification and SSAE16, SOC1/2/3 audit reports.

2. **Built-in redundancy:** Rackspace provides dedicated hardware and network support for enabling redundancy across its global datacenters. Rackspace has built its datacenters with the latest hardware, RAID-enabled servers, Cisco firewall and highly managed backup systems that help to quickly recover in case of datacenter outage or counter any disaster situation.
3. **100% network uptime:** Rackspace offers almost 100% network uptime for all services. The service-level agreement provides assurance to customers they can rely on. Rackspace infrastructure services are always available so that consumers can just focus on their businesses.
4. **All-time access to cloud engineers:** Apart from regular customer support, Rackspace also provides support for various cloud operational tasks for reducing the engineer's workload. Rackspace has a dedicated team of engineers to support the cloud operations of the user's organization. It also assists to design the user's cloud architecture for optimal utilization of Rackspace's cloud resources. It provides 24 × 7 × 365 support.

3.1.3 Google Compute Engine

Google Compute Engine (GCE), launched in 2013, is the IaaS feature of Google Cloud Platform. GCE's cloud instances support almost all types of Linux- and Window-based operating systems. It provides hassle-free and easy-to-understand cloud console interfaces for all its users.

GCE's performance and quality of services (QoS) are also very high compared with those of other providers. In addition, the time taken by GCE in instance creation is quite less and its application launching is also very fast.

GCE also provides integration with other services according to business requirements such as BigQuery, Google Cloud Storage and Google Cloud SQL.

3.1.3.1 Salient Features of GCE

GCE offers some salient features that give it a very competitive edge over other IaaS providers. Some of those features are as follows:

1. **Pricing and sub-hour billing:** GCE offers a very attractive feature known as sub-hour billing that other IaaS providers do not offer. In GCE, machine types are charged for a minimum of 10 min, and after 10 min the user just needs to pay for 1 min increment of usage, which means it is a true pay-per-use model. This makes the GCE offering very lucrative to all consumers.
2. **High network throughput:** Google leverages its own infrastructure for offering IaaS. The same infrastructure is used by Google's other products such as YouTube and Custom Search Engine, which ensures that consumers also experience the same high performance and availability without any delay. GCE also enables the facility to replicate the database across regions.
3. **Multi-region images:** In GCE, every OS image acts as a global recourse, which is managed by a global repository. Global repository contains all the OS images and custom images of different customers as well.
4. **Faster boot times and auto-restart of virtual machines (VMs):** Provisioning of VMs takes very less time in GCE. Within 30 seconds of login, the VM is ready to use, which makes it a very impressive GCE feature.

5. **Live migration:** Sometimes cloud providers need to perform some maintenance and performance-testing activities across all their datacenters and host servers. Because of this planned activity, consumers face some downtime in the offered services. During the downtime, the cloud providers force their consumers to reboot their VMs for completing maintenance activities. GCE, on the other hand, provides graceful live migration facility from one datacenter to another, which is very transparent to its consumers. GCE also provides automatic restart facility just after the scheduled maintenance event.

3.1.4 Microsoft Azure Services

Microsoft Azure is a well-reputed cloud computing service provider in the IT market. It provides all the major cloud services related to infrastructure and platform. Earlier, it was popularly known as Windows Azure when it provided only cloud platform services. Microsoft Azure supports compute, data, app and network services.

In Microsoft Azure, the creation and management of a VM can be done in the following ways:

1. Window Azure Management Portal
2. PowerShell scripting
3. Secure Shell (SSH)

3.1.4.1 Salient Features of Microsoft Azure

Following are some of the key features of Microsoft Azure:

1. **Integrated service environment:** Microsoft Azure was already popular with its Platform as a Service (PaaS) offerings when it recently came up with its IaaS. This way, by providing layer-by-layer services, it has built a highly integrated service framework. Along with fundamental infrastructure services such as networking, storage and VMs, Azure provides integration with high-performance computing (HPC), identity management, media, commerce, software development kits, caching, messaging, commerce and data management services.
2. **Flexibility:** A VM provides an on-demand scalable computing infrastructure. Whenever there is a need, you can choose flexible resources and easily create a VM with pre-installed operating systems such as Linux and Windows that can run a business application. You have also an option for creating customized VMs by providing your own machine images.
3. **Business analytics and reporting:** Analyzing data and making business strategy accordingly are primarily the focus areas of every type of business. Microsoft Azure supports advance big data analytics and reporting features with a combination of Hadoop (big data processing tool), SQL database and VM; you can process a huge amount of data and can get a detailed report according to your business requirement.

3.1.5 GoGrid

GoGrid is a renowned cloud infrastructure service provider. It already has a very good track record for providing IT infrastructure–related services for various companies across the globe.

GoGrid cloud hosting enables customers to develop scalable business services along with taking care of load balancing, elasticity, and control automation and self-service portal.

3.1.5.1 Salient Features of GoGrid

Following are some of the key features of GoGrid:

1. **Secure and dedicated infrastructure:** The GoGrid Hosted Private Cloud resides on a dedicated infrastructure. It offers private machine instances that are comparatively more secure and dedicated to the user's infrastructure without any multi-tenancy arrangements to provide more security assurances to its customers.
2. **Infrastructure on demand:** The Web-based self-service portal allows the user to provision VMs, cloud storage, load balancers and private virtual local area networks (VLANs). The user's infrastructure will be up and running in record time. The usual procurement process for hardware that took six to eight weeks or longer has now become instantaneous. The user's company's strategic projects can begin immediately.
3. **Cost saving:** GoGrid's Hosted Private Cloud allows the user to convert the large capital expenditure of building a private cloud in-house to an affordable monthly cost. Large established businesses as well as cutting-edge technology companies rely on GoGrid for their critical infrastructure.

3.2 Key Benefits of Cloud Infrastructure Services

Following are the key benefits of selecting a cloud infrastructure provider:

1. **No upfront investment:** Whenever any organization plans to set up IT infrastructure, it needs to make huge investments in purchasing high-performance servers, network setup, cabling, high-speed bandwidth, administration, cooling and most importantly separate isolated land for setting up the ground requirement for the entire infrastructure. All the initial upfront costs could be nullified if using a cloud on-demand resource. Consumers pay only monthly bills as per utilization just like they would for any other utility.
2. **Full utilization of resources:** Traditional servers are almost underutilized, with server resource utilization being below 50% in datacenters. As we already know, cloud infrastructure services enable virtualization technology, which helps increase the performance and consolidation of underutilized server resources, mitigate the cost and provide effective utilization of all infrastructure resources.
3. **Instant scalability:** Traditional infrastructure cannot be scaled up an on-demand basis because of its limitations, whereas cloud infrastructure service provides instant on-demand scalability. You do not need to think and plan in advance for future scalability.
4. **Reliability and business continuity:** Yours could be either a large global company or a small start-up, but your customers could be located around the world. In traditional infrastructure, it is quite difficult to serve broadly distributed customers with the same network performance and continuity, with cloud infrastructure service. However, you can get 100% assurance of high-performance infrastructure and constant uptime for your business.

5. **Global reach of the offered services:** Cloud infrastructure services also offer fast content delivery and storage services. They offer the fastest delivery of any static and dynamic content through multiple datacenters located across the globe.
6. **Rapid changes and agility:** Traditional infrastructure takes approximately several weeks or months to get the server ready. A lot of time for server procurement, delivery, running and setting up the systems. With cloud infrastructure services, however, you can provision an on-demand server, irrespective of the number, be it one or be it thousand. All servers can be ready within few minutes as per your required configurations. You can change the settings of the server and customize according to your latest requirement, which brings agility at the infrastructure level.

3.3 Comparison Between Infrastructure Service Providers

Table 3.1 presents some technical and functional aspects of five different cloud infrastructure service providers.

Table 3.1 Functionality comparisons between different cloud infrastructure providers

Cloud Providers	Amazon Web Services	Rackspace Cloud	Microsoft Azure	Google Compute Engine	GoGrid
X-AAS	IaaS	IaaS	IaaS/PaaS	IaaS	PaaS/SaaS
Virtualization	OS level running Xen	OS level running Xen	OS level	Application container	Application container
Service Type	Compute storage (S3)	Compute storage	Compute storage framework	Compute Web	Compute Web application
Programming Framework	Linux Amazon machine image	N/A	MS .NET language	Python or Java	Apex Script or Visual Force (GUI)

3.4 Identification of Business Requirement for Choosing Any Cloud Infrastructure Provider

Cloud adoption is the buzzword in the IT market with many businesses having received tremendous success at optimized costs after cloud adoption. Before planning for cloud adoption, however, the first step is to ask: "Does our business really need cloud adoption?" This is the first and most important criterion to consider before approaching a cloud computing service provider. You must know for sure if you should migrate to cloud services or whether your organization really needs a cloud infrastructure service.

This section helps identify if you need cloud adoption.

If the answer to the following question is "Yes," then cloud infrastructure services definitely could be the best solution for your organization.

1. Is your business expecting a huge amount of upfront investment in IT infrastructure setup?
2. Is your business experiencing unavailability or less availability of services?

3. Is your business experiencing underutilization of resources?
4. Is your business finding difficulty in instant scalability and disaster recovery?

After identifying true business needs, we are going to study how cloud infrastructure can be set up.

3.5 Cloud Infrastructure Setup Procedure

Following is the standard procedure for setting up a cloud infrastructure service:

1. **Selecting an infrastructure provider:** Once you have clearly identified your organizational requirement and prepared your list about which type of cloud services you wish to use, you could easily select any infrastructure cloud provider that aligns with your requirement and offers cheaper prices along with QoS. You must read some customer's feedback and case studies of that particular cloud provider before making a final decision. Security, interoperability, flexibility and service level agreements (SLA) are some important factors you must evaluate while selecting a cloud infrastructure service provider.
2. **Designing architecture:** Designing optimal architecture is the responsibility of the system architect and senior cloud engineers. The architectural design varies according to the requirements of the organization. A cloud infrastructure provider generally provides many services such as different types of storage options, different types of instances options and different types of backend database support, content delivery service, and big data and analytics-related services for handling enormous amount of data. Therefore, it is totally up to the system architect to intelligently design optimal architecture so that maximum benefits can be gained from the cloud with minimal use of resources to save huge monthly expenditure.
3. **Launching the services:** Once architecture is ready, it is time to launch the services according to specification. It takes from a few minutes to a few hours to launch all the services and do the required setting. For better practical understanding, following is a scenario of using the AWS cloud provider to launch the infrastructure services:
    - Select Amazon machine images or provide your own machine image.
    - Select the instances type.
    - Select network, subnet or private IP, if required.
    - Select security group.
    - Launch the database instances (if applicable).
    - Back the instances with EBS (elastic block storage or S3 and both).
    - Migrate the application onto instances.
    - Select CDN or Scalable DNS services (Route 53).
    - Set cloud watch for monitoring.
4. **Monitoring all resources:** Monitoring of all used cloud computing resources is an extremely important criterion in designing the roadmap for reducing further costs and making optimal utilization of resources. In the preceding section, cloud watch is a useful service for resource monitoring. Some third-party applications also provide detailed monitoring of services.

3.6 Platform Service Providers

This section analyzes the most popular and successful PaaS (Platform as a Service) providers and their offerings. The main consideration of PaaS offerings is to provide online a fully integrated development environment (IDE) for developing all types of businesses and personal applications. PaaS offerings are generally preferred by application developers and software and web designers. Some of the prominent PaaS providers are discussed in the following subsections.

3.6.1 Google App Engine

Since around 2008, Google App Engine (GAE) has come to considerable day-light theirs days. It gives the platform for development, deployment and hosting of Web application by Google-managed datacenter. It uses significant amount of virtualization for application process and for running multiple servers. Currently, GAE supports Java, Python and Go languages.

3.6.1.1 Architecture of GAE Hosting

Figure 3.1 clearly shows that irrespective of a multi-tenant environment, Google App Engine runs isolated. Although each application shares the resources along with other multi-tenant applications, the data and security of each tenant is private not shared. Application users cannot directly enter your application because communication ports are blocked for them.

3.6.1.2 Salient Features of GAE

Following are some of the salient features of GAE:

1. **Easy to start:** Developing applications with GAE is quite easy. All you need to do is write your application code, test it on your local machine and upload it onto GAE. Once uploaded, Google takes care of scalability. GAE provides very simple console management interface for managing your application tasks. You can manage all application management–related tasks with some simple clicks.

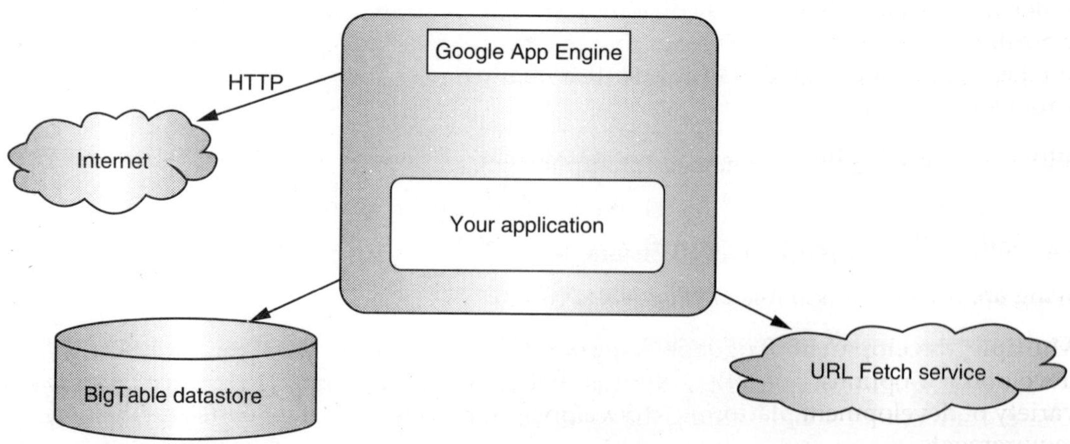

Figure 3.1 | GAE architecture.

2. **Automatic scalability:** All you need to do is write your application code and Google will take care of scalability because automatic scaling is a built-in feature of Google App Engine; the number of uses does not matter.
3. **Leveraging Google's infrastructure:** Because Google has already proven its capability for handling scalability, performance and security, by being a GAE user, you get all of Google's critical features for your project as well. This is the greatest advantage of a GAE user. Google has extremely scalable and high-performance systems. Being a GAE user, you inherit same security, privacy and data protection policies that Google apply for its own application development; for example, YouTube. Google takes care of all security issues of your applications and has measures in place to protect your code.
4. **Trial period option:** With GAE, you can create and publish your application freely so that people can use it free of cost. One application with a free account can use up to 1 GB of storage and afford almost 5 million page views per month. If you feel you require more, you can go ahead with the flexible billing options and allocate your resources within your budget.
5. **Multi-language support:** GAE now supports application development with Java, Python, Go and PHP. Developers have the option of going with any development environment according to their skill sets and business requirements.

3.6.2 Microsoft Azure

As we have learned, the IaaS services of Microsoft Azure was earlier known as Windows Azure and it has had a successful track record for providing PaaS. Earlier only the .Net based development platform was provided but now Microsoft Azure also supports Java, iOS, Node.js and Android-based development platforms.

3.6.2.1 Microsoft Azure PaaS Provider

Microsoft Azure provides a cloud operating system and does the same work as a traditional desktop operating system but on a bigger scale and for distributed applications. The Fabric Controller works exactly like a kernel of your desktop operating system; this fabric layer is capable of supporting thousands of servers running and working together as a unified unit. Microsoft Azure takes care of the whole platform so that the user can focus on the development of their applications only.

Figure 3.2 shows the differences between a traditional Windows server and Microsoft Azure.

3.6.2.2 Salient Features of Microsoft Azure

Following are the salient features of Microsoft Azure:

1. **Multiple development language support:** Microsoft Azure provides multiple language development options like .NET, Node.js, PHP, Python, Java and Ruby. Developers have a variety of development platforms to develop applications according to their key skill sets and requirements.

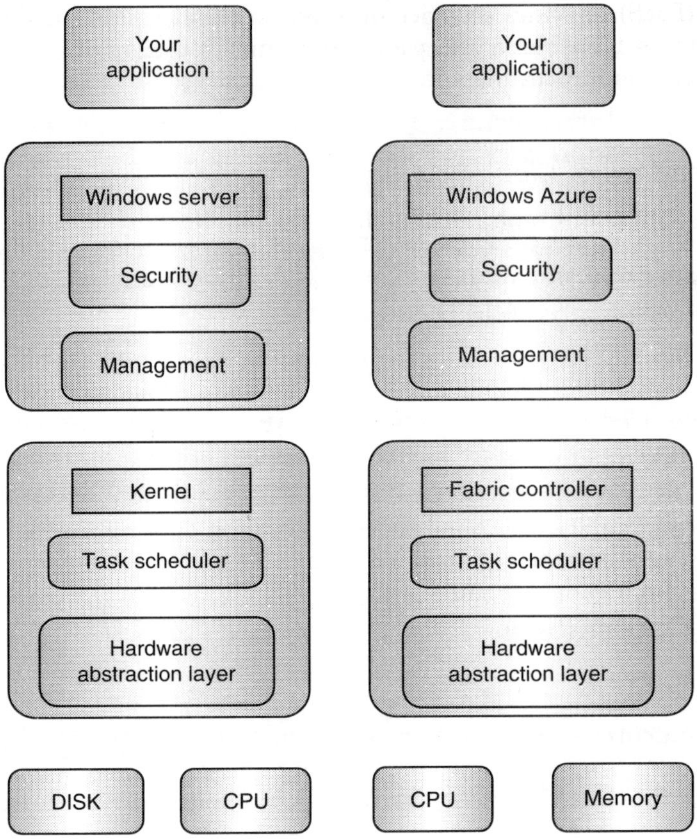

Figure 3.2 | Traditional Windows server and Microsoft Azure.

2. **Faster response to customer needs:** Microsoft Azure provides familiar development tools (Visual Studio and Eclipse) to get you started quickly. It is recommended for testing and debugging applications locally before deploying them to the cloud.
3. **Automated service management:** Microsoft Azure provides automated service management features that protect you from any chance of hardware failure and disturbance because of schedule maintenance.
4. **Cloud business formation with Microsoft:** Because Microsoft support enables you to access all global datacenters and content delivery networks, your business can expand easily with the support of high CDN and worldwide datacenters. Microsoft also coaches you and provides you some training toward building your application for the cloud.

3.6.3 Cloud Foundry

Cloud Foundry is the first open source PaaS developed by VMware. Cloud Foundry is an individual project of Pivotal Software jointly funded by the EMC Corporation and VMware.

Cloud Foundry (PaaS) provides a choice of different cloud providers, developer frameworks and application services. It enables a very easy and prompt application development scenario staring from development, deploy testing and scaling the applications.

3.6.3.1 Salient Features of Cloud Foundry

Following are the salient features of Cloud Foundry:

1. **High performance dynamic routing:** Cloud Foundry provides the unique feature of sharing the routing tier, which works for all application in real time. It is also integrated with real-time logging API.
2. **Buildpack support:** Cloud Foundry enables a very simple approach for integrating software stacks called buildpacks. Using one "push" command, these buildpacks are deployed quickly.
3. **Data and Web services brokers:** Cloud Foundry offers one common mechanism for finding accessible data and Web services, and these services can be a collection of on-premises data services or possibly marketplace of partner-provided services, as available in http://run.pivotal.io.
4. **Active application health management:** Cloud Foundry provides dynamically adjusting and reporting throughout the application development, so that you can see the current status and progress of applications any time.

3.6.4 Salesforce.com

PaaS enables you to develop any business application as simply as opening your browser and start developing it any time. Salesforce.com PaaS offerings are completely aligned in PaaS offerings. Salesforce.com carries the same trust and speed for deploying application in cloud, which is quite faster and more hassle free than on-premises development and deployment.

3.6.4.1 MVC Design Pattern of Salesforce.com

Model view controller (MVC) is the most successful pattern of software architecture that divides the software architecture into three categories – model, view and controller – and segregates representation of information.

SFDC (Salesforce.com) developer considers the MVC approach for developing cloud-based applications and has the following three modules (Fig. 3.3):

1. **Model:** Whenever there is any change of state, the model updates or notifies the views and controllers. Objects, fields and relationships are examples of a model layer in the MVC.
2. **View:** View is the representation of schema and data. A component named as VisualForce represents data to users. VisualForce pages, Page Layouts and Tabs are example of View in the MVC model.
3. **Controller:** The controller layer represents user actions when users interact with VisualForce. Workflows, Apex Classes and Triggers are examples of controller in the MVC model.

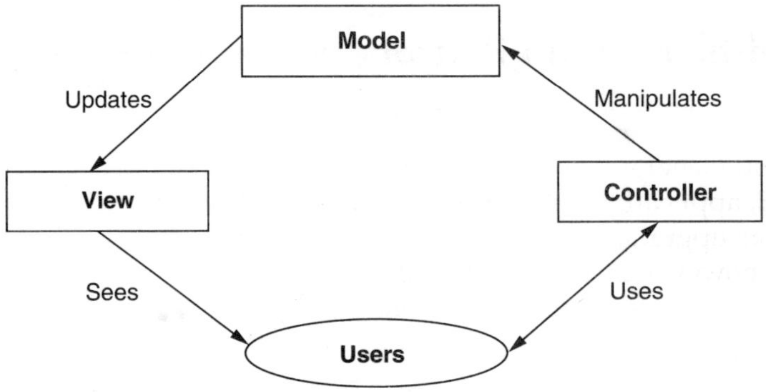

Figure 3.3 | Model view controller.

3.6.4.2 Salient Features of Salesforce Platform Services

Following are the salient features of Salesforce.com:

1. Salesforce provides built-in PaaS services, which means the application services, operational services, platform services, touch services, social services all are together in one console management.
2. Salesforce PaaS accelerates mobile application development for enterprise applications; whatever application you built with Salesforce can run on mobile instantly without any additional coding efforts.
3. Developers can build multi-tenant applications that are hosted on Salesforce's server.
4. Salesforce PaaS offers a very cost effective model for application development and delivery.

3.6.5 Engine Yard

Engine Yard is a Web development platform specifically designed for developers who work on PHP, Node.js and Ruby on Rails. Engine Yard platform service runs on top of other infrastructure services; for example, Engine Yard platform can run on AWS infrastructure very easily. Using Engine Yard, many operational-related task can be performed very quickly, such as managing snapshots and cluster, automated backups, load balancing and data administration–related tasks. In short, we can say that Engine Yard provides a complete platform for cloud application management.

3.6.5.1 Salient Features of Engine Yard

Following are some salient features of Engine yard:

1. Provides dedicated instances without multi-tenancy.
2. Has more granular control on your VM instances.
3. Is based on the pay-per-use model.
4. Provides integration for public and private project repositories; for example, Git.

3.7 Key Benefits of Cloud Platform Services

Following are the key benefits of cloud platform services:

1. **No upfront cost:** Generally, when an application is developed, some costs are involved in purchasing IDE, application deployment engine, maintenance, new licenses of development software, regular upgradation and finally hosting an application on renting platform. After PaaS adoption, however, businesses do not need to worry about capital investment involved in application development and hosting process.
2. **No operational cost:** Because development platform is provided by the PaaS provider, it also removes the overall maintenance cost, including controlling and managing all computing resources. The PaaS provider takes care of all hardware-, software- and application-related security and manages software patching and provides regular updates.
3. **Lower risk:** By eliminating the capital investment involved in developing and operating applications for thousands or millions of users, PaaS actually gives zero risk to their customers. The customers can rebuild and test all versions of their applications as per their requirement and all they need is good-quality Internet connection and a Web browser for tapping massive computing resources and pay as per usage.
4. **Reliability:** PaaS providers enhance the reliability of end-to-end application development, where in case of any hardware and software fault, the transition takes place in the background without user interruption. The PaaS providers take care of fault tolerance as they have built upon industry standards and comply with SLAs, which gives assurance to users of all-time availability of a development platform.
5. **Management:** PaaS gives a better and modified service by automating the management and provisioning of resources. This is done by keeping all the resources centralized for deployed resolution. There is no need to maintain a datacenter or production environment, which comes as relief to the client.

3.8 Comparison of Platform Service Providers

Table 3.2 is the comparison table of all major platforms as service providers.

Table 3.2 Comparisons of platform as service providers

Name	Status	Language Support	Scaling Options	Hosting
Google Application Engine	Production	Go, Java, PHP, Python	Horizontal and auto-scaling	Public
Microsoft Azure	Production	.Net, Java Node, PHP, Python and Ruby	Vertical, horizontal and auto-scaling	Public
Salesforce.com	Production	Apex	Auto-scaling	Public
Cloud Foundry	Beta	Groovy, Java, Node, Ruby Scala	Vertical, horizontal	Public and private
Engine Yard	Production	Java, Node, PHP, Ruby	Horizontal and auto-scaling	Public

3.9 Identification of Business Requirement for Choosing Any Cloud Platform Provider

Similar to IaaS, if we plan for PaaS adoption, we must have a clear idea about whether PaaS adoption is applicable for our organization or industry.

Unlike for IaaS service, when we think about PaaS service, it means we already have either an on-premises or on-cloud (provided by IaaS provider) IT infrastructure. It is now time to plan about application development.

1. **Selection of application development type:** Following are the types of application development. If your requirement is aligned with any one of the following, then you can select any PaaS provider according to your budget.
    - **Social application development platforms:** This type of application development is the most preferable one nowadays, when your application utilizes the collaborative platform of other social network sites such as Facebook, Twitter and MySpace. Social network sites provide APIs (application programming interfaces) that enable the integration of user application with the social media platform.
    - **Web-based application add-on platforms:** This add-on offering helps in the customization of existing applications or software component; for example, Google offers some APIs for utilizing its docs, calendars and other services. It is just like adding some additional services to our existing applications.
    - **Standalone business application platforms:** Business application development platforms enable the development of complex, scalable and large business applications that require high availability, reliability and security. PaaS providers can reduce overall development environment costs incurred when purchasing software license, regular updates and patches, maintenance and services.
    - **Open computing platforms:** If you are testing any Web application or developing an application for research purpose, then there are lots of available open source cloud PaaS tools that could be very useful without investing any capital. If you are using open source development platform, then there is also a huge scope for contributing toward developing standards, any module development or coding.
2. **Evaluation of PaaS provider:** All cloud platform services are not the same. One platform solution cannot be fit for all types of customer requirements. After identifying your application development time, select a suitable PaaS provider that fits your development requirements. Following are some key points to be evaluated before finalizing a PaaS provider.
    - **Multiple language support:** While selecting any cloud platform provider, multiple language or database options must be evaluated. Suppose you are developing an application with one programming language today, tomorrow you may have different programming languages or databases. In that case, your existing platform provider must support different types of programming languages and databases.
    - **Multiple infrastructure support:** According to your business needs, you may select different infrastructure providers that can align with your current business requirement. In that case, your PaaS provider must be capable of supporting multiple types of infrastructure providers, irrespective of your infrastructure deployment model, such as private, public, hybrid cloud or your on-premises traditional infrastructure.

- **Customer support:** Knowing which type of customer support the PaaS provider offers is the foremost consideration before making a final choice about a PaaS provider. There could be many situations where you require expert help or guidance for deployment and management of applications. You must look for 24 × 7 customer support if you are running critical business applications and you should also check the previous track record of support and feedback of the customers.

3.10 Cloud Platform Setup Procedure

Once you have set up your IT infrastructure either on premise or with cloud infrastructure services, the next step is to select the PaaS provider.

If you have already built your IT infrastructure on a cloud, there is a possibility that your cloud provider also offers platform services with integration of infrastructure services, in which case it would be easier for you to collaborate with the cloud provider and leverage maximum utilization of the provider.

After identifying your application development requirement and selecting a PaaS provider on the basis of the considerations mentioned in the previous section, you can go ahead with the platform setup procedure.

3.11 Cloud Application Development

Cloud application development can be done with any PaaS provider directly. You need to sign up with a particular PaaS provider and start developing your business applications.

The following example considers an application development scenario with Google App Engine.

Steps to develop your application with Google App Engine are as follows:

1. Login to the Google Application Engine account with your existing Gmail ID or create a new one.
2. Go to the Create Application tab.
3. Provide your Application Identifier name and Application Title.
4. Go to the management console of your application and make the required settings where applicable.
5. Select your development language in App Config Tool. Currently, Python configuration, Java configuration, PHP configuration and Go configuration options are available.
6. Select your preferred development language.
7. Upload the app and update Task Queue configuration.
8. Update the DoS protection configuration.

The preceding steps are essential to start the application development procedure with Google App Engine. After deploying your application, there is an option of downloading the source code and logs for debugging your code and you can set command line arguments for fast and interactive interaction with applications settings.

3.12 Software Service Providers

This section discusses the most popular and successful cloud Software as a Service (SaaS) providers and their offerings. Various advanced and traditional applications come under SaaS. The SaaS providers develop applications according to current market demands and customer requirements. SaaS-based applications are generally preferred by all Internet and computer users.

Some of the SaaS pr oviders are discussed in the following subsections.

3.12.1 Free Cloud Panda Antivirus Online

Panda antivirus is also known as the best free online cloud-based antivirus (Fig. 3.4). It has several advantages: less system resources are used, there is no need of updates, collective intelligence of many servers is used, offline protection is provided through the local cache. But that local cache cannot maintain the database of viruses and worms out of circulation or considered dead.

Figure 3.4 | Panda antivirus SaaS. (From www.pandasecurity.com)

3.12.2 iCloud.com

iCloud is a specific product for Apple users. It connects the Apple devices to the cloud and is available for free. It allows a 3GB storage account on the iCloud Drive. It also has premium sign-up plan. Users can upload images after sign up and store photos, music, develop applications, movies, media player, etc., online. Users can work as in a public cloud computer.

3.12.3 Mint.com

Mint is a cloud-based personal finance tool to manage the user's money, where users can create an easy account and access all their balances and transactions together on the Web over their Web devices

(Fig. 3.5). The first Mint service was launched in September 2007. In just short span, Mint has received prestigious Web awards from the likes of CNN Money, Business Week, PCMag and Time Magazine.

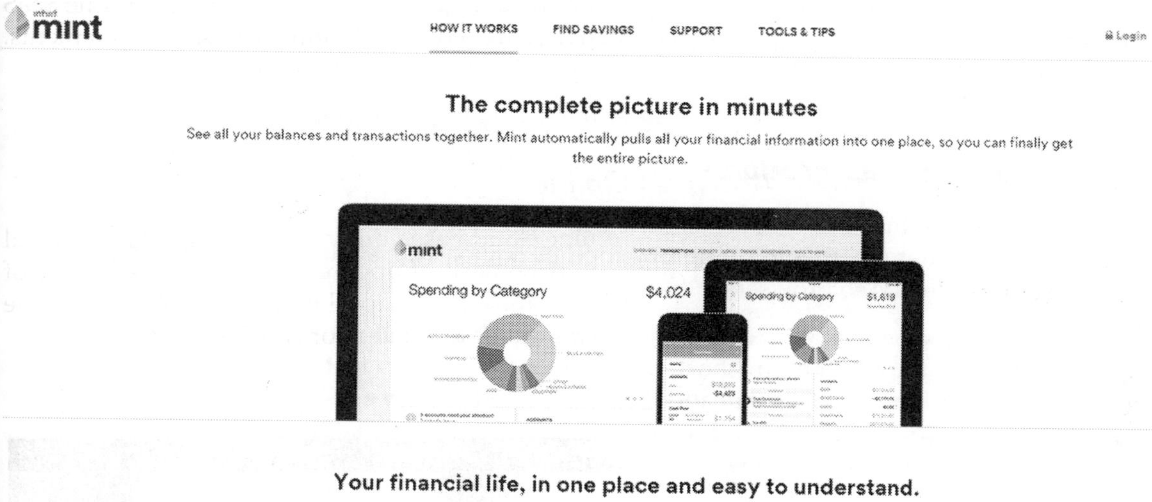

Figure 3.5 | Mint.com. (Reprinted with permission © Intuit Inc. All rights reserved.)

3.12.4 eyeOS

This is yet another efficient online desktop (Fig. 3.6). It provides an online desktop environment where the user can use his or her desktop online, which means that the user can store files and see files any time, and working here gives the user the same feel as working on the home desktop.

Figure 3.6 | eyeOS application. (From www.eyeos.com)

3.12.5 Cloudo

Cloudo is a free cloud computer that lives in a user's browser where users do not need to worry about the task of configuring anything new. Everything is set as perfectly as it can be in this environment. This provides a stylish, attractive interface to users with added centralized backup and perfect security.

3.12.6 Advanced SaaS Products

In past couple of years, the SaaS model has garnered lot of user attraction because anybody can use SaaS products no matter whether a computer expert or novice. One should have only basic understanding of Internet and Web browsers.

In the SaaS model, an application is hosted on a remote datacenter and customers use it through a Web interface over the Internet. In short, a user does not need to install an application or software in his or her desktop or computer, and there is no need to worry about software management and patches installation. It is just used as an online service. Some advanced SaaS products are described in the following subsections.

3.12.6.1 Workday

Workday is a leading SaaS provider that perfectly fits global business requirements. It provides Web-based ERP solutions for managing the employee data, time tracking, expenses management and procurement.

Workday also offers financial management–related and human capital management–related solutions for any kind of business. It works like any traditional ERP system but on on-demand basis over the Internet. More than 50 top Fortune 500 businesses and 280+ mid-size organizations have selected Workday.

3.12.6.2 Salesforce CRM

Salesforce is a pioneering company for developing CRM-based solutions according to an organization's needs.

It provides on-demand customer relationship management software (CRM) over the Internet. Salesforce CRM provides all the advanced features (e.g., mobile apps and real-time visibility of data) that no traditional CRM software provides.

Salesforce also offers several other cloud SaaS products such as Sales Cloud, Service Cloud, Chatter Cloud and some are PaaS products.

3.12.6.3 Google Docs

Google Docs is a free, online, easy-to-use application (Fig. 3.7) with which we can create documents, spreadsheets and presentations. We can also edit, update, delete and store online, just as we do in our system. These documents can be accessible at any point of time and from any location just as we check our Google mail.

Figure 3.7 | Google docs SaaS. (Google and Google logo are registered trademarks of Google Inc., used with permission.)

Google Docs also helps in enabling a collaborative project development environment where many authors can work simultaneously from various locations.

3.12.6.4 Microsoft Office 365

Office 365 is a very good example of SaaS, and in short span, it has received lot of attention in the SaaS market (Fig. 3.8).

Office 365 is a combination of various services such as Office professional Plus, email support, Exchange Online, Lync Online, SharePoint Online and many other collaborative features, and for accessing these, all we need is Web browser and an Internet connection.

It has been designed in such a way that it can support all types of collaborations and communication activities within an organization.

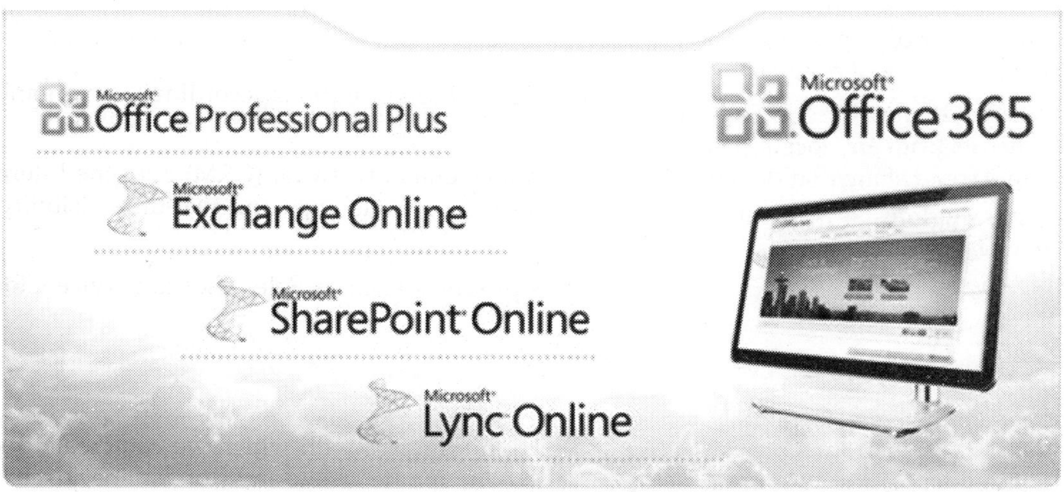

Figure 3.8 | Microsoft Office 365 SaaS. (From www.microsoft.com)

3.13 Benefits of SaaS

Following are the key benefits of SaaS:

1. **SaaS payoff:** Customers are no longer required to purchase any hardware or software and they are free from the pain of installation and maintenance of software application. Accessing application as easy as using our mailbox every day.
2. **Low financial risk:** There is an initial license fee for many traditional on-premise applications. Post implementation, there is a fee for maintenance and support as well. The upgradation of the product to a newer version has some cost. SaaS is somewhat different in that there is no initial IT infrastructure or development fee and the maintenance costs are predictable, which results in low overall cost. Once the subscription ends, the client is free to either renew or end it.
3. **Easy deployment:** An on-premise implementation could be a costly and time-consuming process. Add to this, you have to spend a lot of time on the installation and customization of the application. Consultation fees could further increase the costs. Nowadays, organizations cannot afford lengthy and complex projects. Most SaaS instances can be provided within minutes and can be configured fast with branding, processing flows and many settings with reports.
4. **Comprehensive support:** Many SaaS vendors provide pricing (tiered) for separate levels of support and service agreements. This way, you can have the best package without paying more. Unlike a traditional software license, the SaaS model includes comprehensive support in the subscription fee. This also includes maintenance, upgrades and modifications. There are no extra hidden costs, and there is no worry about the hardware maintenance and failures.
5. **Relief for IT staff:** SaaS does not put any extra demands on the IT team as there is no technology infrastructure or application to support. For small and medium level businesses, SaaS is an optimal solution. If you need any additional assistance, SaaS vendors offer services either directly or through consult partners.
6. **High security:** With SaaS vendors, there is an assurance of good security as they employ encryption and security protocols for integrity of the data with the newest security protocols in every layer of application. SaaS vendors host their applications in high-performance datacenters with a lot of encryption and security features.
7. **Access from anywhere:** A SaaS application makes it possible for gaining access to data and documents from any location with availability of an Internet connection. Remote and mobile workers could share that data information by using any mobile device.
8. **Regular upgrading:** In regular terms, SaaS vendors upgrade their software for the comfort of the users so that they do not have to put too much effort in installing and upgrading the applications.

3.14 Comparison Between Software Service Providers

The comparison between SaaS providers is not feasible as is for PaaS and IaaS providers because there are more than 100 SaaS providers in the market now and every month some new SaaS provider comes up with some new application offerings.

SaaS applications are just according to our current business or perusal requirements. Whatever applications or service we want, we can use it directly online.

Summary

This chapter has given us a detailed understanding of existing IaaS, PaaS and SaaS providers with respect to the current IT market scenario. We have learned individual benefits of each of these service providers and their salient features. The chapter has also showed us how to build our own infrastructure with the AWS cloud and to develop a cloud application with GAE.

After knowing all the macro- and micro-level details of cloud providers, it is time to learn about virtualization, the main cloud enablement technology. The next chapter explores the conceptual details of virtualization.

Multiple Choice Questions

1. What are the most important elements to access cloud services?
   (a) Cloud service and system
   (b) Login credentials and service name
   (c) Web browser and internet connection
   (d) Service level agreement (SLA)

2. Which type of software service is offered by Workday?
   (a) CRM
   (b) ERP
   (c) Desktop app
   (d) Online doc store

3. Which of the following PaaS supports net development environment?
   (a) GAE
   (b) Cloud Foundry
   (c) Salesforce
   (d) Azure

4. Which of the following PaaS is open source cloud platform?
   (a) GAE
   (b) Salesforce
   (c) Cloud Foundry
   (d) Azure

5. Which of the following IaaS provider implements Xen virtualization?
   (a) AWS
   (b) GCE
   (c) Rackspace
   (d) GoGrid

6. Which cloud service can solve the problem if your business is expecting a huge amount of upfront investment in IT infrastructure setup?
   (a) SaaS
   (b) PaaS
   (c) IaaS
   (d) Online services

7. Which of the following cloud service provider consists of Big Table datastore component?
   (a) AWS
   (b) GCE
   (c) Azure
   (d) GAE
8. Which of the following cloud service provider consists of Fabric controller component?
   (a) AWS
   (b) GCE
   (c) Azure
   (d) GAE
9. Which of the following cloud platform provider supports Apex language development?
   (a) Azure
   (b) Salesforce
   (c) GAE
   (d) Engine Yard
10. Which type of cloud service has largest providers?
    (a) IaaS
    (b) PaaS
    (c) SaaS
    (d) All of the above
11. With which cloud service provider live VM migration is available?
    (a) Amazon Web Service
    (b) Google Compute Engine (GCE)
    (c) Microsoft Azure Service
    (d) Rackspace

Review Questions

1. Explain the key benefits of a PaaS provider.
2. How can we develop cloud applications with GAE?
3. Explain the procedure of an infrastructure setup with Amazon's public cloud.
4. What should be the evaluating criteria for opting a PaaS provider?
5. Explain the technical and functional aspects of five different cloud IaaS providers.
6. Explain how the benefits of SaaS products are different from PaaS products.
7. Explain about Microsoft Azure PaaS and its salient features.
8. What should be the business requirement for choosing any cloud infrastructure service?
9. What do you understand by Office 365 and Google Docs? Which type of cloud services are they and why?
10. Why is AWS cloud the most preferred choice for all mid-size and big organizations?

Answers to Multiple Choice Questions

1. (c), **2.** (b), **3.** (d), **4.** (c), **5.** (a), **6.** (c), **7.** (d), **8.** (c),
9. (b), **10.** (c), **11.** (b)

CHAPTER 4

Virtualization Techniques

Learning Objectives

After reading this chapter, you will be able to:

- Analyse the details of virtualization concept.
- Understand different types of virtualization techniques and products for improving system efficiency.
- Learn the concepts of VLAN, VSAN, VM migration, consolidation and management.
- Explore cloud interoperability standards and existing solutions.
- Understand virtual application appliance and its benefits.

4.1 Virtualization Technology

Virtualization is a key concept in cloud computing. It is a massively growing aspect of computing and IT and has been around for many years in some form or the other. It is the creation of a new virtual version of any product or service; for example, disk partitions in the hard drives that we use in our computer system for storage. We may have only one physical hard disk, but we can create two, three or more partitions virtually.

Virtualization is the separation of a resource or request. Let us take an example of virtual memory. Computer software increases access to more memory than is physically installed via the background exchange of data to disk storage. The combination of virtualization technologies – or virtual infrastructure – offers a layer of abstraction between computing, networking hardware, storage and various applications that run on it. The location of virtual infrastructure is non-disruptive because user experiences are mostly unaffected, though virtual infrastructure provides administrators the advantage of managing pooled resources across the enterprise, permitting IT managers to be more receptive to dynamic organizational needs and to better leverage infrastructure investments.

4.1.1 What Is a Virtual Machine?

A virtual machine (VM) is a closely detached software device that could run its own operating systems (OS) and applications as if it is running on a physical computer. A VM exactly works like a physical computer and contains its own virtual RAM, hard disk, CPU and network interface card.

4.1.2 Guest Operating System

Guest OS is an operating system running in a VM environment or on a different physical system.

4.1.3 Virtual Machine Monitor

Virtual machine monitor (VMM) is a software that runs in a layer between a host operating system or hypervisor and one or more VMs that offers the VM abstraction to the guest OSs by full virtualization. The VMM transfers a VM abstraction identical to a physical machine so that standard OS (e.g. Windows 2000, Linux, Windows Server 2003, etc.) can run just as it would on physical hardware.

4.1.4 Hypervisor

A hypervisor is a thin layer of software that usually provides virtual partitioning abilities that run directly on hardware, but underneath higher-level virtualization services. It is also called the "bare metal" method.

4.1.5 Hosted Virtualization

Hosted virtualization is a virtualization method where virtualization and partitioning services run on top of a typical OS (the host). In this method, the virtualization software depends on the host OS to offer the services to dialog directly to the underlying hardware.

4.2 Overview of x86 Virtualization

x86 virtualization is the most common kind of virtualization. Let us see the effect of x86 virtualization before and after virtualization.

4.2.1 Before Virtualization

Following are the characteristics of x86 system before virtualization as described in Fig. 4.1.

1. There is one OS image per machine.
2. Software and hardware are tightly bound.
3. Multiple applications that run on the same machine usually create complexity.

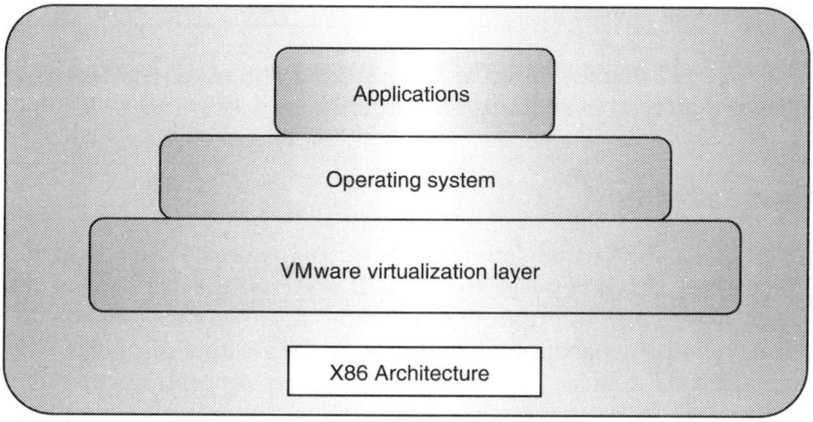

Figure 4.1 | Before virtualization.

4. Resources are not used optimally.
5. Infrastructure is neither flexible nor economically effective.

4.2.2 After Virtualization

Following are the differences after virtualization in x86 system as described in Fig. 4.2.

1. Provisioning of VMs can be done on any system.
2. OS and application work as a single unit.
3. OS and applications are independent of hardware.

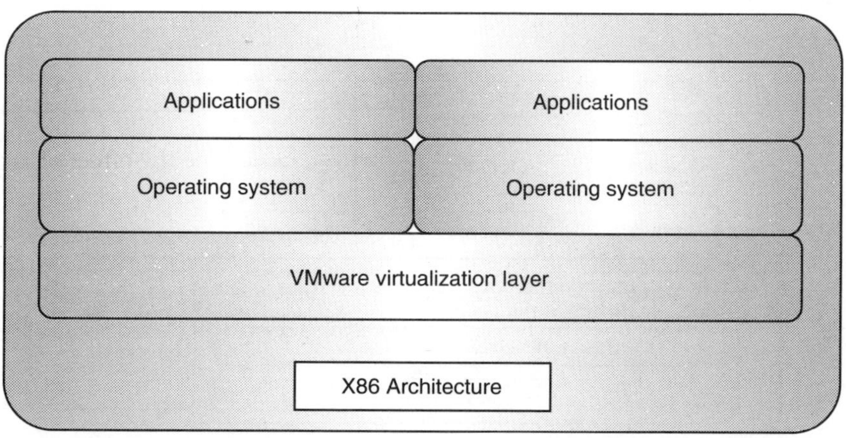

Figure 4.2 | After virtualization.

4.3 Types of Virtualization

There are several types of virtualization techniques and still more techniques are being evolved. Let us see some common type of virtualization techniques.

4.3.1 CPU Virtualization

The common name for CPU virtualization is x86 virtualization. With x86 virtualization, an extra layer of virtualization is added between the OS and underlying hardware as described in Fig. 4.2. This virtualization layer enables multiple OS instances to run simultaneously inside VMs on a single computer, dynamically partitioning and sharing the existing physical resources such as CPU, memory, storage and I/O devices. As desktop and server processing capability have constantly increased year after year, virtualization has proved to be a dominant technology to make simpler software development and testing, to enable server consolidation and to improve business continuity and datacenter agility. Totally abstracting the OS and applications from the hardware and encapsulating them into portable VMs has enabled virtual infrastructure features that are simply not achievable with hardware alone.

While following x86 virtualization, it can be used in hosted architecture or hypervisor. A hosted architecture installs and executes the virtualization layer like an application on the top of the running OS and associates with underlying hardware configurations. Apart from this, hypervisor architecture executes the virtualization layer straight on a pure x86-based system (on bare metal). Because it has straight access to the hardware resources instead of going over an OS, a hypervisor is more capable than a hosted architecture and provides better scalability, robustness and performance. Examples of such architectures are VMware Player, Workstation and ACE.

As described in Fig. 4.3, hypervisor runs just above the hardware. The working scenario of hypervisor may differ according to the underlying architecture and method of implementation. All VMMs run on the hypervisor and manage the running a guest OS. The core responsibility of VMM is that processor, memory and other resources are effectively divided among all guest OS to virtualize the system.

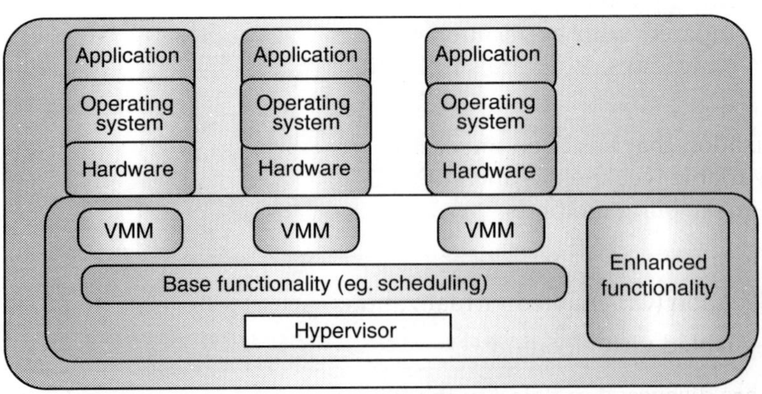

Figure 4.3 | Hypervisor with VMM that hosts VMs.

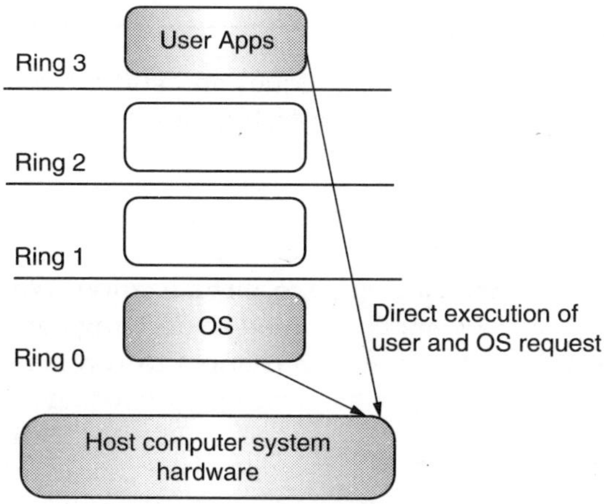

Figure 4.4 | x86 Privilege-level architecture without virtualization.

4.3.1.1 Challenges of x86 Hardware Virtualization

x86 OS is supposed to run directly on the bare metal hardware, so they logically consume the entire system hardware resource. As shown in Fig. 4.4, the x86 architecture provides four levels of privilege known as Ring 0, 1, 2 and 3 to OSs and applications to manage access to the computer hardware. All user-level applications usually run in user application mode (Ring 3), the OS requires direct access to the memory and hardware resource. The OS executes all its privileged instructions in Ring 0. Virtualizing the x86 architecture needs placing a virtualization layer under the OS (which is supposed to be in the most privileged Ring 0) to produce and manage the VMs that provide shared resources.

There is still a more complex condition. When sensitive instructions are not executed in the user level (Ring 0), then it is difficult to virtualize them. Figure 4.4 explains how to solve this type of critical virtualization.

4.3.1.2 VMware Solution of x86 Hardware Virtualization

VMware resolved x86 hardware challenges to increase binary translation techniques that enable the VMM and OS to run in the user-level ring (Ring 0) for segregation and high performance with high privilege compared with applications that run in Ring 3 and have less privilege than the VMM in Ring 0. Nowadays, VMware's full virtualization method using binary translation is the standard.

Every organization that has been increasing virtualization solutions has the liberty to develop solutions with variable weaknesses and strong points. To virtualize the x86 architecture, following are the three main enabling methods:

1. Full virtualization
2. Paravirtualization (OS-enabled virtualization)
3. Hardware-enabled virtualization

These methods are discussed in detail in the following subsections.

4.3.1.2.1 Full Virtualization

With the help of VMware, we can virtualize any x86 OS with direct execution techniques and binary translation. In Fig. 4.5, VMware translates kernel code to switch non-virtualizable instructions with new sequences of instructions. In between, to provide high-performance virtualization, the user-level code is executed on the processor. This type of grouping provides full virtualization; for example, the guest OS is completely abstracted from the primary hardware by the virtualization layer. The guest OS is not responsive because it is being virtualized and requires no alteration. Full virtualization requires no hardware assistance or OS assistance for virtualizing complex and privileged instructions. The hypervisor interprets all OS instructions and caches the results for future usage, though user-level instructions run original at local speed.

Full virtualization provides the topmost isolation and security for VMs, and it also supports migration and convenience as the same guest OS instance can be easily virtualized. Examples of full virtualization include VMware's virtualization products and Microsoft Virtual Server. This virtualization technique is also popular as **type 1** hypervisor.

4.3.1.2.2 Paravirtualization (OS-Enabled Virtualization)

"Para" is a Greek-origin word that means "alongside." We can call paravirtualization as "alongside virtualization." The importance of paravirtualization is the effective collaboration and communication between the hypervisor and the guest OS.

Paravirtualization, as revealed in Fig. 4.6, involves modifying the OS kernel to swap non-virtualizable instructions with hypercalls that communicate straight with the virtualization layer hypervisor. Unlike to full virtualization, working of paravirtualization is different. Using paravirtualization, higher-performance gain and lower overheads than full virtualization can be achieved, and the OS has no idea that it is being virtualized.

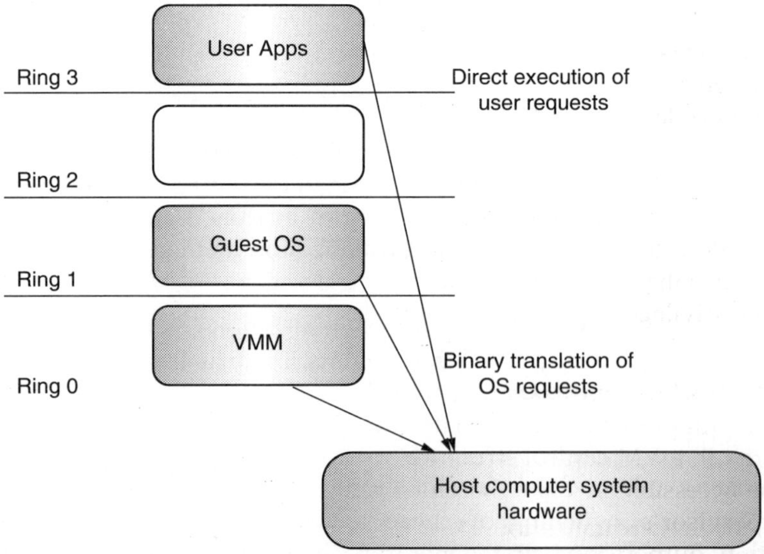

Figure 4.5 | Binary translation approach for x86 virtualization.

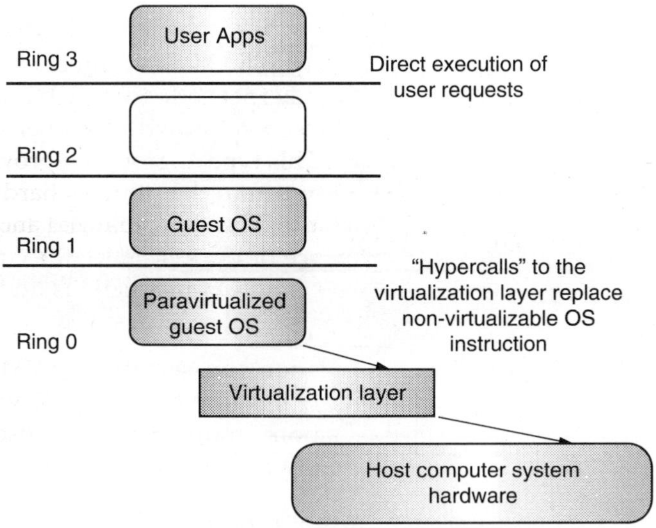

Figure 4.6 | Paravirtualization approach for x86 virtualization.

Paravirtualization may require maintainability or support difficulties in production environments; therefore, it also needs OS kernel-level changes. The Xen (open source project) is a very good example of paravirtualization that virtualizes the memory and processor with the help of a customized Linux kernel and virtualizes the I/O with the help of guest OS device drivers. Although it is extremely tough to assemble the binary translation support essential for full virtualization, customizing the guest OS to support paravirtualization is comparatively easy. VMware has implemented some features of the paravirtualization method through the VMware product in the form of VMware tools and enhanced virtual device drivers.

The I/O device drive of paravirtualization is VMXNET. It also gets the benefit of host device capacities to offer decreased CPU utilization and enhanced throughput. This type of virtualization technique is also popular as **type 2** hypervisor.

4.3.1.2.3 Hardware-Enabled Virtualization

Nowadays, hardware vendors are quickly accepting virtualization and increasing new features to simplify virtualization techniques. This is also known as first-generation virtualization. Popular first-generation virtualization products are Intel virtualization technology (VT-x) and AMD-V, which had some privileged commands with advance execution that enable VMM to run under Ring 0 mode.

As described in Fig. 4.7, sensitive and privileged calls are set to repeatedly catch the hypervisor. It removes the requirement for either binary translation or paravirtualization. The current state of guest OS is stored in a VM control structure or VM control blocks. Processors with Intel VT and AMD-V became accessible in 2006; therefore, new systems have these hardware assist features. Because of hypervisor's switching overhead and inflexible programming model, VMware's binary translation outperforms first generation hardware assist implementations. The strict programming model in the first generation provides some possibility for software flexibility in

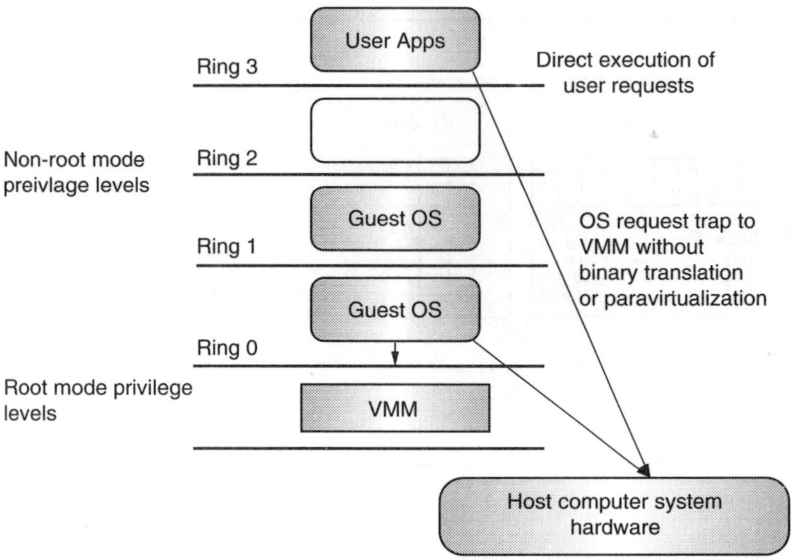

Figure 4.7 | Hardware assist approach for x86 virtualization.

managing either the frequency or the cost of hypervisor to guest transitions. Because of this, VMware takes advantage of this first-generation hardware specification in restricted condition such as for 64-bit guest support on Intel processors. This virtualization technique is also popular as **type 3** hypervisor.

4.3.2 Memory Virtualization

Memory virtualization is the next major component after CPU virtualization. This associates allotment of physical memory and dynamical allotment among all VMs. VM memory virtualization is same as virtual memory feature offered by a modern OS. Applications have an adjacent address space that is not necessarily joined to the underlying physical memory in the system. The OS's responsibility is to hold the mappings of virtual page numbers to physical page numbers and store it in the page tables. All recent x86 CPUs contain a memory management unit (MMU) and a translation look aside buffer (TLB) to optimize virtual memory performance.

To run multiple VMs on a single system, an extra level of memory virtualization is compulsory. In other words, one has to virtualize the MMU to hold the guest OS. The guest OS continues to manage the mapping between virtual addresses and guest memory physical addresses, but the guest OS does not have the privilege for direct access to the actual machine memory. The VMM is accountable for mapping of guest physical memory to the actual machine memory, with the help of shadow page tables to speed up the mappings. As shown with the red line in Fig. 4.8, the VMM uses TLB hardware for mapping virtual memory directly to the machine memory for avoiding excessive two levels of translation on every access.

The moment guest OS switches the mapping address of virtual memory to physical memory to allow direct lookup, the VMM also quickly updates in the shadow page tables. MMU virtualization

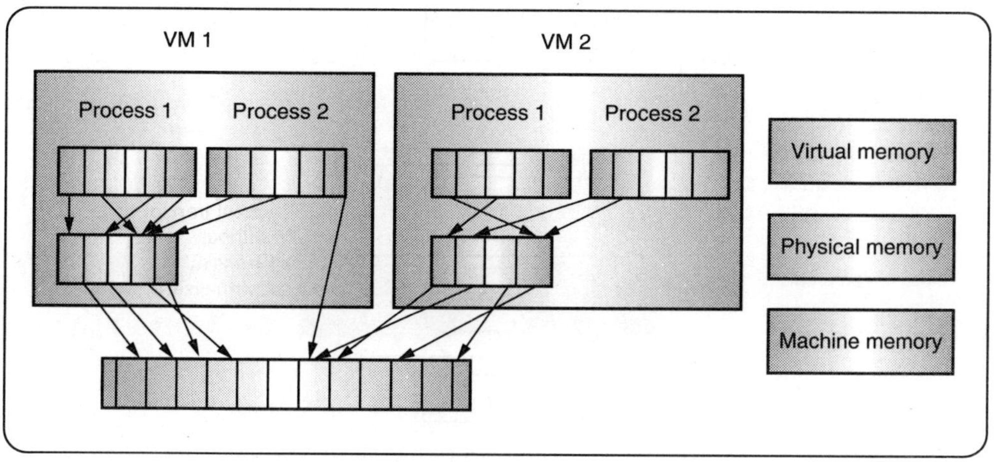

Figure 4.8 | Memory virtualization.

also creates various problems for all types of virtualization methods but to resolve the issue, second-generation hardware–assisted virtualization methods are used.

4.3.3 Device and I/O Virtualization

Device and I/O virtualization are the most critical sections. These include handling the routing of I/O requests between the shared physical hardware and virtual devices. Software-based I/O virtualization and management allow a rich set of features and easy management, whereas hardware-based I/O virtualization has a direct pass-through to the hardware. But software-based I/O virtualization combines with networking, for example, virtual NICs and switches create virtual networks between VMs without the network traffic consuming bandwidth on the physical network.

NIC also allows multiple physical NICs to display as one and failover transparently for VMs, and the VMs can be relocated effortlessly to different systems using VMotion while keeping their existing media access control (MAC) addresses. The solution to efficient I/O virtualization is to reserve these virtualization advantages and make CPU utilization lowest. The hypervisor virtualizes the physical hardware with set of virtual devices to each VM as described in Fig. 4.9. These virtual devices efficiently translate the VM's request according to the instruction of the system hardware. This standardization on consistent device drivers also helps with VM standardization and mobility across various platforms as all VMs are configured to run on the same virtual hardware despite the actual physical hardware in the system.

4.3.4 OS-Level Virtualization

In OS-level virtualization, the virtualization layer is exactly between the OS and the application programs that run on the OS. The VM runs applications, or sets of applications, that are written for the specific OS being virtualized.

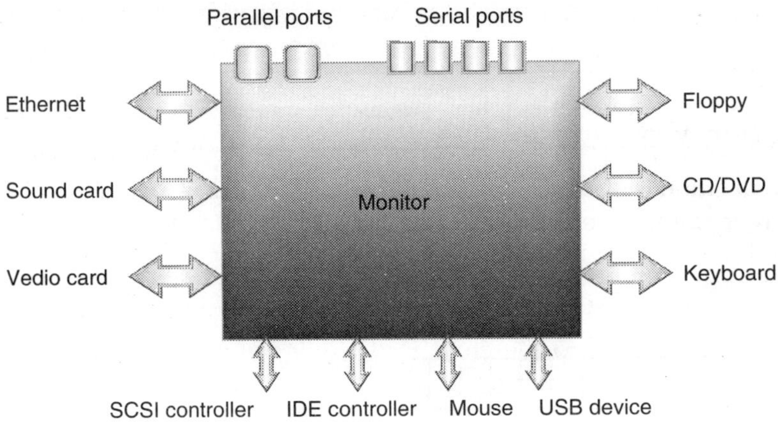

Figure 4.9 | Device and I/O virtualization.

4.3.5 Network Virtualization

When all the separate resources of a network are combined and the condition that allows the network administrator to share them among all network users is called the *network virtualization*. This is done by splitting the resources' bandwidth into channels and permitting the administrator to allocate these resources as and when required. This permits each user to access all of the network resources from their computer. These resources can be files and folders on the computer, printers or hard drives. This efficient approach makes the life of the network administrator much easier, and it makes the system seem much less complex to the human eye than it really is.

4.3.6 Server Virtualization

This is the key area of virtualization, whereby several "VMs" are produced on one server, which means that multiple tasks can then be allocated to the one server, saving on processing power, cost and space. This also means that network tasks that are active on the server still appear to be on a distinct space, so that any error can be identified and fixed quickly.

4.3.7 Client (or Desktop) Virtualization

Client or desktop virtualization is like a separation of a personal computer desktop environment from a physical machine through the client server model of computing.

The desktop virtualization model enables the use of VMs to give permission to multiple network subscribers to preserve individualized desktops on a single, centrally located computer or server. The central machine may operate at a house, business or datacenter. The consumer may be distributed physically, but everyone must be linked to the central machine by any type of Internet connection.

There are basically two types of desktop virtualization:

1. **Remote (server-hosted) desktop virtualization:** In this model, the operating environment is hosted on a server in the datacenter and retrieved by the end user across a network.

2. **Local (client-hosted) desktop virtualization:** In this model, the operating environment runs locally on the user's physical PC hardware and involves multiple essences of client-side virtualization techniques that can monitor and shield the execution of the end user system.

4.3.8 Application Virtualization

Application virtualization is also known as *application portability* or *application service virtualization.* It is the execution of running software from a remote server rather than on the user's computer. Dynamic link library (DLL) programs are good examples of application virtualization. DLL sends all the virtualized application's calls to the server's file system. Because software is run from the server, no changes are made to the local computer's OS file system or registry. Computing resources are merely allocated according to the changing requirements in real time. The advantages of application virtualization are as follows:

1. Cost savings on software and OS licenses.
2. Cost savings on hardware.
3. Capability to handle bulky and fluctuating work volume.
4. Capability to leverage resources without negatively impacting users.
5. Capability to run multiple versions of an application program concurrently on a single computer.
6. Enhanced system scalability and reliability.
7. Easy-to-manage migration and upgradation of application.
8. Optimal utilization of underlying hardware resources.

Application virtualization is beneficial in miscellaneous scenarios such as e-commerce, business simulations, banking, stock trading, insurance administration and supply chain management.

4.3.8.1 Virtualization Applications in Enterprises

An enterprise application is used to define applications – or software – that a business would use to support the organization in resolving enterprise problems. When the term "enterprise" is shared with application, it usually refers to a software platform that is bulky and too complex for individual or small business use.

Enterprise applications are typically designed to interface or integrate with other enterprise applications used within the organization and to be deployed across a variety of networks (intranet, Internet and corporate networks) while gathering strict requirements for administration security and management.

Enterprise applications are usually designed and deployed by a dedicated IT development team within the organization; however, an enterprise can outsource some or all of the development of the application and get it back in-house for deployment.

Today, using enterprise application service providers (ASP) is more dominant. Here, the enterprise application is established by a third-party application service provider and rented to the enterprise as an on-premise or hosted service. This is also frequently referred to software-as-a-service (SaaS) or Web-based applications.

Some of the more common types of enterprise applications include the following:

1. Payment processing.
2. Automated billing systems.
3. Email marketing systems.
4. Content management.
5. Call center and customer support.
6. Customer relationship management (CRM).
7. Enterprise resource planning (ERP).
8. Business continuity planning (BCP).
9. Business intelligence.
10. Enterprise application integration (EAI).
11. HR management.
12. Messaging and collaboration systems.
13. Enterprise search.

4.3.8.2 Application Virtualization Technologies

Application virtualization can be paired with storage virtualization and server virtualization to make a full-fledged virtualized environment. Application virtualization splits the application configuration layer from the OS. It authorizes applications to run on clients – including desktops, servers and laptops – without being installed and to be managed from a central location. This has vast implications for everything from patch.

4.3.8.2.1 Microsoft SoftGrid

Microsoft SoftGrid application virtualization converts applications into virtualized, network-available services resulting in dynamic distribution of software that is never installed, never conflicts and reduces costly application compatibility testing. A few of the benefits of Microsoft SoftGrid comprise the following:

1. Simplified OS migrations and patching.
2. Minimized application conflicts and regression testing.
3. Integrated business continuity for applications.
4. Secured desktops.

4.3.8.2.2 Citrix

Citrix offers a new method to application delivery, which gives IT a strategic solution to hold business growth and change. Starting from the datacenter and working out near the end user, there are four critical best practice objectives that Citrix emphasises on with its product:

1. Protected access to applications.
2. Controller application at their source.

3. Monitor the end user experience.
4. Optimize applications over the network.

4.4 Virtualization Products

Some considerations when selecting commercial virtualization products are reliable technology, performance, technical implications and user interface. Here we are discussing some brief information about most demanding virtualization products that are used by many industries for enabling virtualization.

4.4.1 Category of Virtualization Products

All virtualization products fall in to three categories only, as we have discussed in detail about three techniques of virtualization, those techniques are also popular as type1, type2 and type 3 virtualization. Following is a list of products according to the types of categorization.

4.4.1.1 Type 1 Virtualization

Type 1 hypervisor directly runs on bare metal hardware, there is no need of installing OS, type 1 hypervisor itself works like an OS. Another name of type 1 virtualization is bare metal virtualization.

Following are the examples of type 1 virtualization:

1. **VMware ESX and ESXi:** VMware ESX and ESXi offer the features of scalability, although VMware bare metal hypervisor could be expensive to maintain, but there is a free version of ESXi also available with limited features.
2. **Citrix Xen server:** Xen is one of the most popular and successful open source products. It was originally developed by the Cambridge University research team in 2003 but was acquired by Citrix in 2007. Xen supports almost all types of Linux distributions; it is basically a type 1 hypervisor as explained earlier.
3. **Windows Hyper-V server:** Windows Hyper-V supports only the Windows platform. It was earlier known as Windows server virtualization. Hyper-V lacks much of the advanced characteristics that VMware's products have but there is one specialty when it comes to tight Windows integration. Microsoft's hypervisor technology may be the best hypervisor for organizations that do not need too many complexities.

4.4.1.2 Type 2 Virtualization

Type 2 hypervisors are very easy to set up, these hypervisors runs directly on OS or any hosted OS like any other software or application. In a type 2 hypervisor, resources are provided by the underlying OS. Following are some of the commonly used type 2 hypervisors:

1. **Oracle VM virtual box:** Oracle VM is a widely used hypervisor and well suited for many needs. Oracle VM virtual box provides cost-effective and good performance features. It supports

both desktop and server virtualization and shares many features with other products such as VMware vSphere and Microsoft Hyper-V.

2. **Kernel-based virtual machine (KVM):** KVM provides complete virtualization solutions for Linux distribution OS. It is the product of the open source community since 2007. In short span, it has become most widely deployed open source hypervisor for open source environment. KVM is the preferable choice for researchers and much used in research-based projects. Red hat enterprise virtualization (RHEV) is also based on KVM.
3. Virtuozzo, Sun VirtualBox, Microsoft Virtual PC, VMWare Workstation, VMware server and Parallels Desktop are also popular type 2 hypervisors, here we are going discuss in detail about VMware server hypervisor.

4.4.2 VMware Server

VMware is the name of the company who is pioneer in making virtualization products. VMware server provides a greater initial experience to virtualization with an easy-house, stable, hosted virtualization platform that supports a wide range of OS and hardware. VMware server permits rapid provisioning of VMs by supporting over 30 flavors of guest OS, including Windows Server 2008, Windows Vista and various Linux distributions. Consuming proven and stable technology, VMware server controls the built-in virtualization capabilities in the newest generation server.

4.4.3 Benefits of VMware Server

To understand the various benefits of virtualization, we take a closer look at VMware server hypervisor. Following are the benefits of VMware server:

1. Provides extra servers infraction of time without spending on new hardware.
2. Increases the CPU utilization of a physical server.
3. Runs Linux, Solaris, Windows, Netware OS and applications on a similar physical server.
4. Transfers VMs from one physical server to another without re-configuration.
5. Captures the full state of a VM and rolls back to that configuration at the click of a button.
6. Gives the choice to access enterprise-class product support.
7. Moves VMs to VMware vSphere.

4.4.4 How does VMware Server Work?

VMware server installs and executes an application on the top of a host Windows or Linux OS. A thin virtualization layer divides the physical server so that multiple VMs can be run simultaneously on a single server. Computing resources of the physical server are preserved as a constant pool of resources that can be assigned to VMs in a controlled manner.

In VMware server, each VM is strictly isolated from other host machines (Fig. 4.10). Data never outflow and overlap across VMs. Each VM host is completely independent of each other.

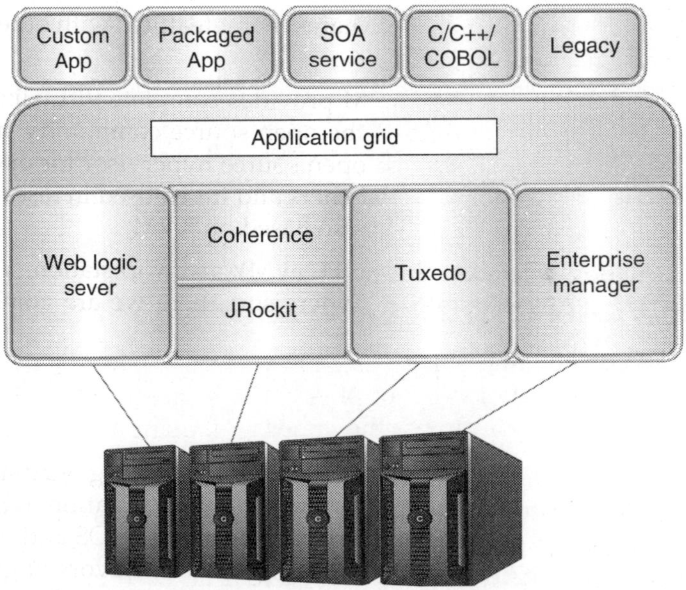

Figure 4.10 | VMware server partitions a physical server into multiple VMs.

4.4.5 How Can Anyone Use VMware Server?

VMware server is available for immediate download at http://www.vmware.com/products/server.

With VMware server, you can do the following:

1. Easily estimate the software if it is ready-to-run in VMs without installation and configuration.
2. Enhance server provisioning by developing a VM once and deploying it multiple times.
3. Simplify IT testing of patches, new applications and OS by facilitating systems administrators to test in a secure VM environment and be able to roll back to a previous state by using the snapshot feature.
4. Easily re-hosting of traditional server OSs such as Windows NT Server and Windows 2000 Server in a newly installed OS using VM.
5. Influence ready-to-run, pre-built, virtual appliances that contain virtual hardware, OS and application environments from the Virtual Appliance Marketplace.

4.4.6 Type 3 Virtualization

Type 3 virtualization is based on the most advanced of technologies because it is directly embedded into the system's BIOS. It works as an emulator that emulates a piece of hardware for its VM.

1. **HyperSpace:** Phoenix is an innovative company that made "HyperSpace" hypervisor, which is embedded in BIOS of the system. Currently, HyperSpace supports only Window XP platform and it can virtualize certain programs such as media player, browser and email.

These programs are presented the moment your turn on your laptop or desktop because they live at the BIOS level below the OS.

2. **Intel VT-x:** Intel's hardware assist virtualization also falls in the type 3 virtualization category. It helps mitigate the overheads of software virtualization. Intel VT first came into picture in 2005 and can be found today in Intel VT-x processors, I/O (VT-d) for virtualization in chipsets and Intel VT (VT-c) for networking device. Type 3 virtualization technology enables high performance because it is directly implemented on the BIOS level.

4.5 Concept of VLAN (Virtual LAN) and Benefits

Virtual LAN is a logical segmentation of local area network (LAN) into different set of broadcasting domains. Because the segmentation is not physical it is called *virtual*. Different users in the same location or in different locations can use the same LAN. Using VLAN can have the following key advantages:

1. **High performance:** Generally, switches and routers need more processing time for incoming traffic because as the traffic passes through the routers, latency increases and the network performance decreases. If VLAN is used, then there is no need of extra routers since VLAN creates broadcasting domains.
2. **Virtual workgroups:** In current scenario, most of the communication within the organization takes place in small workgroups (e.g. development, team, marketing team, accounting team). To manage broadcast and multi-cast functionality within the workgroups, VLAN can be used to enable communication.
3. **Cost effective:** The cost of routers can be reduced when VLANs are used like broadcasting domains.
4. **Easy administration:** Traditional LAN has many access management issues, including LAN cabling, new station setup and addressing, and configuration of hubs and routers. While using VLAN this access management effort can be reduced because user movement within VLAN requires no reconfiguration of routers and hubs.
5. **Enhanced security:** VLAN is also used to set firewalls, restrict access permission for outside access, adding an extra layer of security for intrusion detection and controlling broadcast domain.

4.6 Concept of SAN (Virtual SAN) and Benefits

When a logical partition is created within a physical storage area network (SAN), it is known as virtual storage area network (VSAN). Virtualization technology enables division and allocation of entire storage area network into more logical SANs. Figure 4.11 illustrates a storage area network.

A SAN provides high-speed data transfer across different servers and storage devices. It also mitigates traditional network problems.

SANs allow applications that move data to perform better; for example, by having the data sent directly from the source to the target device with minimal server intervention. SANs also enable

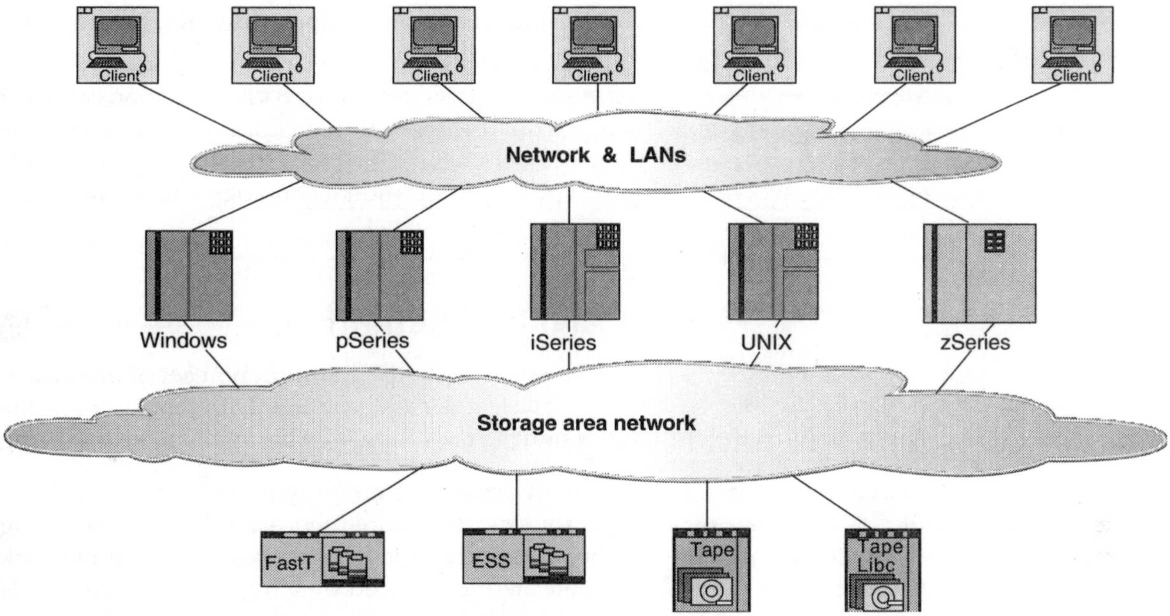

Figure 4.11 | Storage area network.

new network architectures where multiple hosts access multiple storage devices that are connected to the same network. The use of SAN can potentially offer the following benefits:

1. **Enhanced application availability:** Storage is kept separate of applications and can be accessed through different Web sources for enhancing availability, maintainability and accessibility.
2. **Higher application performance:** Application performances increase because the entire storage processing is accessed through a dedicated network and not through the servers.
3. **Centralized and consolidated storage:** SAN enables easy management, scalability and high availability.
4. **Data transfer and vaulting to remote sites:** Replication of data is enabled for quick disaster recovery and malicious attacks.
5. **Simplified centralized management:** Single image of storage media simplifies management efforts.

4.7 VM Migration

VM migration refers to the movement or transfer between different physical machines without any discontinuity. A physical machine could be located at same datacenters or different datacenters across the globe as well. Figure 4.12 shows VM migration.

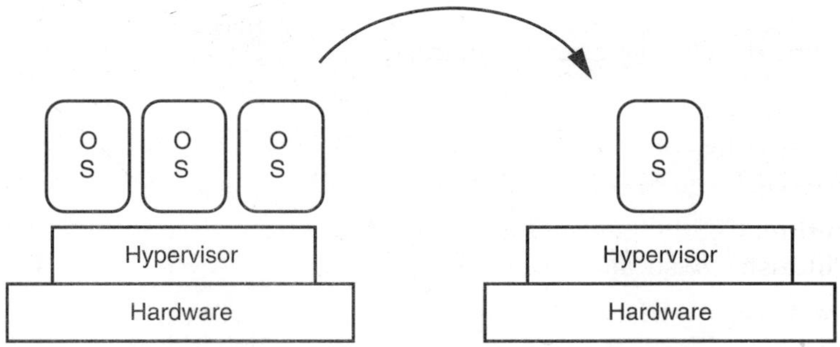

Figure 4.12 | Virtual machine migration.

4.8 VM Consolidation and Management

Consolidation refers to a combination of different workloads from individual machines or applications into lesser number of machines or a single machine. Consolidation has many forms. From multiple servers, heterogeneous workloads can be moved to single larger server. Many workloads can be consolidated under a single OS, which further reduces OS images. Many applications, for example, email systems or database instances could be combined into one system.

Server utilization efficiency can be increased significantly if consolidation is used. For solving problems related to data, applications and servers complexity, which can cause issues for users, server virtualization can be used. It can be used for masking details of server resources during resource sharing optimization. Figure 4.13 illustrates VM consolidation clearly.

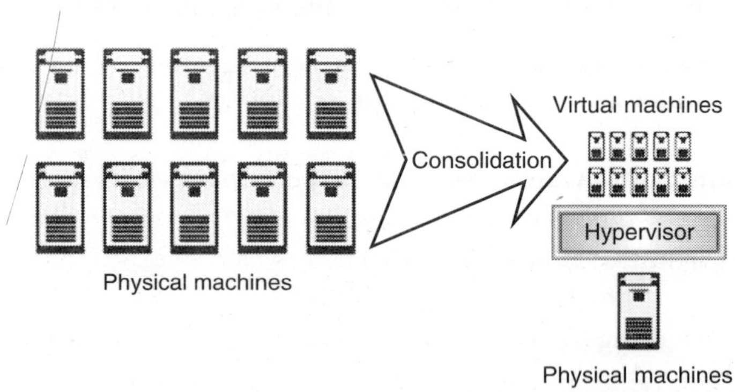

Figure 4.13 | Virtual machine consolidation.

4.9 Cloud Interoperability Standards

There is a strong need for the development of integrated interoperability authentication among all providers. Several organizations such as the Cloud Computing Interoperability Forum (CCIF) have been working on solutions to address cloud interoperability challenges. The Cloud Standards Customer Council (CSCC) provides the opportunity to convert and synchronize client needs and specified requirements into standards of development cloud firms and also for cloud users. It provides standard research materials and documents. It also provides use cases as assistance and service to other firms.

Following are some developing open standards for solving cloud interoperability challenges:

1. **Application solution:** Existing implemented cloud APIs need to become interoperable; therefore, all cloud providers need to agree on a common policy and management scheme. Unified cloud interface (UCI) is a developing interface for the unification of various cloud APIs.
2. **Platform solution:** CCIF, Open Cloud Computing Interface (OCCI) Working Group, Storage Networking Industry Association (SNIA).
3. **Infrastructure solution:** Distributed Management Task Force (DMTF), Open Virtualization Format (OVF), Open Grid Forum (OGF), OCCI, IEEE P2301, P2302.

4.9.1 Need of Interoperability: To Avoid Vendor Lock-In

In today's cloud deployment scenario, there is a need for interoperability standards among all cloud platform providers so that the customer can easily migrate from one provider to another without any vendor lock-in issue.

The whole application, database, IDE and virtual infrastructure design must be portable enough to move across any cloud provider to give flexibility of choice and portability to consumers to move any time whenever they wish to switch cloud providers.

4.9.1.1 Categories of Interoperability

When consumers wish to migrate from one cloud provider to another, interoperability falls into these categories:

1. **Data and application portability:** It means by running applications and data, consumers should be able to migrate easily from one cloud provider to another without any lock-in issue.
2. **Platform portability:** It means application development environment or IDE should be capable enough to run over any type of cloud infrastructure.
3. **Infrastructure portability:** It means virtual server or machine images should have the freedom of portability. They should be able to migrate from one cloud provider to another.

4.9.2 Open Virtualization Format

The OVF specification explains an open, flexible, portable, optimal and extensible format for the packaging of software that has to be run in VMs. The key characteristics of the format are as follows:

1. **Open standard:** OVF has evolved with the collaboration of various key vendors in the industry and it is being developed as a totally accepted standard of portable VMs.
2. **Portable VM packaging:** OVF supports all types of virtual hard disk formats that can be associated with any type of hypervisor, which may or may not be popular. OVF is quite extensible, too, so it is likely to be compatible to all types of format that may evolve come in future.
3. **Optimized for distribution:** On the basis of the latest industry standards, OVF integrates content verification and integrity checking according to public key infrastructure.

4. **Multiple VM support:** OVF extends its service offering for both single VM and multiple VM configuration packages. It provides multi-tier services that contain several independent VMs.
5. **Vendor and platform independent:** OVF is totally platform and vendor independent and is not dependent on host machine, any virtualization platform or a guest OS.

4.9.3 Existing Interoperability Solutions: AppZero, IBM Cloud and Others

In this section, some existing interoperability solutions are discussed.

4.9.3.1 AppZero

With the help of AppZero, enterprise application can be easily moved to any type of cloud; for example, public, private or hybrid. It works on the principal "any application, any server, any cloud," which means any application can move to any type of virtual server that is running under any type of cloud infrastructure provider.

4.9.3.1.1 Salient Features of AppZero

Following are the key features of AppZero:

1. It works on the Zapp extraction technology where only the movement of application and repackaging makes applications ready to run on any OS of any virtual server within the cloud according to organizational requirement.
2. It is really a very easy-to-follow approach for enterprises; they just need to pick the application and move it.
3. AppZero itself is the easiest way to transfer server applications from on-premises infrastructure to the cloud. The same technology can be utilized to move applications from old OS to newer ones.
4. AppZero uses application images but not server or machine images.
5. AppZero is the market's only cloud independent, application on-boarding migrator. This application automates extraction and movement of server side applications in lesser time than needed by other methods without any change in application.

4.9.3.2 IBM SmartCloud

The IBM SmartCloud Orchestrator is a management platform for open, flexible cloud management and for managing heterogeneous hybrid environments. The account and capacity management of cloud services is done by this software, which integrates metering usage.

4.9.3.2.1 Salient Features of SmartCloud

Following are the characteristics and advantages of IBM SmartCloud:

1. Automation and all standard changes in cloud services executed through orchestration engine and self-service portal.
2. Enabling dynamic cloud service delivery.
3. Developed on open source interoperability standard.

4.9.3.3 RightScale

RightScale offers software as a service (SaaS) for managing the resources of cloud providers.

4.9.3.3.1 Salient Features of RightScale

Following are the key features of RightScale:

1. Helps design, deploy, operate and govern various types of cloud resources on multiple cloud providers.
2. Partners with prominent private cloud providers of industry such as Apache CloudStack and OpenStack to facilitate enterprises for building and managing their own private cloud.
3. Enables users to manage hybrid cloud infrastructure as well by migrating all types of workloads between their private and public clouds infrastructure.
4. Provides segregate and reporting among different clouds and teams with accounts. We can also set permissions for users with role-based access controls.

4.9.3.4 NetApp

NetApp provides single storage portable data management service across public and private clouds. Users can move storage securely anytime with any provider without any vendor lock-in. This service falls under hybrid cloud solutions.

4.9.3.4.1 Salient Features of NetApp

Following are the key features of NetApp:

1. Provides easy-to-create hybrid cloud strategy with the support of more than 175 cloud service providers across the globe.
2. Leverages open source cloud solutions such as OpenStack and CloudStack.
3. Provides high speed, availability and scalability in data storage.
4. Ensures secure data transfer between private to public cloud or vice-versa.

4.9.3.5 Scalr

Scalr is an open source community project. It is mostly related to the management of a multi-cloud infrastructure. It supports all types of popular cloud public and private environments including Amazon EC2, Rackspace, Google Compute Engine, Eucalyptus, OpenStack, CloudStack and OpenNebula.

4.9.3.5.1 Salient Features of Scalr

Following are the key features of Scalr:

1. It provides the ability to transfer workloads across multi-cloud providers.
2. It provides the advantage of all common features available in all cloud providers.
3. It provides a single unified user interface for accessing all cloud resources.

4.9.4 Virtual Application Appliance

Virtual application appliance is a self-contained, pre-configured software application system that can directly run on hypervisor, such as VMWare, VirtualBox, Xen HV and KVM.

Machine image is one of the most common examples of a virtual application appliance. It is used by major cloud providers such as Amazon Machine Image (AMI) used for creating new instances.

4.9.4.1 Benefits of Virtual Application Appliance

Following are the main benefits of virtual application appliances:

1. **Packaged solution:** Packaging a solution as a virtual appliance can be very useful as it combines integration solutions to build application which is ready to use immediately with no additional setup requirements.
2. **Simple installation:** A virtual appliance reduces unnecessary complicated installation procedures. The installation process is simple compared with traditional software applications that are installed on top of an OS.
3. **Simplified deployment:** A software appliance bundles all application-related dependencies into one integrated, self-contained unit. All application dependencies encapsulate together. This encapsulation makes the software deployment process simpler by freeing users from having to worry about resolving complex OS compatibility issues, various library dependencies or some adverse interactions following other installation and applications.
4. **Enhanced isolation:** Virtual appliances usually run applications in isolation from each another. If the security of any virtual appliance is affected by any means, or if the virtual appliance crashes, other isolated virtual appliances will not be affected.

Summary

In this chapter, we have learned details about each virtualization technology including basic concepts and various types of virtualization that are common today. Virtualization is the key technology in cloud computing; therefore, learning about virtualization important for gathering skills in cloud computing.

We have seen details of type1, type 2 and type 3 virtualization and different virtualization products, including a detailed discussion of VMware server. We have also understood VLAN, SAN, VM migration and consolidation and cloud interoperability standards, existing interoperability solutions. The next chapter discusses cloud databases and file systems.

Multiple Choice Questions

1. Guest OS is an operating system running in a/an __________ or on a different physical system.
   (a) OS environment
   (b) VM environment

(c) Same machine
(d) Different machine

2. Hypervisor is also known as __________.
   (a) Virtualization method
   (b) OS virtualization method
   (c) Bare metal method
   (d) x86 virtualization method

3. When all the separate resources of a network are combined and the condition that allows the network administrator to share them among all network users is called __________.
   (a) Network virtualization
   (b) OS virtualization
   (c) Virtual LAN
   (d) x86 virtualization

4. Separation of a personal computer desktop environment from a physical machine through the client server model of computing is known as __________.
   (a) Network virtualization
   (b) Desktop virtualization
   (c) Memory virtualization
   (d) x86 virtualization

5. Paravirtualization is also known as __________.
   (a) OS-enabled virtualization
   (b) x86 virtualization
   (c) Hypervisor
   (d) None of these

6. Microsoft SoftGrid is an example of __________.
   (a) Network virtualization
   (b) Desktop virtualization
   (c) Memory virtualization
   (d) Application virtualization

7. Which type of virtualization does Window Hyper-V server represent?
   (a) Type 1
   (b) Type 2
   (c) Type 3
   (d) OS

8. KVM is an example of __________ virtualization.
   (a) Type 1
   (b) Type 2
   (c) Type 3
   (d) OS

9. Intel VT –x, Intel's hardware assist virtualization, is ____________ virtualization.
   (a) Type 1
   (b) Type 2
   (c) Type 3
   (d) OS

10. Which type of cloud interoperability does AppZero help in?
   (a) Application interoperability
   (b) Platform interoperability
   (c) Infrastructure interoperability
   (d) Software interoperability

11. Scalr is an open source community project. It is mostly related to the management of ____________.
   (a) Single-cloud infrastructure
   (b) Multi-cloud infrastructure
   (c) Single-cloud platform
   (d) Multi-cloud platform

12. Packaged solution is one of the most important features of ____________.
   (a) Desktop virtualization
   (b) Cloud interoperability
   (c) Memory virtualization
   (d) Virtual appliance

Review Questions

1. Explain the challenges of x86 hardware virtualization and the three solutions provided by VMware.
2. Explain paravirtualization with a diagram. How does paravirtualization perform better than full virtualization?
3. Explain the principles of memory virtualization.
4. What do you understand by application virtualizations? Explain any application virtualization product.
5. Explain type 2 virtualization with the help of VMware server.
6. Explain the concept of VLAN and describe its benefits.
7. What are the different categories of cloud interoperability and what are the evolving solutions for it?
8. What do you understand by virtual application appliance? Explain the benefits of virtual application appliances.

Answers to Multiple Choice Questions

1. (b), **2.** (c), **3.** (a), **4.** (b), **5.** (a), **6.** (d), **7.** (a), **8.** (b),
9. (c), **10.** (a), **11.** (b), **12.** (d)

CHAPTER 5 Cloud Databases and File Systems in Cloud

Learning Objectives

After reading this chapter, you will be able to:

- Understand the concepts of cloud database.
- Understand different types of NoSQL databases.
- Understand file system concept.
- Understand technicalities of the Google file system (GFS) and the Hadoop distributed file system (HDFS).
- Understand MapReduce programming model.
- Understand different operations that use MapReduce programming.

5.1 Cloud Database

Cloud database is a database that runs on a cloud computing platform like Amazon EC2, Rackspace and GoGrid.

There are two ways to deploy a database – users can either run the database inside a secured virtual machine (VM) or subscribe for particular database services managed by a cloud service provider. Currently, there are some SQL-based and some NoSQL-based database offerings.

5.1.1 Operation Model for Cloud Database

Figure 5.1 describes two primary methods of running a database on the cloud.

5.1.1.1 VM Image

Cloud platforms allow users to purchase VM instances for a limited time. A cloud provider facilitates more security for running databases inside a VM. If users have their own VM image, then they upload it and run the database inside that or do so through preinstalled databases. Oracle, for example, provides preinstalled image with the Oracle database 11g for Amazon EC2 instances.

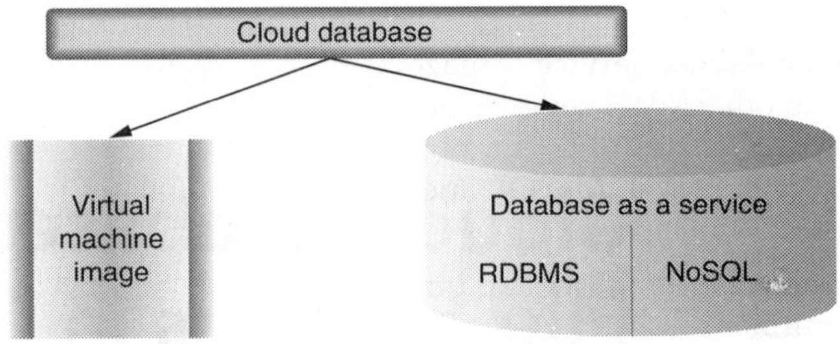

Figure 5.1 | Operation model for cloud database.

5.1.1.2 Database as a Service

Some cloud platform and infrastructure service providers offer database services just as other services offerings, in which case we do not need to launch any instance or individual VM for database installation. All database licensing, updating and configuration are managed by the cloud provider. Application owners have to, each month, pay-per-use of database volume. AWS provides many database services offering to their customers including relational database services (RDS) and NoSQL services such as Amazon RDS, Amazon DynamoDB, Amazon SimpleDB and Amazon Redshift.

The traditional application owner prefers RDS, and in RDS, users have many choices such as MySQL, Oracle, SQL Server or PostgreSQL database engines. All enterprise licensing issue and updates are taken care of by the provider.

5.1.1.2.1 Architectural and Common Characteristics

Following are some architectural and common characteristics of the database as a service offering:

1. Database services provide easy-access Web interface for end users. Database configuration is done by a Web console interface, but some cloud providers offer command line interfaces for managing database operations. AWS, for example, provides Web console interface for launching database instances, taking snapshots, backup and monitoring of database instance.
2. Database services providers offer more flexibility and transparency to users. The service provider is entirely responsible for database installation, patch update and regular maintenances of the respective database. These services offer user transparency during software stack selection, including operating system, database and other third-party software installation.
3. Database services automatically handle high availability and scalability issues. Scalability features differ between cloud providers because some providers offer auto-scaling and some offer API for scale or some offer both, but all giant cloud providers assure 99.9% availability of services.

5.1.2 Types of Cloud Database

It is also important to differentiate between cloud databases that are relational as opposed to non-relational or NoSQL (not only SQL). In this regard, the details of each type of cloud database are discussed in the following subsections.

5.1.2.1 Cloud Relation Databases

Many cloud providers offer RDS nowadays. Some popular and most adopted RDS across the globe are as follows:

1. **Amazon relational database service:** Amazon RDS is very popular and widely adopted Web service. It looks like other AWS services and provides easy management consoles for operating RDS on cloud. Amazon RDS is a highly cost-efficient and secured service. Currently it supports Oracle, SQL Server, MySQL and PostgreSQL database. Amazon RDS specifically offers two types of RDS instances.
   - **On-demand instances:** An on-demand instance offering is a pay-per-use instance with no long-term commitment.
   - **Reserved DB instances:** Reserved DB instances give the flexibility of one-time payment for the DB instance if the database usage is predictable. There is also an offer of 30%–50% price cut over the on-demand price.
2. **Google cloud SQL:** Google cloud SQL is a MySQL database service that is managed by Google, and the entire management, data replication, encryption, security and backups are handled by Google's cloud infrastructure. Google claims maximum availability of its data because its data centers are located across every region of the world. Google cloud is also integrated with the other Google cloud services discussed in Chapter 3. Google cloud SQL is a very flexible, easy-to-use service, which enables connecting and managing cloud SQL with an existing application, just as is done with MySQL.
3. **Heroku Postgres:** Heroku Postgres is a relational SQL database offered by Heroku. It is accessible through all programming languages supported by Heroku. It basically provisioned as an add-on service. Heroku Postgres offers fully reliability of services, which means around 99.99% uptime and 99.999999999% durability of data. One of the advance features of Heroku Postgres is Dataclips, which enables users to send the results of the SQL query via the URL.
4. **HP cloud relational database for MySQL:** HP cloud RDS automate application deployment, configuration management and patch-up task database. It currently supports command line interface (CLI), but an easy-to-use Web-based console interface through APIs is expected soon. It also provides database snapshot facility in multiple availability zones for providing more reliability. It is also built atop an OpenStack-based MySQL distribution, which provides database interoperability from one cloud provider to other.
5. **Microsoft Azure SQL database:** Earlier it was known as SQL Azure. It is the most important component of the Microsoft Azure cloud service; however, it can be operated as a standalone cloud database also. The database can be synched easily with other SQL server databases within the cloud infrastructure of the company or organization. With Microsoft Azure SQL database, the performance of database can be predicted irrespective of whether the service chosen is basic, standard or premium.
6. **Oracle database cloud service:** Oracle database cloud offers two options for users: one is a single schema-based service and another is fully configured Oracle database installed virtual machine. Oracle database can be quickly provisioned, and the user can spin up a database instance with just a few clicks. It also provides flexibility in the management option: self-managed service or fully managed by Oracle.
7. **Rackspace cloud databases:** Rackspace cloud databases are based on open standards. These currently support MySQL, Percona and MariaDB databases. Rackspace cloud provides high database performance using container-based virtualization. It provides automated configuration, which reduces operational costs and team effort. Rackspace cloud is built on top of an open source technology like the OpenStack cloud platform. Rackspace cloud is also connected to SAN storage, which provides built-in data replication for high data replication.

5.1.2.2 Cloud NoSQL Databases

NoSQL database is "not only SQL" database. The evolution of NoSQL database started in early 2009 and has been growing rapidly since because of some limitations with relational databases. NoSQL database is categorized as a non-relational database.

5.1.2.2.1 Limitation with Existing Database

There are certain limitations with our traditional database system and they cannot fit into the current scenario of big data-related application because data is growing exponentially in every industry. Traditional databases are not capable of handling such data growth, which is now in terabytes (TB) and petabytes (PB). Following are some of the key limitations that became the reason behind the birth of NoSQL databases. Traditional databases are unable to:

1. Store data in TB/PB; even a good processor cannot process millions of rows.
2. Process TB of data on a single machine.
3. Be scalable after a certain limit.
4. Provide fault tolerance capability because they have a single point of failure.

5.1.2.2.2 Types of NoSQL Database

There are basically four types of NoSQL databases:

1. **Key-value store:** Based on table keys and values (e.g. AWS DynamoDB).
2. **Document-based store:** Document-based database stores records that are made of tagged elements (e.g. MongoDB, CouchDB).
3. **Column-based store:** Data divided into multiple columns and every storage block contains data of each column (e.g., Apache HBase, Cassandra).
4. **Graph-based store:** A network graph storage that uses edges and nodes for storing data (e.g. Neo 4j).

Following are the most popular and widely adopted NoSQL databases:

1. **Amazon DynamoDB:** Dynamo DB is one of the most popular NoSQL databases of Amazon, which is based on the key-value data store. It was first developed for an internal purpose like handling customer-related big data applications. DynomoDB is built on the top of a single solid device (SSD) architecture; therefore, it scales according to the data in the system. It provides very high-quality reliable throughput and single-digit millisecond latency, which is preferred in building fast gaming and analytics-based applications.
2. **MongoDB:** MongoDB is one of the most popular and fast growing NoSQL databases. It can be managed easily on a cloud infrastructure; therefore, various hosted MongoDB services are available. MongoDB is written in C++ and comes under the category of open source document databases, which belongs to the NoSQL database family. Using MongoDB search queries can be done by fields, range queries and regular expression.
3. **Apache Cassandra:** DataStax is the leading commercial company behind Cassandra. Founded by the Apache chairman of the Cassandra project, DataStax employs most of the project's committers and provides an enterprise-ready and tested version of Cassandra in its Edition 4.5. Cassandra delivers fast performance, high availability and scalability with dynamic schema.

It is designed specifically for handling real time data analytics-related high workload without a single point of failure. It offers high data availability and quick scalability to many enterprises.

4. **CouchDB:** CouchDB is one of the most appreciated projects of the Apache Foundation. The term "couch" represents "cluster of unreliable commodity hardware." CouchDB NoSQL database is completely Web oriented. It stores the data in the JavaScript Object Notation (JSON) document format, which can be accessed using the JSON API, and query of index can be done with the help of Web browsers. CouchDB works for all types of Web and mobile apps. Also, the data of the Web applications can be replicated and distributed using incremental policies of CouchDB. It offers great reliability, availability and scalability as well.
5. **Apache HBase:** Apache HBase is mostly used in Hadoop-related projects (Hadoop is explained in Section 5.2.3). HBase is another sub-project of the Apache Foundation, which is strongly associated with the Hadoop ecosystem. HBase is used to write and update data in real time and can be placed as the traditional database. It can contain as many columns for a row key as required; however, there can be exactly one value for per row for every column. HBase also provides various APIs which supports many operations using application programming languages.
6. **Neo 4j:** Neo 4j is the most popular graph database used in various mission critical applications. It is the preferred choice of many start-ups and mid-size organizations across the globe. Its highly robust and scalable database comprises ACID (Atomicity, Consistency, Isolation, Durability) properties. Because Neo 4j provides high-availability clustering with a graph query language, the customer can easily import the data into the CSV format. It also supports advance monitoring.

5.2 Cloud File System

As we have already learned in Chapter 1, cloud is an advanced concept of distributed computing; therefore, to understand cloud file system, we must know that what distributed file system is.

5.2.1 Distributed File System Basics

Distributed file system (DFS) is basically used for storing huge amount of data and provides accessibility of stored data to all distributed clients across the network. The objective of the DFS is to provide a system for all the geographically distributed users as a common file system for data sharing and storage.

DFS comprises various software components that run as a single system entity on multiple systems. An Internet search engine is the most common example of DFS, which is used for indexing millions of Web pages. There are a number of DFS that solve this problem in different ways. Some popular file systems are:

1. Andrew file system (AFS)
2. Network file system (NFS)
3. Coda

4. Microsoft distributed file system (DFS)
5. Apple filing protocol (AFP)
6. Google file system (GFS)
7. Hadoop distributed file system (HDFS)

Of all the file systems listed earlier, NFS is the most commonly adopted DFS. It grants remote access to a logical volume that resides on a single machine and makes some segment on its local file system which provides accessibility to different distributed clients. Mounting of a remote file system can be done easily with the client's file system and can be viewed as a local drive.

NFS is one of the oldest file systems because of which it has some limitation as well. Here all the data resides on one machine, so it does not provide much reliability of data because it has only a single point of failure. NFS generally experiences the power of overloading if large numbers of clients access data simultaneously. To handle these challenges GFS and HDFS follow different approach.

5.2.2 Concept of GFS

Google invented and implemented a scalable DFS to handle their huge internal distributed data exhaustive applications and named it the Google File System. In 2002–03, Google launched its file system based on DFS architecture but added some advance features that are driven by Google's unique workload and environment.

5.2.2.1 Google File System Architecture

A cluster of a Google file system contains a single master and multiple chunk servers that are associated with many clients. The master holds the metadata of chunk servers. All the data processing happens through these chunk servers. The client first contacts the master and retrieves the metadata of the chunk server, which is then stored in the chunk servers. So the next time, client directly connects to the chunk servers. Figure 5.2 describes the GFS architecture.

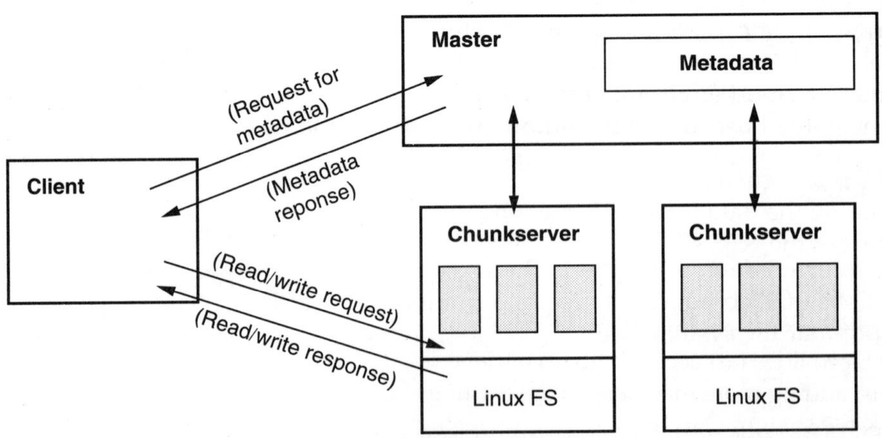

Figure 5.2 | GFS architecture.

Following are the details of each component of GFS:

1. **Chunk**: A chunk is very similar to concept of block in a file system, but chunk size is larger than the traditional file system block. The block of chunk is 64 MB. This is specifically designed for the Google environment.
2. **Master:** Master is a single process that runs on entirely separate machine for security purposes. It only stores metadata-related information, chunk location, file mapping information and access control information. The client first contacts the master for information about metadata and then connects to that particular chunk server.
3. **Metadata:** Metadata is stored in the memory of a master; therefore, master operations are much faster. Metadata contains three types of information:
   - Namespaces of file and chunk
   - Location of each chunk
   - Mapping from file to chunk

5.2.3 Concept of HDFS

HDFS is a DFS based on GFS that provides high throughput access to application data. It uses the commodity hardware with the expectation that failures will occur and provides portability across heterogeneous hardware and software platforms. HDFS is acquired by Hadoop Apache open source project, which is very popular these days for its ability to handle big data.

The Hadoop core consists of two modules:

1. **Hadoop distributed file system:** Used for storing huge amount of data.
2. **MapReduce programming mode:** Used for processing of large set of data.

Hadoop provides a DFS, called HDFS, and a framework for the analysis and transformation of very large data sets using the MapReduce paradigm. HDFS is designed to store very large data sets (terabytes or even petabytes) reliably and to stream those data sets to high bandwidths for user application. Hadoop is an open source implementation of the MapReduce programming and HDFS written in Java. Files are stored in a redundant fashion across multiple machines to ensure their durability to failure and high availability to very parallel applications. That is why Hadoop is very useful in a cloud environment; it can easily process vast amounts of data. HDFS supports the cloud environment because of the following reasons:

1. HDFS is designed to store vast amounts of information in terabytes or petabytes, which means spreading the data across a large number of machines. It also supports much greater file sizes than does the NFS.
2. HDFS provides data reliably. If individual machines in the cluster malfunction, data will be available due to its replication policy.
3. HDFS provides fast accessibility to retrieve stored information. Scalability can be achieved any time by just adding more machines to the existing cluster and machines can be removed easily anytime.
4. HDFS integrates with MapReduce programming model easily, which allows data to be read and computed on system locally.

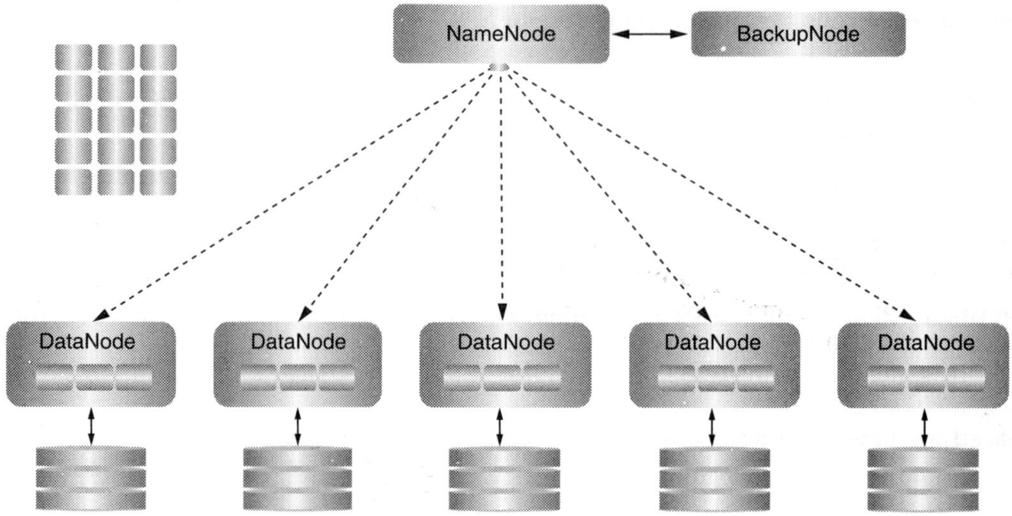

Figure 5.3 | Architecture of HDFS.

5.2.3.1 Architecture of HDFS

The working architecture of HDFS is almost similar to GFS. Figure 5.3 shows details about the architecture of HDFS.

An HDFS cluster consists of multiple commodity machines that can be classified into the following three types:

1. Name node (runs on master machine)
2. Secondary name node or backup node (runs on separate machine)
3. Data node (runs on slave machine)

The working of an HDFS is the same as master slave architecture. Here the master is the name node that contains the metadata of the cluster, but the processing occurs through data nodes. The client first connects to the metadata and receives information about the data node and the next time directly connects to the data node. GFS works the same way as well. The different colors in Figure 5.2 represent data replication across the cluster. By default the replication factor is three times, but it can be adjusted to higher or lower levels also; therefore, the fault tolerance feature is automatically enabled with HDFS.

5.2.3.2 Features of HDFS

Following are some technical features of HDFS:

1. **Durability:** Replication of each block of file thrice on different data nodes makes the cluster robust against data loss due to node failure. It is unlikely that Yahoo! has ever lost any data like that. The probability of losing a block is less than 0.005 in a year.
2. **Placement policy:** For a huge HDFS architecture deployment, nodes are replicated across the multiple racks and one common switch is shared among all nodes that are connected

by two or more switches. The HDFS placement policy also ensures that there are no more than two replica of the same block in the same rack.

3. **Replication management:** In HDFS, whenever a replica becomes under-replicated, it is managed by the replication priority queue. Replication management handles priority issues of replica, if there is only one replica of one block then this replica would have the highest priority over other blocks that may have two or three replications.
4. **Load balancing:** The balancer is a default application program deployed on HDFS. Disk space utilization is balanced across HDFS with the help of this program.
5. **Data integrity:** The data integrity is provided by the use of checksum. When a client writes a block to the HDFS, checksum is calculated for the block and saved along with the data. When the same block is read in the future, the respective checksum is checked and if there is a mismatch, an error is thrown and NameNode is notified. The corrupted data block is then replaced with the correct one immediately.

5.2.4 Comparison of Features

Some key differences between HDFS and GFS are given in Table 5.1. The table includes both similarities and differences.

Table 5.1 Comparison between HDFS and GFS

Features	GFS	HDFS
Architecture	Clustered based, asymmetric parallel, object based	Clustered based, asymmetric, parallel, object based
Process	Stateful	Stateful
Communication	RPC/TCP	RPC/TCP and UDP
Naming	Central metadata server	Central metadata server
Synchronization	Follows write-once-read-many policy, various producers but only one consumer	Follows write-once-read many policy,
	Provides locks on objects to clients	Provides locks on objects to clients
Consistency and replication	Replication on server side, checksum policy and replication of data objects	Replication on server side, checksum policies and replication of data objects
Fault tolerance	Failure an exception	Failure may be expected
Security	No dedicated security mechanism	No dedicated security mechanism
Read rate	6 MB/s per client	1.02 MB/s per node
Write rate	2.2 MB/s per client	1.02 MB/s per node
Garbage collection	Yes	No
Inter-cluster data copying	No	Yes
Data integrity	Checksum	Checksum

5.3 Cloud Programming Model

An existing programming model such as PHP, Java, .Net, Ruby or any other programming language for developing Web or e-commerce-based application can be used with the help of various cloud services. Apart from these, some programming methodology is used with programming languages that support processing extremely vast amounts of data called big data. The MapReduce programming model is one of the greatest inventions in programming. Let us understand MapReduce programming in detail.

5.3.1 Understanding MapReduce Programming

The MapReduce programming model was introduced by Google in 2004. Since then, it has been used for large-scale batch data processing-related tasks. MapReduce is generated from very old list processing programming languages such as Lisp (previously LISP), which is based on the concept of data parallelism and modeling of data based on key-value pairs. MapReduce is used for writing applications that rapidly process vast amounts of data. It has two main functions:

1. **Mapper:** A function that processes a key-value pair to generate a set of intermediate key-value pairs.
2. **Reducer:** A function that merges all intermediate values associated with the same intermediate key.

Figure 5.4 represents key-value operations during the MapReduce function.

The map function takes a value and outputs key-value pairs. For example, if we define a map function that takes a string and outputs the length of the word as the key and the word itself as the value, then "map(moon)" would return 4:moon and "map(universe)" would return 8:universe.

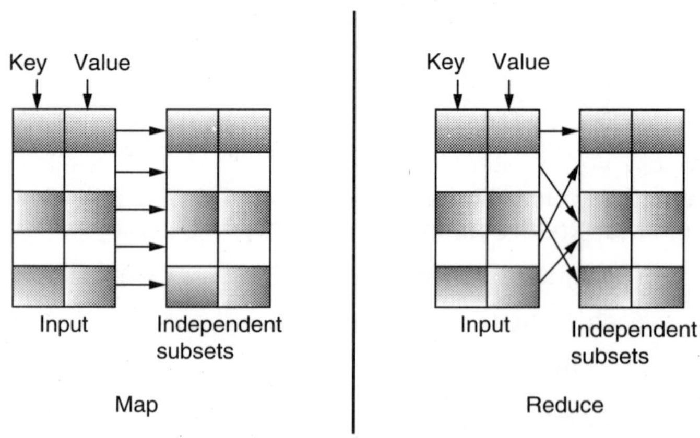

Figure 5.4 | MapReduce function.

In the preceding example, we saw that map function only requires an input value to compute the output value. This allows us to run map function values in parallel and process huge amount of data sets simultaneously. We get the following type of intermediate output from the map function. The MapReduce framework groups all of the values together by key, so if the map functions output the following key-pair values:

- 3: you
- 3: not
- 3: why
- 4: what
- 4: that
- 4: hello
- 5: never
- 5: where
- 8: servants
- 8: research

They get grouped as:

- 3: [you, not, why]
- 4: [what, that, hello]
- 5: [never, where]
- 8: [servants, research]

After this, each of the previous line will be passed as an argument to the reduce function:

- 3 : 3
- 4 : 3
- 5 : 2
- 8 : 2

The reductions also work in parallel to leverage the real power of MapReduce programming. Here we are considering an example of MapReduce which is about counting the number of times words occur in a corpus. Suppose you have a copy of some data and you want a list of every word on the webpage from Internet as well as how many times it occurred. Following steps are required to process such file through MapReduce function:

1. The first step is to take the entire document into word or notepad file, break the entire page into words and pass each word as an input to mapper function.
2. The mapper function counts the values of each word, after which all the values are combined in the grouping phase and a list of each value is made.

3. The reduce phase then takes a key (the word), counts the value of each word (the number of times it appears) and sum up the list.
4. Finally reducer produces the word count as an output.

5.3.2 Operation Using MapReduce Programming

In this final section, we will understand the kind of problems we can solve by using MapReduce programming. MapReduce is used to perform the following types of operations:

1. Problems that can be converted easily into key-value pairs.
2. Common operations on all types of data sets.
3. Some common operations on a group of data.

Some commonly used cases of MapReduce programming are as follows:

1. **Log analysis:** MapReduce with counting or summation function.
2. **ETL process:** MapReduce with counting or summation.
3. **Building of inverted indexes:** MapReduce with collect and combine function in proper order.
4. **Data query analysis:** MapReduce with filtering or parsing function.
5. **Data validation:** MapReduce with filtering or parsing function.
6. **Data analysis:** MapReduce with sorting function.
7. **Graph processing:** MapReduce with iterative message parsing function.
8. **Data aggregation:** MapReduce with iterative message parsing function.
9. **Unique value counting:** MapReduce with distinct value function.
10. **Text analysis:** MapReduce with cross-correlation function.
11. **Market analysis:** MapReduce with cross-correlation function.

Summary

In this chapter, we have learned details about cloud database, operational models and architectural considerations. We have understood how both relational and NoSQL databases work in a cloud environment. We have seen details of a cloud file system, mainly GFS and HDFS with detailed architecture. We have also discussed the MapRreduce programming model and various operations that use it.

In the next chapter, we will learn about cloud security details and the existing security solutions of cloud computing services.

Multiple Choice Questions

1. Google file system contains _______.
   (a) A single master
   (b) A single chunk server
   (c) Multiple masters
   (d) Multiple chunk servers

2. Which type of database is Cassandra?
   (a) SQL
   (b) NoSQL
   (c) Relational
   (d) None of these

3. Which one of the following options is a graph database?
   (a) Amazon RDS
   (b) CouchDB
   (c) MongoDB
   (d) Neo 4j

4. Which one of the following databases is mostly used in Hadoop-related projects?
   (a) Apache HBase
   (b) Amazon RDS
   (c) Apache Cassandra
   (d) Apache DynamoDB

5. Which file system is provided by Hadoop?
   (a) GFS
   (b) HDFS
   (c) NFS
   (d) DFS

6. In HDFS, cluster name node runs on _______.
   (a) Separate machine
   (b) Master machine
   (c) Slave machine
   (d) Both master and slave

7. Which one of the following databases is based on the key-value data store?
   (a) Amazon DynamoDB
   (b) Neo 4j
   (c) Amazon RDS
   (d) Oracle database cloud service

8. Which type of database is Amazon RDS?
   (a) Relation database
   (b) NoSQL database
   (c) Graph database
   (d) Key-value database

Review Questions

1. What do you understand by a cloud database and what are the operation models for a cloud database?
2. What are the architectural and common characteristics of cloud relational databases? Explain any two cloud relational databases.
3. Explain the architecture of HDFS and differentiate between the different features of GFS and HDFS.
4. What do you understand by NoSQL databases and what are the reasons to adopt NoSQL database?
5. What are the different types of NoSQL databases? Explain Apache Cassandra and CouchDB database in brief.
6. Explain the MapReduce programming with the help of any example.
7. What are the possible operations that can be performed using MapReduce programming?

Answers to Multiple Choice Questions

1. (a), 2. (b), 3. (d), 4. (a), 5. (b), 6. (b), 7. (a), 8. (a)

CHAPTER 6

Cloud Security and Existing Security Solutions

Learning Objectives

After reading this chapter, you will be able to:

- Provide realistic picture of the current cloud security scenario.
- Understand the detailed analysis of cloud security concerns and various categories of cloud risks.
- Learn about the popular vulnerability assessment tool for cloud.
- Know about VM security challenges.
- Understand cloud computing security architecture.
- Understand open source security solution products in cloud.

6.1 Cloud Security Fundamentals

Cloud security is the first and foremost concern of every industry using cloud services. A cloud vendor must ensure that the customer does not face any difficulties such as loss of data or data theft. There is a possibility that a malicious user can go through the cloud by impersonating a legal user, thereby infecting the cloud services and hence affecting various customers sharing the malicious cloud services. Data integrity, privacy issues, authentication issue, data loss, user-level security and vendor-level security are some of the basic concerns of cloud computing. These fundamental problems in cloud computing scenario can be defined as cloud risks.

6.2 Cloud Risk

When infrastructure, applications, data and storage are hosted by cloud providers, there is a huge chance of risk in each type of service offering. This is known as a cloud risk. Several aspects apart from cost and offered services must be evaluated before choosing a particular cloud provider. Security is of utmost importance while considering a cloud computing environment. Sometimes, the physical location of the servers may also be a factor for sensitive data.

Organizations such as the Cloud Security Alliance (CSA) offer certification to cloud providers that meet their criteria. The CSA's Trusted Cloud Initiative program was created to help cloud service providers enable industry-recommended standards, secure access, compliance management, interoperable identity and follow best practices. Several cloud risks should come under supervision before moving data and services to the cloud. Section 6.3 categorizes various cloud risks, their associated types and existing open source cloud security solution products.

6.3 Cloud Risk Division

Cloud risks have been the biggest concern since the start of the cloud computing era. These risks can be divided into the following four major categories:

1. Policy and organizational risks
2. Technical risks
3. Legal risks
4. Other risks

These categories will be discussed in detail in the following subsections.

6.3.1 *Policy and Organizational Risks*

Following are policy and organizational risks:

1. **Lock-in:** When applications, data and services are dependent on only one cloud provider, it is known as a lock-in problem. Lock-in is one of the biggest problems of a cloud computing environment. There could be SaaS lock-in, PaaS lock-in and IaaS lock-in. Lock-in problem occurs because of high customization of services according to user demand.
2. **Loss of governance:** The cloud provider may sub-contract or outsource services to third parties (unknown providers) that may not compromise the same guarantees (such as to provide the service in a lawful way) as issued by the cloud provider. Or there is a possibility that the control and operational management of the cloud provider may change, and with that the terms and conditions of their services may also change. Loss of control and governance could lead to the impossibility of fulfilling the security requirements, lack of confidentiality, integrity and availability of data, and a deterioration of performance and quality of service.
3. **Compliance challenges:** Cloud providers make huge investments for external certifications such as SAS 70, PCI DSS and HIPPA. These certifications give them the reputation in the market that they are following the best security practices. However, in some cases particular certification may also be a problem for accessing cloud services. For example, if a client using AWS cloud wants to use the EC2 service and if the EC2 service does not have PCI compliance, then the EC2 service cannot be used for credit card–related transactions. Although customers could use other AWS services, they are restricted from using this particular service.

4. **Cloud service termination or failure:** There must be 24 × 7 support and high availability of all services, but in the competitive world of IT, an inadequate business strategy, lack of financial support and other factors could lead some providers to go out of business or shut down their service portfolio offering. And it is possible that for a short or medium period of time some cloud computing services could be terminated.
5. **Supply chain failure:** There is a possibility that the cloud provider could outsource some services to other third parties. In that case, any interruption or corruption in the chain or a lack of coordination of responsibilities between all parties involved can lead to inaccessibility of services, loss of data confidentiality, availability and integrity economic and reputational losses because of failure to meet customer demand such as cascading service failure and violation of SLA.

6.3.2 Technical Risks

Following are some technical risks:

1. **Isolation failure:** Because cloud computing works on multi-tenancy and shared resources architecture, there is sharing of computing capacity, storage and network among multiple users. This multi-tenancy also leads toward some threats such as failure of logical or physical separations between memory stacks, storage and routing tables (e.g. side channel attacks, SQL injection attacks and guest-hopping attacks), where the data of multiple customers can be maliciously stored in the same table.
2. **Resource exhaustions:** Cloud service is fully on-demand pay-per-use service. There is a chance of risk in proper allocation of resources to cloud users. Although there are many resource allocation algorithms used for allocating all the resources of a cloud service, insufficient resource provisioning and investments in infrastructure may lead to service unavailability problem or degradation in performance.
3. **Cloud provider malicious insider:** The malicious actions of an insider could possibly have an impact on the confidentiality, integrity and availability of all kind of data, IP, all kind of services and, therefore, indirectly on the organization's reputation, customer expectation and the experiences of employees. Taking care of this issue is extremely important in case of cloud computing because cloud architectures contain certain special characteristics that are at very high risk.
4. **Intercepting data in transit:** Cloud services are based on distributed architecture; therefore, transmission of data takes place across multiple physical machines, from one VM to another, images distribution between cloud infrastructure and remote web clients, VPN environment and such. This risk is more vulnerable when data is being transferred from on-premises to cloud or cloud storage to on-premises. Spoofing, man-in-the-middle attacks and sniffing types of attacks could be possible during data transfer–related activities.
5. **Insecure or ineffective deletion of data:** Whenever a provider is altered, resources are scaled down, physical hardware is moved, data may be available beyond the lifetime specified in the security policy. It may be tough to carry out the procedures stated by the security policy because full data deletion is only imaginable by destroying a disk that also stores data from other clients. When a request to delete a cloud resource is made, this may not result

in true wiping of the data (as with most operating systems). For this, true data spreading is required and special procedures must be followed that may not be supported by the standard API (or at all); therefore, an effective encryption mechanism is required to reduce this risk.

6. **Conflicts between customer hardening procedures and cloud environment:** Cloud providers follow different server or instances hardening mechanisms that are little different from traditional server hardening procedures. For example, AWS EC2 service follows security group and the IAM role for securing and authentication of instances, whereas physical servers such as Linux or Windows follow traditional methods for hardening. Users must clearly understand the hardening procedures of cloud providers and which best practices they are using for hardening.
7. **Loss of encryption keys:** This includes disclosure of secret keys (e.g. file encryption, SSL, customer private keys) or passwords to malicious parties, the loss or corruption of those keys, or their unauthorized use for authentication and non-repudiation (digital signature).
8. **Malicious probes or scams:** Malicious probes or scanning, as well as network mapping, are indirect threats to the assets being considered. They can be used to collect information in the context of a hacking effort. A probable impact could be a loss of confidentiality, integrity, and availability of service and data.
9. **Compromise service engine:** All cloud providers rely either on an extremely specific platform or the service engine that is placed just above the physical hardware and manages customer requests at different levels of abstraction. For infrastructure service providers, this software element can be the hypervisor, for platform service providers, it could be hosted application engines. Hacking the service engine may be useful to escape the isolation between different customer environments (jailbreak) and gain access to the data contained inside them, to monitor and adapt the information inside them in a transparent way (without direct interaction with the application inside the customer environment), or to decrease the resources assigned to them, causing a denial of service (DoS attacks).

6.3.3 Legal Risks

Following are some legal risks:

1. **Risk from changes of jurisdiction:** Customer data may be kept in several jurisdictions, some of which may be high risk. If datacenters are located in high-risk countries (e.g. those that lack the rule of law and have an unpredictable legal framework and enforcement, monocratic police states, states that do not respect international agreements), sites could be attacked by local authorities and data or systems subject to enforced disclosure or seizure.
2. **Licensing risks:** Licensing conditions, such as per-seat agreements and online licensing checks may become unusable in a cloud environment; for example, software is charged at per instances basis so if our cloud-based instance increases, the cost of the software also increases exponentially.
3. **Data protection risks:** It can be tough for the cloud customer (in its role of data controller) to efficiently check the data processing that the cloud provider brings out and hence be sure that the data is handled in a lawful way. There may be data security breaches that are not

intimated to the controller by the cloud provider. The cloud customer may misplace control of the data administered by the cloud provider. This issue is increased in the case of multiple transfers of data (e.g. between federated cloud providers).

6.3.4 Other Risks

Apart from policy, technical and legal risks, following are some other risks:

1. **Backup lost or stolen:** This risk is possible due to inadequate physical security procedures, AAA vulnerabilities, User provisioning vulnerabilities and user de-provisioning vulnerabilities.
2. **Unauthorized access to premises (including physical access to machines and other facilities):** Because of inadequate physical security procedures, unauthorized access in datacenters is possible. Generally, cloud providers have large datacenters; therefore, physical control of a datacenter must be stronger because the impact of a breach of this issue could be higher.
3. **Theft of computer equipment:** This risk is possible because of inadequate physical security procedures. This risk is mainly related to the datacenter, only authenticated person must be allowed to enter in physical datacenters and dual authentication mechanism should be followed to accesses those machines.
4. **Natural disasters:** Natural disasters are possible any time so there must be a perfect disaster recovery plan. Although, the risk from natural disasters is quite less compared to traditional infrastructures because cloud providers offer redundancy and fault tolerance by default; for example, AWS has various physical regions and multiple availability zone option within a region also.

6.4 Cloud Computing Security Architecture

There are several proposed and research-based cloud security architectures in the market. Following is a generic view of cloud computing security architecture:

Figure 6.1 shows an architectural view of the security issues to be addressed in a cloud computing environment for providing security to the customer. We have defined four layers on the basis of cloud computing services categorization. The cloud computing categorization is the same as we have already discussed in detail, that is, Software as a Service (SaaS), Platform as a Service (PaaS) and Infrastructure as a Service (IaaS). This section presents the four layers shown in Figure 6.1 and maps different security issues in each layer.

There are four layers in the generic architecture of cloud, i.e. user layer, service provider layer, VM layer and datacenter layer, which are described as follows:

1. **Data center layer:** This layer is related to traditional infrastructure security concerns. It consists of physical hardware security, theft protection, network security and all physical assets security.
2. **VM layer:** This layer involves VM level security issues, VM monitoring, hypervisor-related security issues and VM isolation management issues.

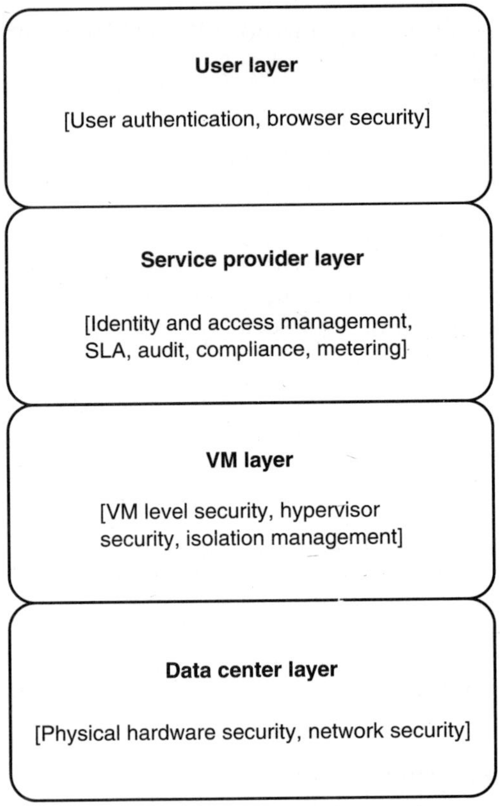

Figure 6.1 | Cloud security architecture.

3. **Service provider layer:** This layer is responsible for identity and access management, service level agreement (SLA), metering, compliance and audit-related issues.
4. **User layer:** This is the first layer of user interaction. It is responsible for user authentication and authorization and all browser-related security issues.

6.5 VM Security Challenges

As discussed in Chapter 2, virtualization is the key technology in cloud computing and because of the evolving nature of virtualization, there are many virtualization-related threats. Over the last couple of years, we have observed some great features of virtualization that can open unwanted security vulnerabilities. Unfortunately, some features are frequently implemented before the linked security consequences are fully understood. Some of the items labeled as threats here could also be considered unbelievable benefits. The objective of listing these items is to increase the alertness of the potential downside, while encouraging people to consider through the implementations with respect to security.

1. **Communication between VMs or between VMs and the host:** VMs serve some key requirements for any organization such as the following:

- Sharing one physical computer resource among multiple companies or organizations.
- Consolidation of different services into one physical computer.
- Providing a general hardware platform to host multiple operating systems.

In virtualization technology, basically the operating system enables the VM layer for logging keystrokes and passing regular screen updates to all guest VMs. These screen updates and key strokes are logged to files out on the host and enables monitoring of secured terminals within the VM.

Some VM technology provides full accesses to all guest VMs and guest VMs can easily access all critical resources of the guest operating system such as the file system level access. There must be a strong layer of isolation and security between guests and the host VM. It is the responsibility of VM users to discuss and understand this isolation issue with their respective VM vendor.

2. **VM escape:** VMs allow us to share the resources of the host computer and provide isolation between VMs and their host.

   In an ideal situation, any program that runs under the VM should not communicate to any other program inside that or any other VM, but because of some architecture limitations or some other bugs, software affect this isolation.

   It may so happen that a program running inside a VM can totally bypass the VM layer and acquire full access to the host system. Such a situation is known as *VM escape*. Because of the host's privileged position, the result may be a total collapse in the security model of the system.

3. **VM monitoring from the host:** It is not normally considered a limitation or a bug when one can start monitoring, changing or communicating with a VM application *from the host*. In this case, the host itself starts controlling; therefore, the host requires more strict security environments compared to each individual VM. The host can affect VMs behavior in the following ways, although it depends on the kind of VM technology being used.

   - Start, stop, pause and restart VMs.
   - Monitor and configure resources available to the VMs, including CPU, memory, disk and network usage of VMs.
   - Adjust the number of CPUs, amount of memory, amount and number of virtual disks, and number of virtual network interfaces available to a VM.
   - Monitor the applications running inside the VM.
   - View, copy and possibly modify the data stored on the VM's virtual disks.

   As all network packets coming from or going to a VM pass through the host; the host is generally able to monitor network traffic for its VMs. This same condition may occur in a co-hosting facility where one host has the privileges to monitor network traffic for all its hosted machines.

4. **VM monitoring from another VM:** Isolation is a basic characteristic of VM technology; it is usually referred as a security defect when one VM can easily monitor another without definite configurations and privilege to do so. The memory protection built into most modern CPUs should be inherited in the hypervisor too. If the hypervisor memory is implemented

properly then individual VM protection takes place automatically. It will not disturb other VM's memory address space. Because VMs do not have direct access to the host file systems, VMs should not be able to directly access the virtual disk of each other's VM on the host machine.

If network traffic is more complicated then there could be an issue with isolation depending on how the network connections are set up with the VMs, but if there is a dedicated physical channel for each host VM, then guest VMs should not be able to sniff each other's network packets.

There could be the case of a virtual hub also, if the VM uses a virtual hub for connecting all VMs host machine, then guest VM may sniff the packets of host VM or other guest VMs using ARP poisoning or some other spoofing technique. Virtualization technology must ensure all possible preventions to such attacks.

5. **Denial of service:** Because various computing resources like CPU, memory, network and hard disk are shared among multiple VMs and host machine. This may create a denial of service attack against another VM.

   This can be avoided by limiting the access of VM resources. There are many virtualization techniques that are used for restricting the allocation of resources to individual VMs. If proper virtualization configuration is implemented, the host machine can prevent denial of service attack among hosts and guest VMs.

6. **External modification of a VM:** In a business application scenario, users' VMs have the privilege of accessing employee databases through a secured application. Database security is more critical in a virtual environment. Database is placed inside a secured VM environment so that any external user is not allowed to access the database outside of the application. If a VM where database is installed becomes accessible from outside because of a malicious attack, then the database can be corrupted or modified and the system trust can be broken.

   This secure VM should be executed by digitally signing every VM and validating the signature before execution. The signing key should be used very carefully and never be placed anywhere else, otherwise it can be compromised.

7. **External modification of the hypervisor:** Because the hypervisor is mainly responsible for the enablement of virtualization while making the process of more self-protected and secure VM, it does not affect the working of any underlying hypervisor. Therefore, the first thing is to protect the hypervisor from any external unauthorized access and changes.

8. **Mixed trust level VMs:** Enterprises must take care of mission critical–related information while leveraging the benefits of virtualization. After applying some seif-protection system and some external security mechanism such as integrity checking, file monitoring, log assessment, firewall protection and antivirus detection, the VM can be more secure in mixed environments.

9. **Resource contention:** Whenever some resource-consuming operations like malware or antivirus scanning, files and patch updates are executed on VMs, the results of these operations produce high loads on the systems and hamper server applications and VDI environments.

To avoid such situations, each VM requires additional significant memory footprint because just like traditional architecture, the antivirus must be installed on each operating system and the same kind of protection is required for each VM, too.

More virtualization-sensitive technology is needed for optimal resource utilization and increasing VM performance so that dedicated antivirus and file scanning should not affect the memory footprint on the virtual hosts.

6.6 Vulnerability Assessment Tool for Cloud

As discussed earlier, security in cloud services is comparatively the most important concern.

Generally, cloud providers take care of all security issues. For example, one of the biggest cloud service provider AWS offers series of administration and security services like Identity and Access Management, CloudTrail, CloudWatch, Trusted Advisor and Directory Services, though it provides one CloudHSM service which stands for Cloud Hardware Security Module. It is a dedicated hardware device which stores cryptography encryption and decryption keys.

Clients always seek some definite assurance that their data must be fully secure while using cloud services. Thereby cloud computing best practices suggest that consumers should enable security in each layer and leverage some third party security service provider also.

To address this important concern, cloud service providers have partnered with third parties to allow these entities to independently test their environment. In the following subsections, some most popular third party cloud security and vulnerable assessment tools in current industry scenario are discussed.

6.6.1 Netskope

Netskope (Fig. 6.2) is a service that monitors cloud app policies for specific groups or users. It monitors user's devices, browser session, location and every activity like sharing, downloading or editing content.

Netskope security solution is quite useful for any organization where employees can use their preferred cloud apps. In addition, any unwanted activity is blocked by Netskope fine-grained policy.

6.6.1.1 Features of Netskope

Following are the key features of Netskope:

1. Creates one policy which can control all your cloud apps.
2. Provides single point of control.
3. Provides more granular level security to all your apps.
4. Provides detailed audit trail report in case of any security breach.

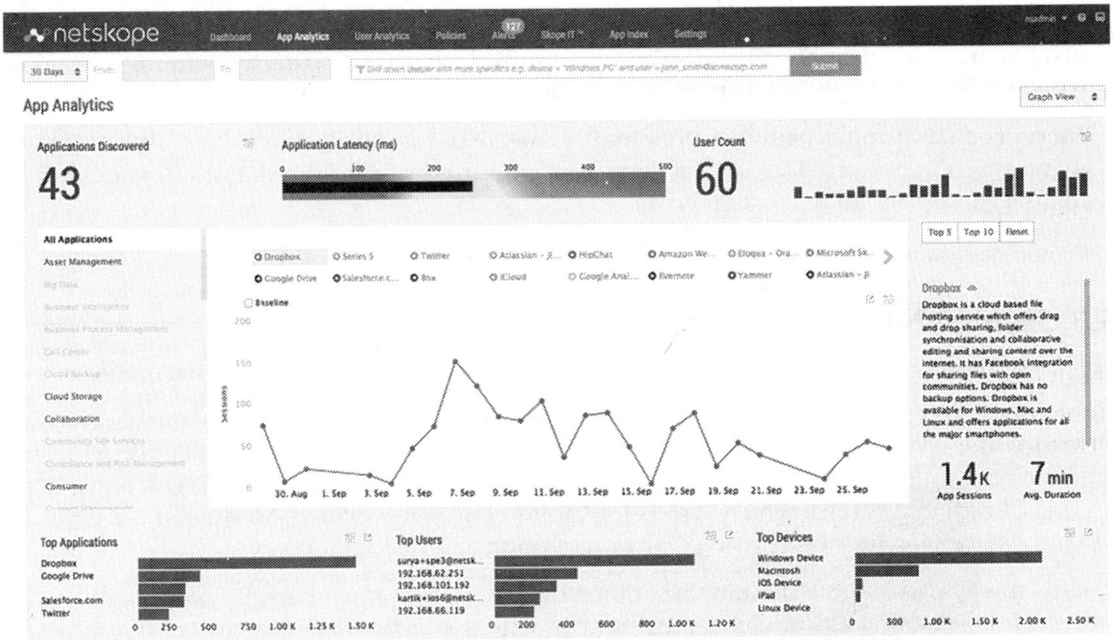

Figure 6.2 | Netskope. (From www.netskope.com)

6.6.2 CipherCloud

CipherCloud (Fig. 6.3) security software encrypts data directly at your business gateway. It is one platform which can protect all your clouds. This is why CipherCloud got tremendous growth and acquired more than 2.5 million business users and 250 million customer records over the last few years.

Figure 6.3 | CipherCloud. (From www.ciphercloud.com)

6.6.2.1 Features of CipherCloud

Following are the key features of CipherCloud:

1. Encrypts data during uploading process and also decrypts during downloading process.
2. Provides security solution for each type of cloud service including database or any kind of cloud app.
3. Provides data loss preventions and also detects malware functions.

6.6.3 Skyhigh Networks

Skyhigh (Fig. 6.4) cloud security service enables IT to quickly and easily adopt the cloud services. With Skyhigh, you can effectively manage your employees to use cloud services while ensuring business compliance of your organization's data privacy, security and internal policies.

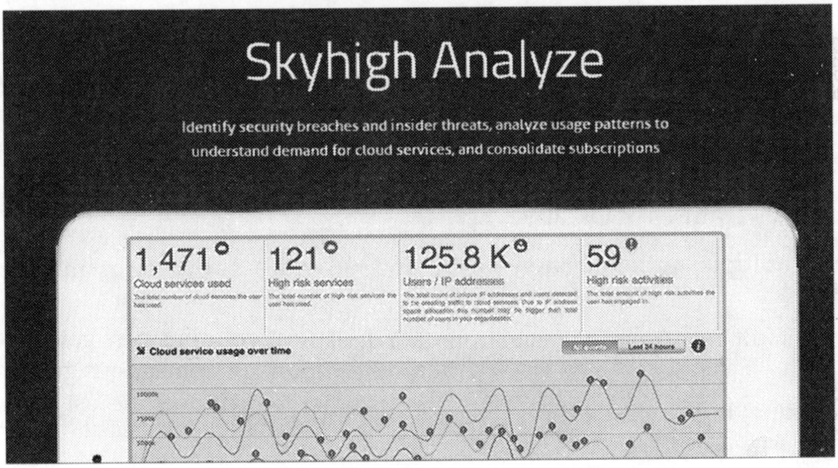

Figure 6.4 | Skyhigh. (*Courtesy*: Skyhigh Networks)

6.6.3.1 Features of Skyhigh Networks

Following are the key features of Skyhigh networks:

1. Uses reverse proxy technology to allow contextual access to the cloud.
2. Provides consistent policies across clouds and grants direct access to clouds without having VPNs or any specific device agents.
3. Implements data loss protection techniques and granular level access, and also encrypts data.

6.6.4 Okta

Okta (Fig. 6.5) is a common solution for all cloud-based business applications. It is pre-integrated with Google, Microsoft, Salesforce.com and other cloud providers.

Okta cloud solution provides single sign on (SSO) for all types of cloud service providers including business app or mobile app. This service eliminates the need of time authentication for each service.

Figure 6.5 | Okta. (From www.okta.com)

6.6.4.1 *Features of Okta*

Following are the key features of Okta:

1. Okta offers multiple authentication factor and provides support for mobile devices and applications.
2. Okta supports full user cycle; organizations can deploy their own LDAP solution without any problem.
3. Okta helps managing access policies from one centralized position to control all cloud-based apps.
4. Okta also provides role-based administration through which we can set more granular level control for each type of access.

6.6.5 *Qualys*

Qualys (Fig. 6.6) security solution covers all aspects of cloud services including asset discovery, network security, Web app security, threat security and compliance monitoring. It proactively checks the vulnerabilities of your network and cloud services.

6.6.5.1 *Features of Qualys*

Following are the key features of Qualys:

1. Qualys can quickly scan all Web apps keeping data safe whenever you are using SaaS, IaaS and PaaS.
2. Qualys security solution uses automation to test the entire Web application more efficiently and fix the vulnerabilities very quickly.
3. Qualys helps in seeing the details of all security attacks through one interactive dashboard.

4. Qualys always verifies system process to ensure the proper enablement of password policies and compliance certificates like PCI, HIPAA, FISMA and others.

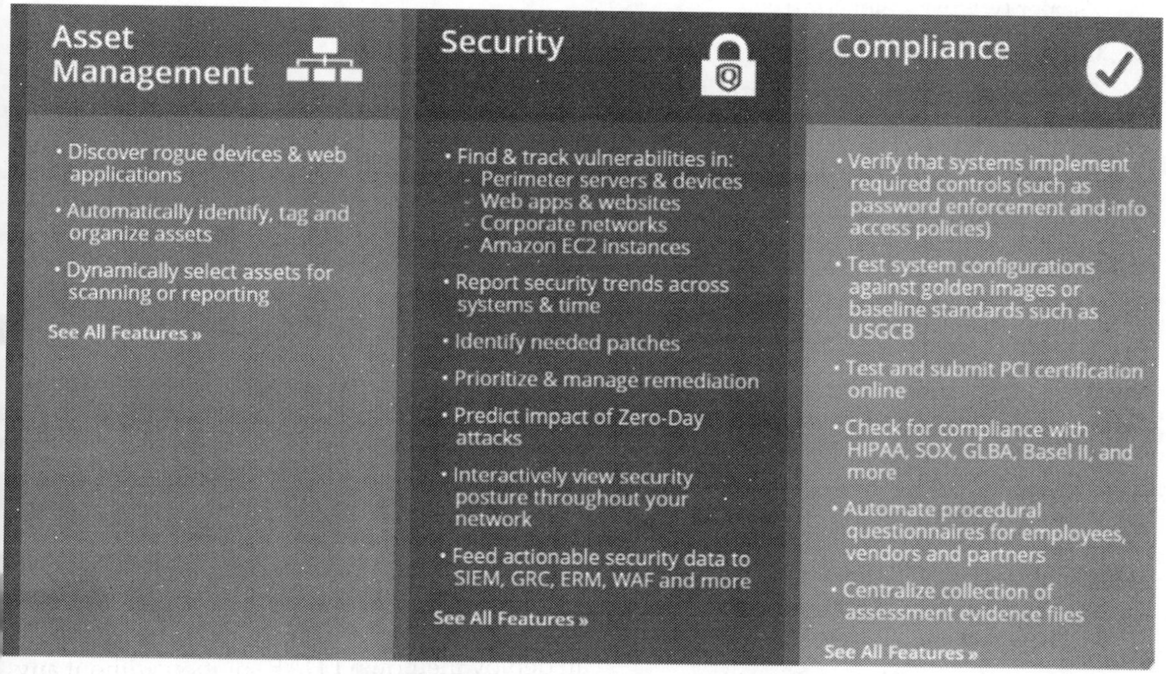

Figure 6.6 | Qualys. (From www.qualys.com)

6.6.6 *Vaultive*

Vaultive cloud security is one of the most trusted solutions. It ensures business to move on cloud and complies with many regulations like HIPAA, PCI, GLBA and others. Vaultive security solution works on the principle of transparency network proxy which means encryption of data takes place the moment data leave the network and reach out to any cloud application.

6.6.6.1 *Features of Vaultive*

Following are the key features of Vaultive:

1. Vaultive encryption engine supports all types of cloud-based services.
2. Vaultive helps in directly encrypting SaaS applications without any modification.
3. Vaultive follows the cloud security best practices where customer always holds the encryption keys.

Following are some evolving cloud security and vulnerability assessment tools:

1. Boxcryptor (www.boxcryptor.com)
2. Zscaler (www.zscaler.com)
3. Certify (www.centrify.com)
4. SilverSky (www.silversky.com)
5. HyTrust (www.hytrust.com)
6. Prevoty (www.prevoty.com)
7. Bitium (www.bitium.com)

6.7 Open Source Security Solution Products in Cloud

There are various security solutions for all types of cloud computing services. Most are commercial solutions developed by some other third-party companies. Users or clients need to pay for those security solution products. Here we discuss some open source solution products that can be downloaded and used by anyone. Following are some prominent open source cloud security solution products:

1. **OSSEC–HIDS (Open source security host-based intrusion detection system):** OSSEC (www.ossec.net) is an open source host-based intrusion detection system (HIDS). According to their Website:

   "OSSEC is a scalable, multi-platform, open source Host based Intrusion Detection System (HIDS). It has a powerful correlation and analysis engine, integrating log analysis, file integrity checking, Windows registry monitoring, centralized policy enforcement, rootkit detection, real-time alerting and active response. It runs on most operating systems, including Linux, OpenBSD, FreeBSD, MacOS, Solaris and Windows."

   OSSEC works on a server–client model. The OSSEC server must be installed on Linux/Unix machines and clients (also called agents) can be installed on any operating system. It could be cloud-based instances as well.

   Multiple installation options are available with OSSEC. It could be installed on a stand-alone machine or multi-host scenario, where one instillation is a server and others are agents. The communication between the OSSEC server and the agent is always encrypted.

   OSSEC works well with cloud instances. The OSSEC server and agents can be installed on AWS instances and can monitor file integrity checking, real-time file monitoring and log inspections.

2. **SNORT:** SNORT is a fully open source network intrusion prevention system (NIPS) and network intrusion detection system (NIDS). It can perform real-time analytics on IP networks. It has three main modes of working – sniffer, packet logger and network intrusion detection. It can be used with AWS EC2 instances also. SNORT host-based IDS supports tracking of

running processes, detection of configuration changes, tracking of file access and detection of any abnormal behavior.

SNORT provides in-flight data encryption for cloud instances; for example, in AWS, all incoming traffic passes through the Elastic Load Balancer, which is used as an HTTPS terminator. It works as proxy traffic for backend IDS instances as HTTP. SNORT is used here for packet analyzing and to decide whether to reject or accept the packet. After transmission, SNORT analyzes the outbound packet and logs the results.

3. **CryptSync:** The best way to protect files is to encrypt them before moving to other servers. CryptSync provides an additional layer of security that makes it difficult for attackers to view files. CryptSync uses two folders that work synchronously. One folder contains current working files that are unencrypted and the other folder contains encrypted files.
4. **Crypton:** Crypton is developed by the SpiderOak and licensed under the AGPL. It enables applications to encrypt data in a Web browser itself before moving to cloud locations. Crypton is a library that allows developers to write secure cloud applications, where all data is encrypted on the client side itself before moving to cloud storage. Crypton supports JavaScript library for Web applications that offer an object storage API. Data storage backend of Crypton is built with compatibility of PostgreSQL, Redis and Node.js.
5. **TrueCrypt:** TrueCrypt is an open-source disk encryption application. It provides real-time and transparent encryption. It creates virtual encrypted disk within a file and mounts it as a real disk. It supports Linux, Mac OS and Windows platforms also. AWS Import/Export supports device encryption using TrueCrypt for import to Amazon S3 and export from Amazon S3.

Summary

In this chapter, we have learned about the most important concern of cloud computing. All cloud service providers and cloud service users first take care of this foremost concern. The chapter has provided a detailed explanation of cloud security fundamentals, cloud risks categories, cloud vulnerability assessment tools according to current industry trends, various VM-related internal security challenges, cloud computing security architecture and some open source security solution products of cloud computing. In the next chapter, we will learn about cloud middleware and some best practices of cloud computing.

Multiple Choice Questions

1. Identify the principle on which CryptSync works.
   (a) Encryption of files before moving to other servers
   (b) Encryption of files after moving to network
   (c) Encryption of files before reaching to other servers
   (d) Encryption/decryption of data during uploading and downloading processes

2. Which one of the following categories does SNORT security tool belong to?
   (a) Host-based intrusion detection system
   (b) Client side data encryption
   (c) Server side data encryption
   (d) Network intrusion detection system

3. How can the denial of service be avoided?
   (a) By network firewall
   (b) By operating system firewall
   (c) By limiting the access of VM resources
   (d) By using intrusion detection system

4. Where does lock-in problem exist?
   (a) In SaaS
   (b) In PaaS
   (c) In IaaS and PaaS
   (d) In SaaS, PaaS and IaaS

5. How many security layers are there in cloud computing security architecture?
   (a) 2
   (b) 3
   (c) 4
   (d) 5

6. Which one of the following categories does OSSEC security tool belong to?
   (a) Network intrusion detection system
   (b) Host-based intrusion detection system
   (c) Client side data encryption
   (d) Server side data encryption

7. Which type of cloud risk is isolation failure?
   (a) Legal risk
   (b) Technical risk
   (c) Policy and organizational risks
   (d) Other risks

8. Which type of cloud risk(s) are data protection risks?
   (a) Legal risk
   (b) Technical risk
   (c) Policy and organizational risks
   (d) Other risks

9. What is the purpose of AWS CloudHSM service?
   (a) Identification and management service
   (b) Directory service
   (c) Dedicated hardware device which stores cryptography encryption and decryption keys
   (d) On-demand cloud security tool for intrusion detection and prevention

10. Which one of the following options is the key feature of Netskope cloud security service?
    (a) One policy can control all your cloud apps
    (b) Network and VM monitoring
    (c) Encryption/decryption of data during uploading and downloading processes
    (d) Open source service

11. Which one of the following options is the key feature of CipherCloud?
    (a) Data prevention
    (b) Data loss monitoring
    (c) Encryption/decryption of data during uploading and downloading processes
    (d) Network and VM monitoring

12. Identify the technology on which Skyhigh security works.
    (a) Transparency network proxy
    (b) Reverse proxy technology
    (c) Single sign on (SSO)
    (d) On-demand

13. Identify the principle on which Vaultive security solution works.
    (a) Principle of transparency network proxy
    (b) Reverse proxy technology
    (c) Single sign on (SSO)
    (d) On demand

14. Which one of the following options is the key feature of Okta security solution?
    (a) On demand
    (b) Anytime accessible
    (c) Single sign on
    (d) VM protection

15. Which one of the following options is evolving cloud security and vulnerability assessment tools?
    (a) SilverSky
    (b) OSSEC
    (c) SNORT
    (d) CloudHSM

Review Questions

1. Which policy and organizational risks are associated with cloud computing?
2. What do you understand by compromise service engine risk?
3. List out some key legal risks associated with cloud computing.
4. Explain the security concerns associated with each layer of cloud security architecture.
5. How do open source products provide security in a cloud scenario? Explain with the help of OSSEC and SNORT.

6. Explain the key features of Okta and CipherCloud security tools.
7. Describe in detail about various VM security challenges.

Answers to Multiple Choice Questions

1. (a),	2. (d),	3. (c),	4. (d),	5. (c),	6. (b),	7. (b),	8. (a),
9. (c),	10. (a),	11. (c),	12. (b),	13. (a),	14. (c),	15. (a)	

CHAPTER 7

Cloud Middleware and Best Practices

Learning Objectives

After reading this chapter, you will be able to:

- Describe the need of middleware in cloud services offerings.
- Understand functionalities and characteristics of cloud middleware.
- Discuss various quality of service (QoS) issues of cloud services.
- Know the detailed process of data migration in cloud computing.
- Understand streaming process in cloud computing.
- Know about the performance monitoring tools in cloud.
- Learn best practices for infrastructure setup and for data and service migration in cloud.
- Learn best practices for cost optimization and cloud capacity management in cloud.

7.1 Concept and Need of Cloud Middleware

7.1.1 *Concept of Middleware*

The computer science term "middleware" is originated from distributed computing systems. Middleware is a set of intermediaries that facilitates different associated components in distributed computing system, which means it allows distributed networked computers to communicate with each other more quickly and easily as described in Fig. 7.1.

7.1.2 *Cloud Middleware*

A cloud computing scenario is separated into two segments: (a) front end (user/client side) and (b) back end (cloud provider side). Front ends have a computer system or thin client and software applications that are required to access the cloud computing system, including a Web browser. Back ends have a cluster of servers, datacenters and high-performance storage devices; however, both ends connect to each other through the Internet.

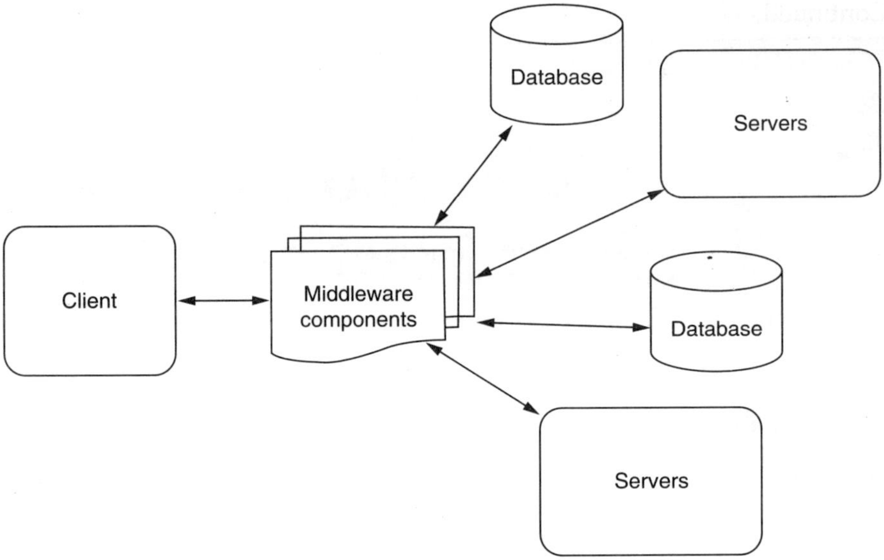

Figure 7.1 | Middleware system.

Cloud middleware is an abstraction layer that hides system complexities and enables a seamless communication mechanism between the cloud provider and cloud computing service users. Nowadays, there are many commercial and open source middleware.

7.1.3 Cloud Middleware Functionalities

Table 7.1 shows the key functionalities and characteristics of cloud middleware, their definitions and benefits.

Table 7.1 Cloud middleware functionalities

Middleware Functionalities/ Characteristics	Definition	Benefits
Data replication	Storing the same data in multiple devices	Improving performance, increasing availability
Scheduling jobs	Resource allocation, job execution	Managing the job queue for a cluster, runtime optimization
Fault tolerance	Transparent takeover of failed machine by another with service continuity	System recovery after outages
Load balancing	Optimizing job distribution on multiple computers	Increased availability and data accesses

(Continued)

Table 7.1 Continued

Middleware Functionalities/ Characteristics	Definition	Benefits
Interoperability	Support interoperation among different cloud services	Simple access to more external services, simple data exchanges process
Security	Support to security (passwords, SSH, X509certificates, LDAP, etc.)	Protection against intruders, securing data exchange
Image disk management	Storing, transferring and cloning image disk	Avoiding loss of data
Resources monitoring	Enabling viewing information about use of resources in real time	Controlling resource usage
Virtualization management	Creation of virtual versions of system, such as OS, storage device or networks	Enabling resource sharing and reliability
User management	Adding, deleting or modifying user's account and authorizations	Controlling user access to cloud services, managing privileges
Control panel	User interface used to execute tasks	Easy manipulation

7.2 QoS Issues in Cloud

Cloud computing services should meet the highest standards of service because they own critical corporate data. If a cloud provider has the following seven standards of quality, it implies that the provider can make any business successful.

1. **High-standard security – enable high security at each level:** As we have learned in Chapter 6, security goes beyond passwords and access policies and that many more factors are involved when it comes to cloud security. Because businesses have multi-dimensional impact, especially when they run on cloud platforms, it is imperative that the cloud service provider must ensure robust policies and all best practices when delivering services. Following are various types of security businesses seek from a cloud provider:
   - Physical security
   - Network security
   - Application security
   - Internal systems security
   - Data backup and replication security
   - Internal policies and procedures
   - Third-party certification and audits

2. **Transparency in service delivery – provide transparent, real time, exact service performance and information availability:** Cloud computing providers should offer detailed information to consumers about service delivery and performance in real time, with the following details:
    - Precise, appropriate and comprehensive information regarding service performance data and planned maintenance activities over weekly or monthly basis.
    - Daily used service, data accessibility and transaction performance report.
    - Prior information regarding maintenance activities.
3. **Accurate multi-tenancy – provide accurate multi-tenant architecture to all consumers** Multi-tenancy is an important characteristic of cloud computing. Instant scalability and high performance can be delivered at a low cost using multi-tenant architecture. Multi-tenancy provides the following benefits to consumers:
    - Competent service delivery with minimal client-side administration, less maintenance and burden.
    - Reliable, well-organized performance and high delivery on large-scale deployed architecture
    - Quick release cycles for new product or version update.
4. **Verified scalability – support millions of users with verified scalability:** When customer start using any cloud computing service, they may scale business application and services a any time. Greater power of scalability reflects bigger consumer community, which can pro vide more high-value feedbacks to cloud providers for making further improvements and innovations. Bigger users' communities also enhance collaboration among customers; the can easily share their project and service experience. Cloud computing platform and infra structure service providers must ensure the following:
    - High and instant scalability to hundreds of thousands of subscribers with some prove history.
    - Resources to guarantee service-level agreements (SLAs), highest standards of servic quality, high performance and dedicated security to every consumer.
    - Automation and continuous delivery in infrastructure to meet changing demands.
    - Performance and reliability as customer numbers increase.
5. **High performance – deliver high-speed performance across the globe:** Consistency an high availability are the key success drivers for cloud providers. It is the responsibility c cloud providers to always ensure high-performance continuity across the globe and provid historical statistics for performance claims such as the following:
    - Number of average transactions per day.
    - Average page response time.
6. **Total disaster recovery:** A disaster recovery process always assures consumers that their da will always be available and secure in case of any crisis or security violation. Disaster recove

depends on quick data backup, retention, archival and retrieval capability across multiple locations of geographically dispersed datacenters. A complete disaster recovery plan includes the following:

- Data backup policies that create multiple backups across the datacenters in near real time at the disk level.
- Multi-level backup strategy should be implemented; data must be stored as a secondary level backup, which means more on hard-disk level.

7. **High availability:** To provide high availability and business continuity, cloud providers must have the latest hardware and networking facilities with verified high-availability infrastructure and software application. To ensure high availability, providers must include the following:
   - Reliable electricity supply, power, cooling and network infrastructure.
   - High-availability infrastructure – networking, server infrastructure and software.
   - Comprehensive availability of each and every historical data and service.
   - N+1 datacenter redundancy model.

7.3 Data Migration and Streaming in Cloud

Data migration in cloud is the process of transitioning some or all services, application and data of any company from on-premises location to the cloud. Certain parameters must be evaluated before moving to particular cloud provider.

7.3.1 Analysis of Cloud Provider

Before finalizing a cloud provider for your business, it is most important that you perform a detailed feasibility check and analysis of the particular provider so that you can be assured of QoS. Cloud analysts should give deep insight to customers about all factors related to cloud providers. Following are some parameters to consider before choosing a cloud provider:

1. Analysis of service offerings
2. Analysis of security offerings
3. Analysis of internal policies
4. Analysis of availability and support
5. Analysis of service level agreements
6. Analysis of infrastructure complexity and user-friendly interface
7. Analysis of disaster recovery and backup recovery plans

7.3.2 Cloud Migration Process

After zeroing in on a cloud provider in accordance with your business needs, ensure a proper strategy for application and data migration on cloud. Following are the steps you may take before cloud migration:

1. Launch cloud instances according to expected server utilization.
2. Select the operating system according to your application hosting.
3. Select different storage options such as block storage and static storage.
4. Install application server and Web server according to your application.
5. Select the cloud database instances or launch your own database image.
6. Transfer the data onto cloud database.
7. Transfer and deploy the application onto application server.
8. Host your application through a Web server and make necessary settings, such as DNS configuration.
9. Enable content caching, if required.
10. Enable content delivery network (CDN) service, if required.

7.3.3 Streaming in Cloud

The cloud streaming solution allows clients to stream their videos without owning a streaming media server. A cloud streaming solution helps clients leverage any type of streaming format and improve end user experience while reducing their time and effort to market. Figure 7.2 shows the end-to-end flow of cloud streaming.

Cloud streaming servers are also connected to content delivery network (CDN) servers for fast content delivery across the globe and encoding or transcoding servers for on-demand media transcoding (for converting source format into a device's playback format, e.g. tablets, smartphones and PCs).

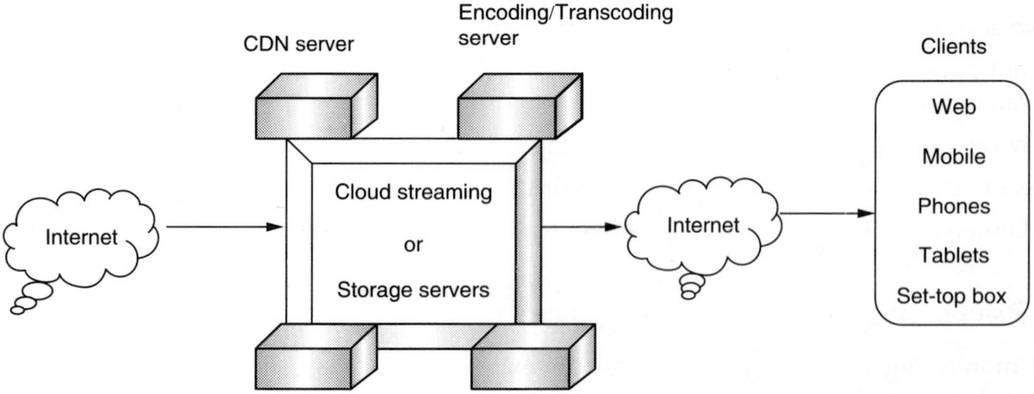

Figure 7.2 | Cloud streaming.

Amazon CloudFront and Amazon Elastic Transcoder are some popular services used along with a streaming service. CloudFront is for content delivery with high transfer speeds, whereas Transcoder is for media transcoding. Cloud streaming is designed for customers with the following requirements:

1. **Video streaming:** Ability to stream multimedia files.
2. **On-demand scalability:** Streaming capacity accessible whenever needed.
3. **Enhanced streaming performance:** High and continuous streaming over the Internet.
4. **Global reach:** Streaming points across the globe.

7.3.4 Working of Cloud Streaming

Following is the working scenario of a cloud streaming setup:

1. Cloud streaming works on an on-demand basis according to the reverse proxy technology.
2. Users do not need to deploy all multimedia files on a streaming server because of this reverse proxy technology. It works as on-demand streaming so you just need to host multimedia files on the HTTP Web server.
3. Because streaming servers are connected through a CDN network, whenever end users request for streaming content, they are immediately redirected to the nearest edge streaming servers. If the edge server does not have the content at that time, it immediately initiates an HTTP byte request for retrieving the content from the central HTTP Web server or cloud storage repository.

7.3.5 Key Features of Cloud Streaming

Following are some of the key features of cloud streaming:

1. Reliable, scalable and high performance streaming.
2. Support for all types of player, for example, on-demand Windows Media, QuickTime, Real and Flash player.
3. Streaming is possible using native platforms.
4. No additional or costly hardware or software setups are required to enable streaming media.
5. Continuous integration with cloud storage for storing multimedia files to ensure 24×7×365 availability.
6. Live streaming facility for live events using any type of streaming format.
7. Secure streaming and access policies according to content, geographic or IP address location.
8. Maintenance of log delivery or FTP of streaming log files.

7.4 Performance Monitoring Tools in Cloud

Cloud monitoring is the best way for an organization to administrate and optimize its cloud resources by taking care of full utilization of resources at maximum efficiency. Cloud monitoring ensures that SLAs are met and performances are optimal.

To monitor cloud resources, some QoS tools and services are used. Cloud QoS monitoring is done with the help of a third-party service or tool (which comes under cloud SaaS model). Cloud providers also offer some internal services for monitoring their internal cloud resources. Various cloud monitoring tools are evolving every year, but this chapter will discuss only a few popular and most adopted cloud monitoring tools:

1. **Zenoss cloud monitoring:** This tool was developed by Zenoss. It supports all types of cloud deployment, which means it can monitor all cloud operations related to public, private or hybrid clouds. It provides cloud monitoring ZenPacks for different cloud vendors. Following are some key functions of Zenoss cloud monitoring:
    - It provides quick monitoring of each cloud instance without installing any agent software before monitoring.
    - It provides detailed reporting of end-to-end cloud operations, sending alerts, facilitates self-service portal.
2. **RevealCloud:** RevealCloud is a cloud virtual server performance monitoring tool developed by CopperEgg. It has the capability to monitor both private and public cloud deployments. RevealCloud is based on cross-correlation analytics that can quickly identify and fix the original causes of any issues while running an application in a cloud environment. It is designed for use in the server side. RevealCloud has the following features:
    - It sends immediate notification to cloud administrators visually whenever problems are detected. It also provides detailed analytics and visibility report.
    - It provides real-time measurements, monitoring server performance every 5 s.
    - It also provides details of system, OS and process monitoring.
3. **Compuware APM:** The application performance management (APM) tool was developed by Compuware and especially designed for detailed monitoring of application performance that runs in cloud environment along the whole delivery chain. APM has the following features:
    - It provides detailed information on the root cause of problems and how much impact it has on the entire system and business.
    - It easily detects the area of faults through its fault domain isolation facility – be it a data center fault, a third-party provider issue, an Internet service provider (ISP) issue, Internet connection issue or even an Internet browser issue.
4. **Amazon CloudWatch:** Amazon CloudWatch is a service adopted worldwide by many AWS cloud users. It is used only for monitoring of all AWS services. Mostly users use Amazon CloudWatch for monitoring of AmazonEC2, RDS and DynamoDB instances. It sets many custom metrics according to the service utilization and can see any log files that the application generates. Amazon CloudWatch has following features:
    - It provides detailed monitoring of resource utilization, custom metrics auto scaling groups, elastic load balancers, DNS health check and application performance.
    - It sets alarm for custom metrics for sending notification via email or messages.
    - It also triggers automated action using alarm conditions; for example, if CPU utilization is more than the threshold, then new EC2 instances are created and vice versa.

5. **Rackspace Cloud Monitoring:** Rackspace cloud monitoring is specifically developed for Rackspace cloud users. It has a set of APIs that facilitates administrators to use or create APIs according to their requirement. Using these APIs, the administrator can automate the notification process via email or mobile, which means all resource monitoring details can be observed any time. Following are the key features of Rackspace cloud monitoring:
   - Effectively monitors overall system status including ping check, SSH check, HTTP check and HTTPS check.
   - Provides deep insight of server resources like CPU, memory, load average, file system, disk and network.
   - Provides Cloud Monitoring Agent's plug-in framework through which you can monitor any aspects of your infrastructure.

7.5 Best Practices of Cloud Computing

Cloud computing adoption has tremendous benefits and can enable massive transformation in the IT service delivery model. On the flip side, most IT infrastructures are unable to execute cloud computing adoption in the best way because of lack of knowledge and experience. Some reports say that 58% of applications running on different cloud adoption models are unmanaged and around 80% of cloud instances are underutilized. Some customer reports also state that 15% of over-utilization causes 7% revenue loss. These problems can be avoided easily if some best practices are followed while using the cloud services. Following subsections discuss some cloud computing services best practices.

7.5.1 Best Practices for Infrastructure Setup

There are some cloud architecture principles for an infrastructure setup. Let us understand these in detail:

1. **Design for failure consideration:** This must be the first and foremost concern of a cloud architect. Whenever any company or organization decides to move to a cloud infrastructure solution, it has to plan about failure. If failure conditions are planned properly, nothing will fail and data will always be available.
2. **Decouple your components:** All the components in cloud infrastructure should be decoupled and isolated from each other; for example, decoupling while setting load balancing applications. Web servers are kept tightly coupled with the application server, but this is not a best practice. Isolation and decoupling are necessary between components. Figure 7.3 shows that each Web server and application server is highly coupled.

   Web servers and application servers can be loosely coupled and isolated by putting a load balancer between them as shown in Fig. 7.4. Any Web or application server can be easily scaled up or scaled down without any dependency.

Web servers

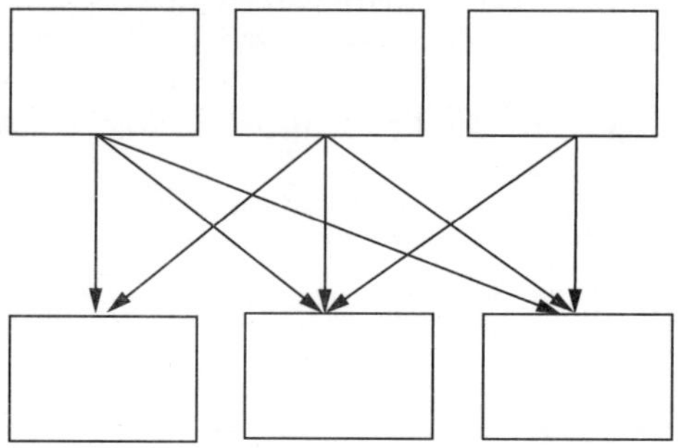

App servers

Figure 7.3 | High coupling.

Web servers

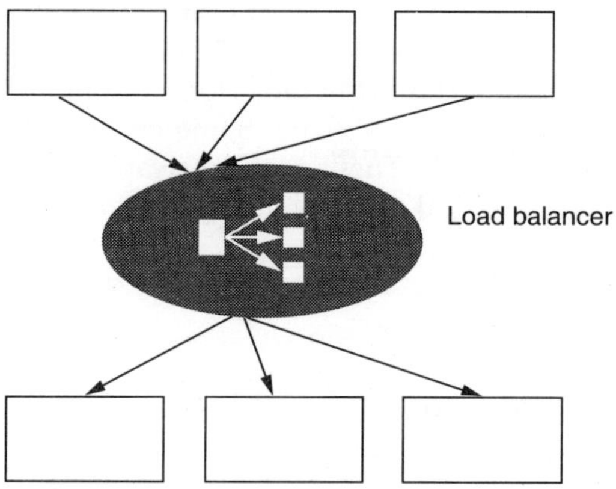

App servers

Figure 7.4 | Decoupled applications.

3. **Enable elasticity:** Elasticity is a revolutionary feature that cloud services offer. While creating the cloud infrastructure, elasticity should be implemented, but before that automation is necessary for the configuration, deployment and building process so that any application can be scaled up or down without human intervention.
4. **Design parallel:** While designing a cloud infrastructure, parallel architecture that is faster and efficient should be implemented. Two possible approaches could be as follows:
   - A server works on a job sequentially for 4 h.
   - Four servers work on a job in parallel for 4 h.

   There is no cost-wise difference, but the second approach is likely to be four times faster; therefore, parallel design is highly recommended.

5. **Build security in every layer:** While designing a cloud infrastructure, building security in each layer is recommended. Because security is the shared responsibility of the consumer and the cloud provider, following are some steps a consumer must take to ensure security:
    - Enforce the principle of least privileges when developing applications.
    - Encrypt data in transitions state.
    - Try to use multi-way to multi-factor authentication.
6. **Leverage many storage options:** Some people have this misconception that cloud storage services like Google Cloud Storage, S3, One Drive or Dropbox can be fitted for all types of data. But this is not true, one type of storage solution does not fit all. Following are some possible storage operations that must be explored for different types of requirement:
    - Object store
    - Block store
    - Relational database
    - NoSQL
    - CDN or edge caching

7.5.2 Best Practices for Data and Service Migration

The data migration approach alone is not sufficient, the best practice is to follow six processes (as shown in Fig. 7.5) whenever any enterprise wants to move data and services to the cloud.

1. **Cloud assessment:** In this phase, an enterprise gathers the business requirement to move to the cloud following the cloud adoption trend in the market. Many businesses have received tremendous success with optimized costs after adopting cloud solutions, but before planning on cloud adoption, the first step is to analyze whether the business really needs cloud adoption. Cloud assessment includes finding out the type of cloud deployment model suitable to the enterprise's business demand and the type of cloud service model that aligns best with the existing business requirement. The following questions should be discussed within the enterprise before making a decision:
    - Does our business need the cloud?
    - What benefits will our company achieve after adopting the cloud service?
    - How much would the budget be?
    - Which cloud deployment model will suit our business need?
    - Which cloud service model will suit our business need?

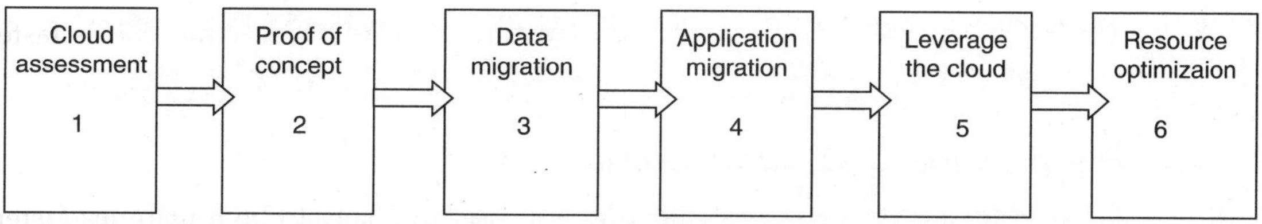

Figure 7.5 | Best practice for data and service migration to the cloud.

2. **Proof of concept:** Once an enterprise identifies the right cloud provider and services, it is time to validate the business case on actual the cloud deployment environment. The functionality can be tested with a small size cloud instance and a small database. In this phase, necessary benchmarks and set expectations should be performed, all legacy software testing, stress testing and system end-to-end performance testing should be conducted. It is mandatory to test the capacity of the cloud service provider and the performance of the migrated application. Following are some tests required while building a proof of concept:
    - Testing of cloud infrastructure.
    - Testing of offered cloud services.
    - Non-functional testing of deployed cloud application.
3. **Data migration:** In this phase, the actual mapping of the cloud resources is done on the basis of the business requirement. Following are the main questions that should be discussed by a cloud architect:
    - How much time and effort would be required to migrate to the cloud?
    - What would be the best storage options available on the cloud?
    - Which database would be the most suitable for existing applications and from a future perspective?
4. **Application migration:** The application migration phase is divided into the two following categories:
    - *Forklift migration strategy:* If an enterprise wished to move its application in one shot rather than in parts, then the forklift strategy is used. This requires very minimal code changes and is preferred for traditional applications, that is, stateless and tightly coupled applications or self-contained applications.
    - *Hybrid migration strategy:* Using hybrid strategy, applications can be moved in parts. This is mostly suitable for huge infrastructure systems because it mitigates the risk of any unexpected behavior.
5. **Leverage the cloud:** Once an enterprise has successfully migrated to the cloud, run the required tests and is assured that everything is working as expected, the next step is to analyze how to leverage other benefits of cloud computing, such as load balancing, auto scaling, content caching, elasticity and automation. Implementation of disaster recovery solution is also important in this phase.
6. **Resource optimization:** Resource optimization is a continuous process. While leveraging all resources of cloud, an enterprise should also consider the optimal utilization of resources and the best, cost-saving model. It should always strive to lower its costs and increase system performance whenever possible. To do this, various cost- and capacity-assessment tools are available.

7.5.3 Best Practices for Cost Optimization

Users are always recommended to use some monitoring tools and services that were discussed earlier in this chapter. Some cost-calculating tools are available that can suggest the best optimal ıtilization of cloud resources. These tools provide detailed reporting of each service costing and ıtilization so that the enterprise can manage it according to its budget with the best utilization of ·esources.

Following is a list of some tools that can suggest the best optimal utilization of cloud ·esources:

1. Cloudyn (http://www.cloudyn.com/)
2. Teevity (http://www.teevity.com/)
3. Apptio (http://www.apptio.com/)
4. Kaavo (http://www.kaavo.com/)
5. Cloudability (https://cloudability.com/)
6. CloudVertical (https://cloudvertical.com/)
7. CloudCheckr (http://cloudcheckr.com/)

\n enterprise should always try to use any one of the above tools for cloud infrastructure cost ›ptimization.

⁷.5.4 *Best Practices for Cloud Capacity Management*

Jsually cloud architects plan for cloud capacity according to business requirements and demand orecasting. Cloud infrastructure service resources falls into three categories: (a) server, (b) storage nd (c) database. Because there are many cloud providers and different pricing models for various loud instances, it becomes difficult to select and plan. To solve this problem of plenty, one way is ɔ survey, analyze and conduct extensive market research among all cloud infrastructure provid- rs and then decide. Another approach that is very successful nowadays and is recommended as best practice is to use a cloud infrastructure service comparison tool such as PlanForCloud. This ɔol works as shown in Figure 7.6 and is described as follows:

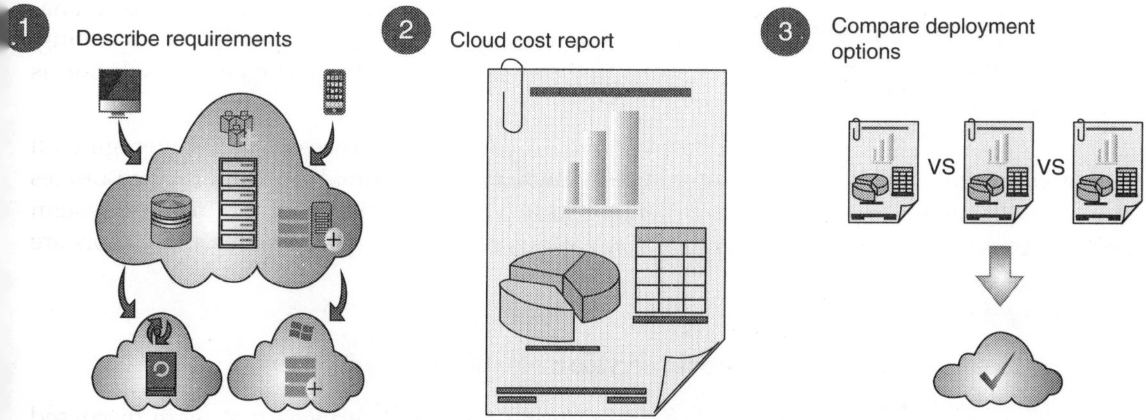

Figure 7.6 | PlanForCloud. (*Courtesy:* RightScale)

1. **Describe requirement:** An enterprise can compare all major cloud infrastructure service providers by selecting the CPU count and RAM that its application may require.
2. **Generate cloud cost report:** After collecting the requirement, a cloud cost report is generated on the basis of various deployment components such as server instance costs/hour, database instance cost/hour, database I/O transaction costs, storage costs, snapshot costs, database read and write request costs, data archiving costs, and internal or external data transfer costs.
3. **Compare deployment options:** Now the detailed report can be studied easily and all specific scenarios and deployment can be compared to help make the right decision and best capacity planning for the future.

Following are some other tools which could be helpful in planning and cloud capacity management:

1. Virtustream Advisor Modeling and Planning Software (http://www.virtustream.com/cloud-software/advisor)
2. Cloudamize (http://www.cloudamize.com/)
3. Cloudyn (http://www.cloudyn.com/)
4. Kloud (http://www.kloud.com.au/)

Summary

In this chapter, we have learned about concept of cloud middleware and the functionalities of cloud middleware. We have understood QoS issues of cloud providers, data migration steps, cloud streaming and features of cloud streaming. We have gained in-depth knowledge about the best practices for cloud infrastructure setup, data and service migration and cost and capacity management. These best practices have given us an architectural view, which is useful for designing and implementing cloud solution for any enterprise. The next chapter will discuss details about private cloud computing platforms and cloud testing.

Multiple Choice Questions

1. Middleware is originated from _______.
   (a) Cloud computing systems
   (b) Distributed computing systems
   (c) Grid computing
   (d) Web technologies

2. What is the first most important thing in data migration in cloud?
   (a) Cloud testing
   (b) Cloud security test
   (c) Legal issues
   (d) Analysis of cloud provider

3. Identify the use of Amazon Transcoder service from the following options.
   (a) Fast content delivery
   (b) Monitoring

(c) Media transcoding
(d) Capacity planning

4. Cloud streaming works according to _______.
(a) Reverse proxy technology
(b) Client server technology
(c) Web technology
(d) None of these

5. Identify the use of Amazon Cloud Watch service from the following options.
(a) Cloud security of AWS resources
(b) Monitoring of all AWS services
(c) Cost optimization of AWS resources
(d) Initial cost estimation of AWS resources

6. All the components in cloud infrastructure should be _______.
(a) Decoupled
(b) Loosely coupled
(c) Highly coupled
(d) None of these

7. How many steps are required for data service migration on cloud?
(a) 4
(b) 5
(c) 6
(d) 7

8. Which types of tools are required for an organization to administrate and optimize its cloud resources by taking care of full utilization of resources at maximum efficiency?
(a) Cost optimization tools
(b) Performance monitoring tools
(c) Cloud security tools
(d) Cost estimation tools

9. During data service migration on cloud, testing of cloud infrastructure and offered cloud services is part of _______.
(a) Cloud assessment
(b) Data migration
(c) Application migration
(d) Proof of concept

10. If an enterprise wished to move its application in one shot on cloud, then it is called _______.
(a) Hybrid migration strategy
(b) Forklift migration strategy
(c) Traditional cloud strategy
(d) None of these

11. What is the purpose of Cloudyn and Cloudability tools?
    (a) Cost optimization tool
    (b) Performance monitoring tool
    (c) Cloud security tools
    (d) Cost estimation tools

12. What is the key purpose of PlanForCloud tool?
    (a) Cost optimization
    (b) Performance monitoring
    (c) Cloud capacity management
    (d) Cloud security

Review Questions

1. Explain the concept and functionalities of cloud middleware.
2. What are the seven quality standards that must be followed by any cloud provider?
3. Explain cloud streaming and key features of cloud streaming.
4. What are the two main application migration strategies on cloud computing?
5. What do you understand by cloud monitoring? Give examples of any two cloud monitoring tools.
6. Explain in detail about the best practices for data and service migration to the cloud.
7. What do you understand by decoupling of cloud application?
8. Explain how to implement the best practices for cost and capacity management.

Answers to Multiple Choice Questions

1. (b), **2.** (d), **3.** (c), **4.** (a), **5.** (b), **6.** (a), **7.** (c), **8.** (b),
9. (d), **10.** (b), **11.** (a), **12.** (a)

CHAPTER 8 Private Cloud Computing Platforms and Cloud Testing

Learning Objectives

After reading this chapter, you will be able to:

- Know about Eucalyptus private cloud computing provider.
- Know about OpenNebulla private cloud computing provider.
- Know about OpenStack private cloud computing provider.
- Know about CloudStack private cloud computing provider.
- Know about Tplatform web infrastructure system.
- Know about Apache Virtual Computing Lab and Enomaly Elastic Computing Platform.
- Understand different types of cloud testing.
- Understand details of application testing strategy in a cloud computing environment.

8.1 Private Cloud Computing Platforms

A private cloud infrastructure is operated solely for an organization, deployed across its infrastructure and used by its employees and some privileged persons. This section discusses a variety of existing private cloud computing providers, although most private cloud computing platforms are based on open source technologies and still evolving in nature.

8.1.1 Eucalyptus

Eucalyptus is one of the most popular and well-adopted private cloud infrastructure providers. Users can provision their own organizational infrastructure resources on an on-demand basis with the help of the self-service portal of Eucalyptus.

The Eucalyptus private cloud is deployed on "on-premise" datacenters and can be accessed by users within the enterprise over intranet. All the critical and sensitive data are always behind the enterprise firewall; thereby, it is more secure and less prone to any external attack.

Eucalyptus also provides hybrid cloud functionalities; it provides some APIs to support the AWS public cloud. The entire framework of Eucalyptus is robust and according to industry standards. Figure 8.1 explains the eucalyptus architecture.

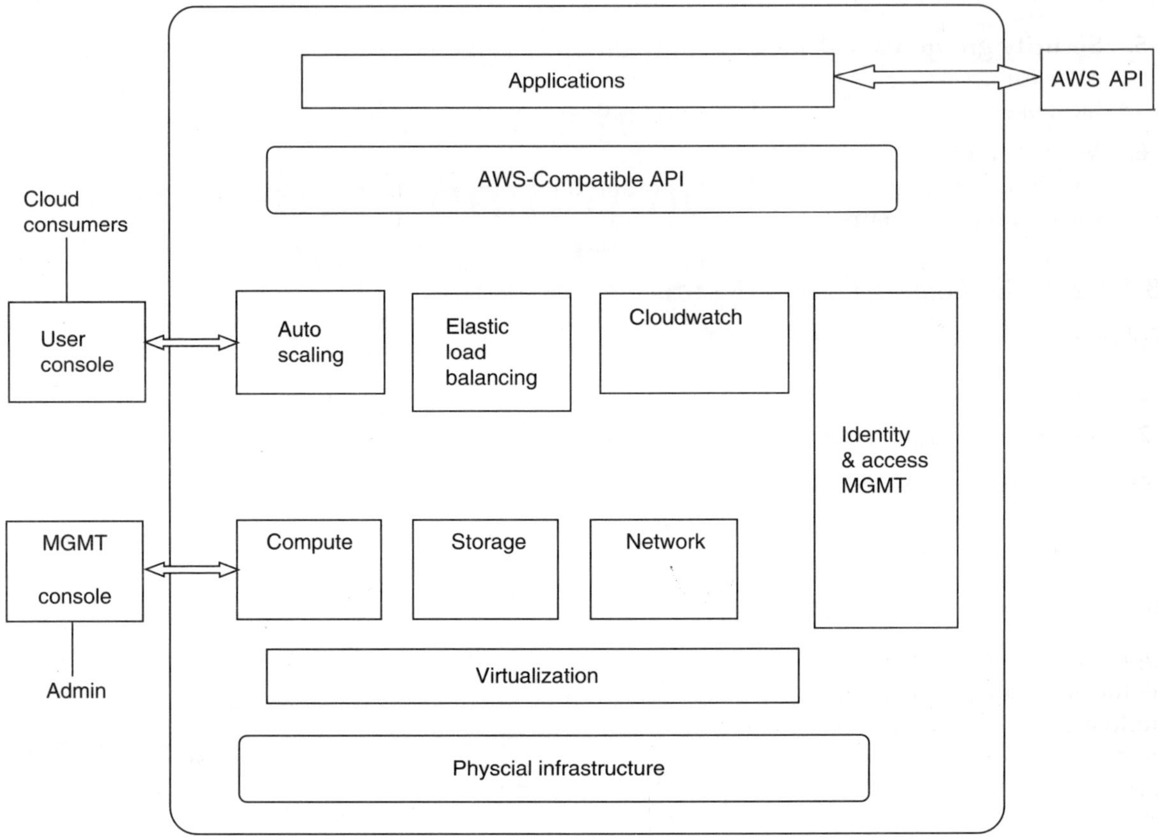

Figure 8.1 | Eucalyptus architecture.

8.1.1.1 Functionalities of Eucalyptus

Following are some key functionalities of Eucalyptus:

1. **Key management:** To validate identity of users, Eucalyptus provides both (public and private) key pairs. Users cannot make an SSH login to virtual machine (VM) without these key pairs to validate a user's identity when logging into the VMs via SSH.
2. **Image management:** To run instances on Eucalyptus cloud, some image operations, such as register, deregister, upload, download, bundling and unbundling of images, are required. All these operations are performed easily by using a simple-to-use image management interface.
3. **Linux-based VM management:** This is a basic functionality provided by any cloud infrastructure provider. Eucalyptus allows users to run their Linux-based VM instances. Users can make all types of operations with the VM, such as run, terminate, reboot or restart using the simple-to-use VM management interface.
4. **IP address management:** Users can associate or disassociate elastic IPs with VM instances so that IP address does not change in case of VM reboot or restart. According to the mode of networking, users can perform all these operations easily using the IP address management interface.

5. **Security group management:** Security group is a specific feature to set customized firewall rules for accessing VM instances. With the help of the Eucalyptus security management interface, users can easily create, delete and give permissions in security groups.
6. **Volume and snapshot management:** Eucalyptus lets users create dynamic block volumes, which are analogous to raw block storage devices that can be attached with VM instances. Users can make snapshots of volumes and can make volumes from snapshots.

8.1.1.2 Major Features of Eucalyptus

Following are some main features of the Eucalyptus cloud platform:

1. It supports hybrid cloud and extends API support with public cloud AWS.
2. It supports multiple hypervisors including KVM and Xen.
3. It has multiple networking modes to support a variety of network architectures.
4. It enables administration and management through command line interface or Web UI.

8.1.2 OpenNebula

OpenNebula is a complete open source package for building all types of cloud deployments including hybrid, private and public clouds. To build a hybrid cloud, the first requirement is to build a private cloud and then the private cloud can be extended to support a public cloud deployment. OpenNebula is one of the oldest open source private cloud infrastructure providers. The OpenNebula infrastructure service provides elastic platforms for instant scalability and high-speed delivery of services. Figure 8.2 represents the user view of OpenNebula.

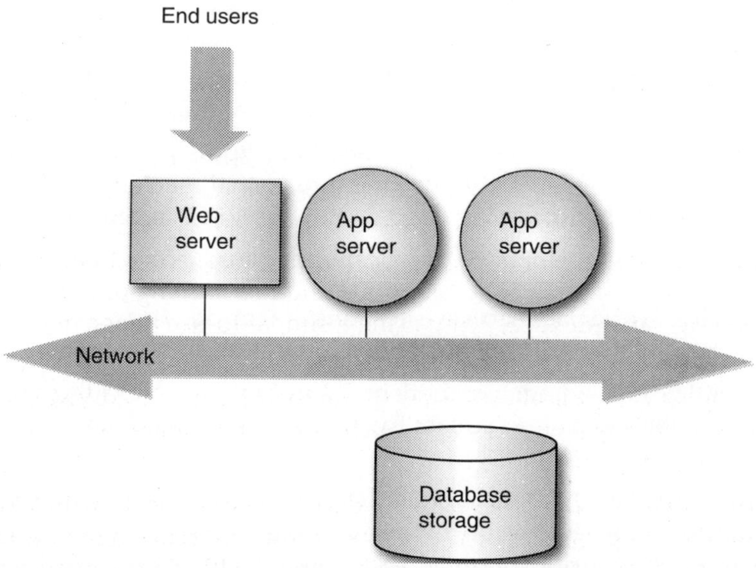

Figure 8.2 | User view of OpenNebula.

Services are hosted in virtual machines and then monitored and controlled by the OpenNebula operations center or control interface. All services can be accessed by OpenNebula's command line interface or cloud APIs.

8.1.2.1 Functionalities of OpenNebula

Following are some main functionalities of OpenNebula:

1. **Infrastructure resources management:** It manages all infrastructure resources such as storage, network and virtualization using automation for enabling the dynamic placement of the multi-tier services.
2. **Virtual machine life cycle management:** VMs are easy to execute and operate. The end-to-end flow is managed by internal VM placement polices. It extends support for interconnecting virtual machine network.
3. **VM images management:** This is the explanation and process of transfer and clone VM images. The registration of the images can be done before execution. VM images are moved to the host and swap disk images are produced. Once the execution is done, VM images can be copied on the repository again.
4. **Security management:** Security policies ensure users that they only use their resources with proper authorization and isolation.
5. **Information and accounting management:** It is necessary to check whether the operations of the servers are correct or not. There are indicators to analyze the expected server operations and results.

8.1.3 Nimbus

Nimbus is an open source software package for building infrastructure as a service (IaaS) offers. Nimbus enables users to outsource their infrastructure services to other consumers that are quite attractive and challenging when someone leverages open source products. Nimbus cloud is an integrated set of tools that supports all types of virtualization, including Xen and KVM hypervisor.

8.1.3.1 Functionalities of Nimbus

Following are the main functionalities of Nimbus cloud infrastructure services:

1. **Workspace service:** Workspace service is responsible for providing computing resources that allows users to deploy their virtual machines and rent out their computational resources.
2. **Cumulus:** Cumulus is a storage component responsible for allocating quota-based storage system. It also enables seamless scalability, which allows users to create multiple storage options.
3. **Nimbus Context Broker:** Nimbus Context Broker is one of the important components in Nimbus architecture. It is responsible for provisioning of resources from multiple clouds with the enablement of all security concerns. Users are able to leverage different IaaS cloud services using the Nimbus Context Broker component.

4. **Sky computing tools:** Sky computing tools are responsible for the on-demand basis scaling of the infrastructure. These tools are executed in multi-cloud environments including private and public clouds. Automatic scalability is also achieved by using sky computing tools.
5. **Open source extendibility:** Nimbus is an open source-based project; it is always expected that developers and contributors should enhance and extend the functionalities of existing Nimbus components. Nimbus has a community of open source contributors where all can connect and discuss more issues.

8.1.4 TPlatform

TPlatform is a Web infrastructure system developed and designed by Bo Peng and co-workers from China.

They designed a new GFS-like file system called "TFS" in which files are divided into variable-size chunks to facilitate massive data processing and implemented some enhancement on MapReduce to improve the system throughput.

This section describes the implementation architecture of TPlatform and presents an overview of the system, followed by detailed system components and some practical issues.

Figure 8.3 illustrates the TPlatform system framework, which consists of three layers – the PC cluster, infrastructure for cloud computing platform and a data processing application layer.

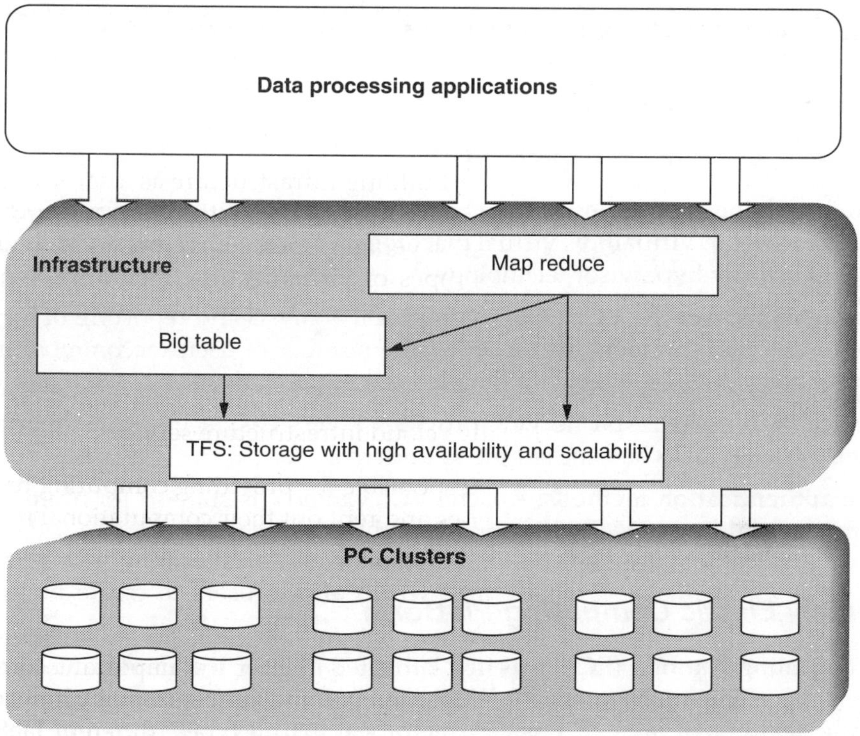

Figure 8.3 | System framework of TPlatform.

1. **Data processing layer:** Data processing layer interacts with users for developing their applications like natural language processing (NLP), Web analysis, classification system or any other data consuming application.
2. **Infrastructure for cloud computing platform:** This layer is a central layer and is responsible for all operations. This layer includes TFS file system with implementation of BigTable and MapReduce programming model.
3. **PC cluster:** PC clusters are a collection of hardware and storage devices that are used in the form of a cluster for big data processing.

8.1.5 Apache Virtual Computing Lab

Apache VCL is an open source private cloud computing platform developed by the Apache Software Foundation. It provides all basic functionalities of private cloud computing deployment to users. The architecture of VCL is a combination of the following four main elements:

1. **Compute node:** It is a combination of physical servers, virtual machines, lab machines and other computing resources.
2. **Management node:** It is a central component of VCL architecture. It consists of physical deployer, virtual deployer and new deployer module.
3. **Database:** VCL database provides resource mapping, resource inventory, reservation requests, user privileges, image profile and metadata.
4. **Web UI:** It is an end-user access point which authorizes registered users.

8.1.5.1 Features of Apache VCL

Following are some key features of Apache VCL:

1. **Multiple provisioning supports:** Apache VCL supports multiple hypervisor technologies including BareMetal, VirtualBox, virtual machines, VMware ESXi and KVM. It gives users the flexibility to use any hypervisor technology.
2. **Log data analysis:** Apache VCL enables graphical analysis and reporting of logs of different resources. Customer can view the report by the number of users' accommodation, total and unique user count, OS, browser with detailed statistical analysis.
3. **Self-service Web portal:** Apache VCL provides a very easy self-service interface for users and administration tasks become simple to understand.
4. **Multiple authentication methods:** Apache VCL extends its support for multiple authentication methods including LDAP, which builds additional security layers for security.

8.1.6 Enomaly Elastic Computing Platform

The Elastic Computing Platform (ECP) was first launched in 2005; it is also known as the first cloud infrastructure service. The initial version of ECP itself became very successful; however, version 3 contains all true features of IaaS. ECP is capable of serving all types of critical IT infrastructure demands. It provides an easy-to-use administrator as well. Figure 8.4 depicts ECP architecture.

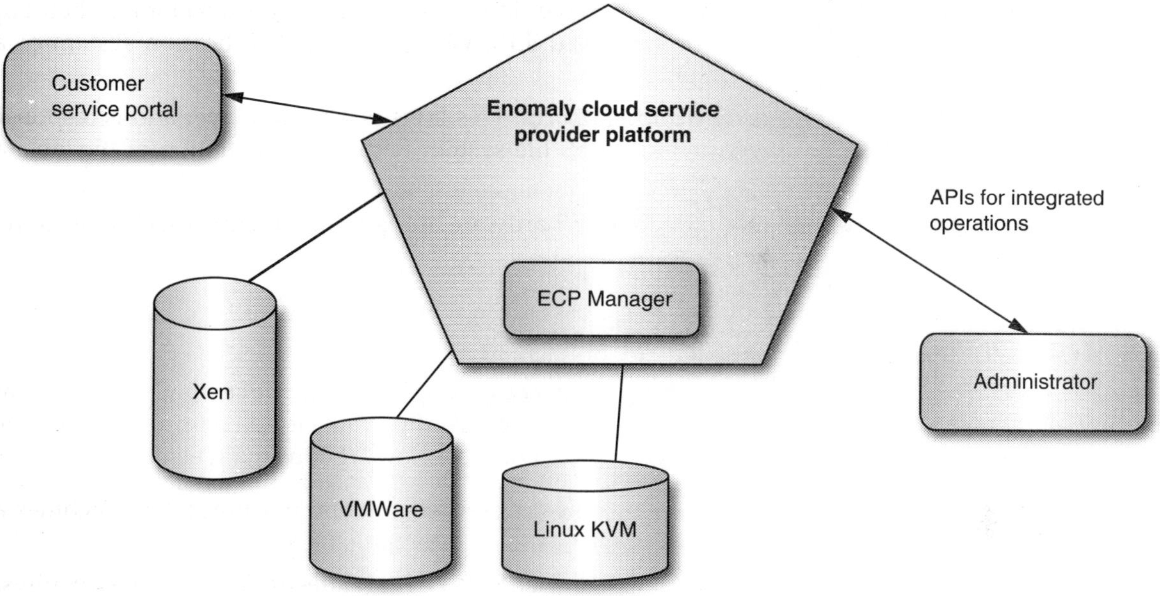

Figure 8.4 | Enomaly Elastic Computing Platform.

8.1.6.1 Features of Enomaly ECP

Following are the key features of Enomaly ECP:

1. **Unlimited scalability:** ECP has multiple datacenters across various geographic locations, which enable unlimited scalability for customers. ECP's self-service managed portal provides an easy-to-use, simple administration portal with real-time monitoring and controlling features.
2. **Strong multi-tenant security:** ECP offers fine-grained strong multi-tenacy for each customer. It enables proper virtual resource isolation and network resource isolation among all customers while serving numerous virtual networks (VLANS) for each customer. It has a solid mechanism to ensure true multi-tenancy.
3. **Automated provisioning:** ECP enables automatic configuration and management for infrastructure deployment, which is the prime need for huge infrastructure nowadays. Users can perform pre-configuration and modifications in VM images even if they are offline so that they can quickly perform migration and configuration.
4. **Rich integration with existing infrastructure:** ECP has a very large set of API support for simplifying user task and provisioning infrastructure resources such as service level agreement (SLA) integration, billing system overview, provision or de-provisioning the virtual resources and controlling all administrative tasks.
5. **Flexible cloud service business and revenue models:** While developing the cost model (pay-per-use model) for infrastructure services, the provider faces the challenge of delivering high-quality service with a cost-effective model. ECP solves this challenge by applying over-subscription and quality of services approaches.

8.1.6.2 Benefits of Enomaly ECP

Following are the key benefits of Enomaly ECP:

1. Support for cloud interoperability and application portability with instant recovery and live migration features.
2. Datacenter resources are quickly accessible for any application without provisioning costs and any distraction of services.
3. Proficient association of SLAs and virtual applications under one common management portal.
4. Automatic scalability in case of unexpected spikes in workload demand.
5. Fully API support for user management, billing and accounting.

8.1.7 OpenStack

OpenStack is the leading private cloud platform provider purely based on open source technologies. OpenStack was the pilot project initiated by Rackspace and NASA with the association of more than 200 companies. The first version of OpenStack was launched in 2010. The objective of this great initiative was to utilize open source software for building a cloud computing platform that can be run on standard hardware.

OpenStack provides an easy-to-control dashboard to manage networking, storage and compute resources and facilitates users to provision resources. Figure 8.5 illustrates the architecture of OpenStack.

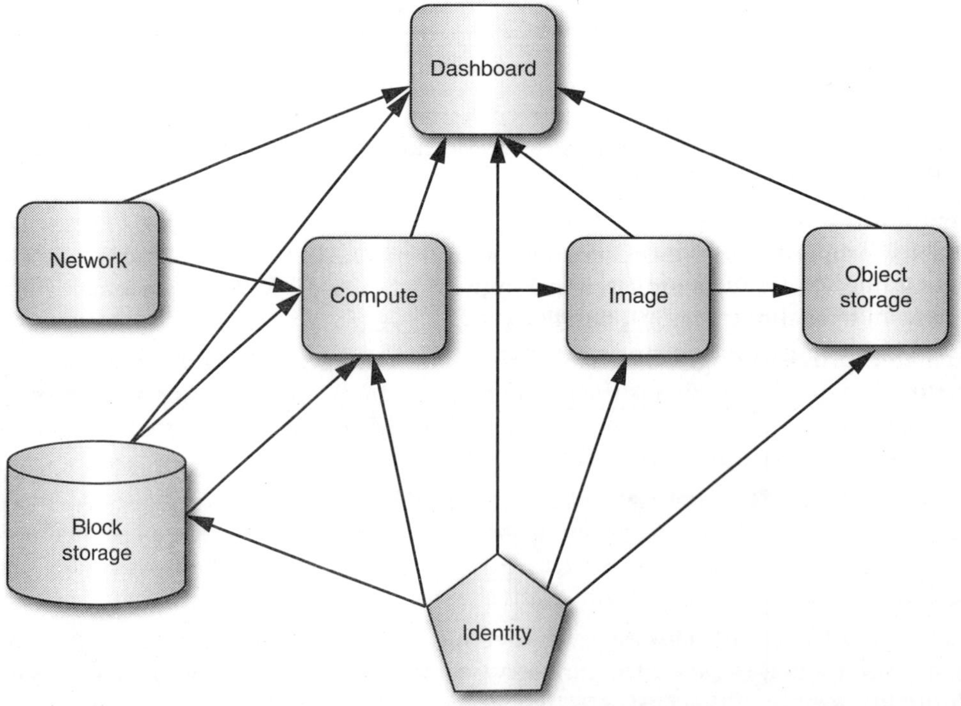

Figure 8.5 | Architecture of OpenStack.

8.1.7.1 Components of OpenStack

OpenStack private cloud is a combination of various interlinked components that are responsible for all the following different operations:

1. **OpenStack compute (Nova):** Nova is the main computing component of OpenStack. Users can provision virtual machines using the Nova service. Users manage virtual computing resources with the help of this service; thereby, it is the most important and basic service of OpenStack.
2. **Object storage (Swift):** This is a storage service for OpenStack. It is an object-based store accessed via HTTP. It also has data replication and scalability features that depend on the size of enterprise cloud deployment.
3. **Block storage (Cinder):** The facility of persistent block storage is achieved by using Cinder. Block storage can be easily attached by running instances.
4. **Identity service (Keystone):** Identity and access management is done by the Keystone service. It is same as the IAM service of AWS EC2 public cloud. It manages all authentication and access services for OpenStack users.
5. **OpenStack image service (Glance):** Image management is performed by the Glance service. It includes registration, storage and retrieval of virtual machine server images.
6. **Dashboard (Horizon):** This component is responsible for communicating with other components such as Nova and Neutron and provides Web-based admin portal for managing and visualizing all other services.

8.1.8 CloudStack

CloudStack is another very successful open source cloud deployment. It was first developed by cloud.com but was later acquired by Citrix. It facilitates building, deploying and managing on-premises private cloud. It also extends API support to public cloud for enabling hybrid cloud capabilities.

The basic installation of CloudStack just requires two machines. Admin server for management can be installed on the first machine and the second machine can work as a cloud infrastructure. Figure 8.6 represents the basic deployment model of CloudStack.

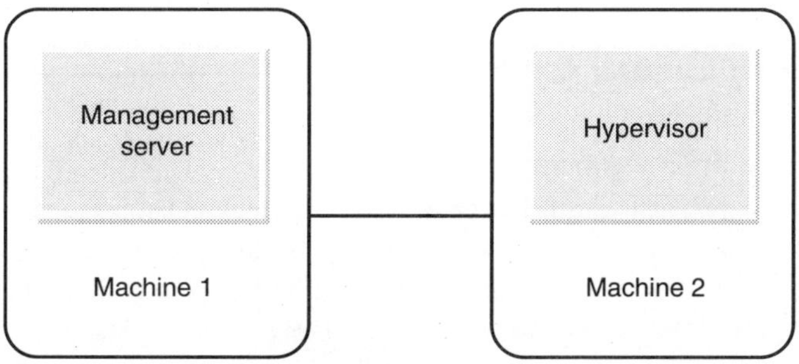

Figure 8.6 | Basic deployment of CloudStack.

8.1.8.1 Functionalities of CloudStack

Following are the main features of CloudStack:

1. **Setting up on-demand cloud:** On-demand elastic cloud computing services can be easily set up using the CloudStack private cloud with end-users resources provisioning.
2. **Multiple hypervisor support:** CloudStack supports multiple hypervisor technologies including Xen, Hyper-V, KVM, vSphere and BareMetal. This feature is specific to CloudStack as the only cloud model that can support all type of hypervisors.
3. **Automation:** CloudStack enables automatic configuration of network, routing VPN, firewall and storage access settings for each virtual machine deployment; therefore, less human intervention is required in administration.
4. **Scalable infrastructure:** CloudStack is capable to manage any number of numbers of servers across the different datacenters. Virtual machines are never affected by any schedule maintenance or in case of any disaster.
5. **High availability:** CloudStack enables high availability using multi-node server deployment, replication and load balancer methods. Users never experience discontinuity in services.

8.2 Cloud-Optimized Linux

Linux distribution is more optimized in a cloud environment. It is observed that Linux OS are mostly acquired by all public cloud providers. We can get easily variety of Linux distribution OS like Ubuntu, RHEL, CentOS, Suse Linux Enterprise Server and BSD versions on cloud platforms offering.

Following are some of the main reasons for the adoption of Linux in a cloud environment:

1. Licensing is not required for open source Linux distribution on a per-unit or per-core basis.
2. Server hardening process for Linux distribution OS is simple.
3. Linux distribution is ideal for virtual appliances.
4. Because of the open source nature, users can enable more security options.
5. Enablement of third-party tools, services and new research to improve performance is easy with Linux distributions.

8.3 Testing in Cloud Computing

Various types of testing environments are offered by cloud providers, which is also known as Testing as a Service (TaaS), but the scope of this section is limited to focus upon cloud interoperability solutions and automated testing frameworks. However, various types of cloud testing scenarios, the need for interoperability, the challenges and existing developing solutions of interoperability will be discussed. This section will propose a practical and feasible architecture for cloud interoperability testing which will benefit the client's business.

8.3.1 Types of Cloud Testing

Following are the three main categories of cloud testing (Fig. 8.7):

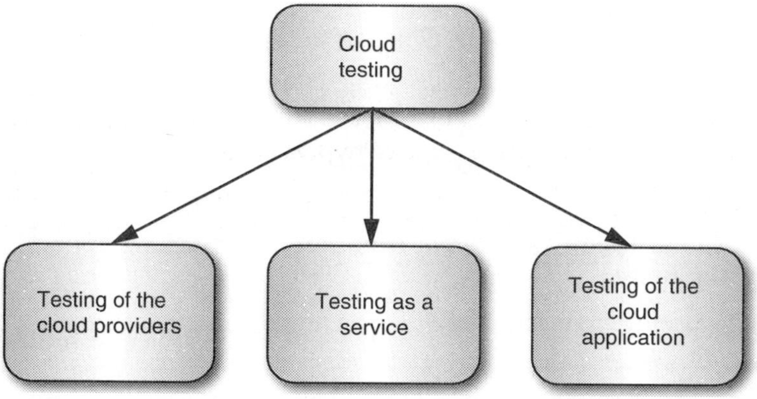

Figure 8.7 | Category of cloud testing.

1. **Testing of the cloud providers:** It employs testing of cloud infrastructure and resources. The cloud itself consists of computing, services, storage and networking components, all of which must interoperate smoothly to guarantee high performance. This testing is conducted by the cloud provider to ensure that all cloud resources such as storage, switching, security, virtual infrastructure, QoS, application delivery are working according to the expected output. TestShell and CloudShell are the good examples of this.
2. **Testing as a service:** Moving the testing process, test assets and test infrastructure from their current state to facilitate either testing in the cloud. It is a model of software testing used to test an application as a service provided to customers across the Internet. By eliminating the need to test the application on the customer's own computer with testers on site, TaaS alleviates the customer's burden of installing and maintaining test environments, sourcing and (test) support. Various SaaS tools, open source testing tools and licensed tools come in this category. Cloud9, D-Cloud and YETI are the good examples of TaaS.
   - **Cloud9** is a platform for automatic testing that parallelizes symbolic execution, an effective, but poorly scalable test automation technique to cloud infrastructures.
   - **D-Cloud** is a research project of testing that can fall either in the category of testing in the cloud or of the cloud. Test cases can be run simultaneously using the D-Cloud test framework; it provides automation in system configuration.
3. **Testing of the cloud application:** This includes testing of application qualification to migrate on cloud. This test ensures that all prerequisites that are required for migration of existing applications on the cloud are properly working. Performance tests for a given load profile (load test), for abnormal stress conditions (stress test), for system availability, for VM Migration and its availability, and for multi-tenant are all examples of application qualification testing before moving to a cloud. PushToTest and SOASTA are the good products available for this.

- **PushToTest** can be used within a continuous integration environment, where the build server can start the cloud testing tool automatically to deploy the system under test and the test code to available test nodes in the cloud. The cloud testing framework runs the test cases, collects results and tears down the cloud instances afterwards.
- **SOASTA** cloud test supports performance and stress testing by leveraging the compute power offered by cloud computing.

8.3.2 Application Testing Strategy in a Cloud Computing Environment

In traditional testing, scalability is generally fixed and testing is limited to fixed numbers of users within the network. Cloud testing is different from traditional testing applications because on-demand scalability is unlimited.

Following are a few testing steps required when an application moves to a cloud environment:

1. **Performance testing:** To identify the response time of the system when multi-users are operating simultaneously, cloud performance testing is required. Customers must test the latency of their application after deploying it in the cloud.
2. **Load testing:** To identify availability and system stability when user count is increasing, cloud load testing is required.
3. **Capacity testing:** When an application migrates to a cloud environment, the highest capacity of existing underlying hardware, bandwidth and network performance should be benchmarked to verify if the existing system is capable of handling unexpected usage scenario. Cloud capacity testing is required for this.
4. **Failover testing:** Cloud failover testing is required to identify system availability and performance in case of datacenter outage or peak loads on all virtual machines. For anticipating these, a simulated test bed is required using the failover testing mechanism.
5. **Application security testing:** To verify application security, cloud security testing must be performed on all applications running in a cloud environment. Some applications may have dependency on other systems, which also need to be tested in cloud application security testing.
6. **Cloud application testing tools:** Following are some commonly used test tools for all the above-mentioned testing steps which are required to verify application behaviour in cloud computing environment:
   - LoadStorm (http://loadstorm.com/)
   - CloudHarmony (https://cloudharmony.com/)
   - Windmill (http://www.getwindmill.com/)
   - SOASTA (http://www.soasta.com/)
   - Selenium (http://www.seleniumhq.org/)
   - BlazeMeter (http://blazemeter.com/)
   - QEngine (http://www.manageengine.com/products/qengine/)
   - BrowserMob (http://bmp.lightbody.net/)

Summary

In this chapter, we have learned about various private cloud computing platforms with a comprehensive architectural approach and key features of each computing platform. We have covered Eucalyptus, OpenNebula, Nimbus, TPlatform, Apache VCL, Enomaly ECP, OpenStack and CloudStack platforms. We have also understood why Linux is more preferred on a cloud environment. We have discussed in detail about the various types of cloud testing, application testing processes and testing tools used in the cloud computing environment. In the next chapter, we are going to learn about advance cloud applications and related supported services.

Multiple Choice Questions

1. How many main categories of cloud testing are there?
   (a) 2
   (b) 3
   (c) 4
   (d) 5

2. Cloud9 testing tool is an example of which type of cloud testing?
   (a) Testing of the cloud providers
   (b) Testing of the cloud application
   (c) Testing as service
   (d) Testing of the cloud service

3. SOASTA testing tool is an example of which type of cloud testing?
   (a) Testing of the cloud providers
   (b) Testing of the cloud application
   (c) Testing as service
   (d) Testing of the cloud service

4. CloudShell testing tool is an example of which type of cloud testing?
   (a) Testing of the cloud providers
   (b) Testing of the cloud application
   (c) Testing as service
   (d) Testing of the cloud service

5. What is the purpose of Keystone service in OpenStack?
   (a) Computing
   (b) Identification and authorization
   (c) Storage
   (d) Image registration

6. Which one of the following options is known as first cloud infrastructure service?
   (a) AWS cloud
   (b) OpenStack
   (c) Mircosoft cloud
   (d) Elastic Computing Platform

7. Identify the functionality of nimbus for Which cumulus service is responsible.
   (a) For allocating images
   (b) For computing
   (c) For allocating quota-based storage
   (d) For identification and authentication

8. What is PC cluster in Tplatform?
   (a) Data processing applications
   (b) MapReduce applications
   (c) Cloud resources
   (d) Collection of hardware and storage devices

9. What is the purpose of OpenStack Nova component?
   (a) Computing
   (b) Identification and authorization
   (c) Storage
   (d) Image registration

10. What is the purpose of cloud failover testing?
    (a) To identify the response time of the system
    (b) To identify system availability and performance in case of data canter outage
    (c) To verify application security
    (d) To identify availability and system

11. What is the purpose of Cloud performance testing?
    (a) To identify the response time of the system
    (b) To identify system availability and performance in case of data canter outage
    (c) To verify application security
    (d) To identify availability and system

Review Questions

1. What do you understand by private cloud computing platform? Explain the architecture of OpenStack and Eucalyptus.
2. Explain the architecture, key features and benefits of ECP.
3. Explain in detail about the cloud computing platform TPlatform.
4. What do you understand by Nimbus and OpenNebula cloud platforms? Explain the key functionalities of both platforms.
5. What do you understand by cloud testing and types of cloud testing?
6. Which testing steps are required when an application is moved to a cloud environment?
7. What are the main reasons for the adoption of Linux in a cloud environment?

Answers to Multiple Choice Questions

1. (b), 2. (c), 3. (b), 4. (a), 5. (b), 6. (d), 7. (c), 8. (d),
9. (a), 10. (b), 11. (a)

CHAPTER 9

Advance Cloud Application and Supporting Services

Learning Objectives

After reading this chapter, you will be able to:

- Know in detail about various advanced cloud applications and their practicalities.
- Provide an overview of all online sharing and collaborative services on the cloud.
- Provide an overview of various third-party services that use cloud platforms such as webmail services and instant messaging.
- Provide an overview of web conference tools and how to create groups on social networks or collaborate via blogs and wikis.
- Understand cloud analytics and software plus services.
- Understand cloud CDN and multi-CDN services.
- Understand mobile cloud computing and InterCloud issues.
- Understand sky computing and cloud governance.

9.1 Advance Cloud Applications

Cloud computing did not evolve merely to serve customers' on-demand computing resource requirements. Several data-exhaustive and critical-computing application processes can also be easily deployed over cloud computing platforms. Such mission-critical application deployment using cloud services helps in various research projects which benefits the scientific community. This section will discuss various types of critical application deployment over cloud.

9.1.1 ECG Analysis in the Cloud

An ECG (electrocardiogram) is a medical test to check heart disease by measuring the ECG waveform generated by heart. ECG analysis and monitoring can be executed effectively by cloud-enabled technologies from any devices at any time. It could be a more optimal and better option than the traditional one. Following are the key benefits of using cloud services for ECG monitoring:

1. Remote monitoring of patient's heartbeat.
2. Data analysis in much less time.
3. Immediate notification and response in real time.
4. Continuous observance with doctors and live consulting.

In the following example (Fig. 9.1), we look at the end-to-end scenario of hosting ECG analysis application as SaaS on AWS public cloud service:

1. A patient is attached to a wireless ECG sensor and a mobile device is connected to the Internet.
2. An attached wireless ECG sensor collects the patient's data and sends it to the mobile device over Bluetooth automatically.
3. Data received from the patient's mobile device are transmitted using client software to the cloud-hosted Web services.
4. A SaaS application is built to extract the waveform from the heartbeat data and then compare the extracted waveforms with a historical reference to analyze variations.
5. This SaaS is hosted on AWS EC2 instances for collecting sensor data.
   - All data are stored using the AWS S3 service.
   - The number of workflow engine instances can be controlled by AWS Elastic Load Balancer.
   - Scalability is handled using the AWS Auto Scaling service, which takes care of large number of simultaneous ECG processing.

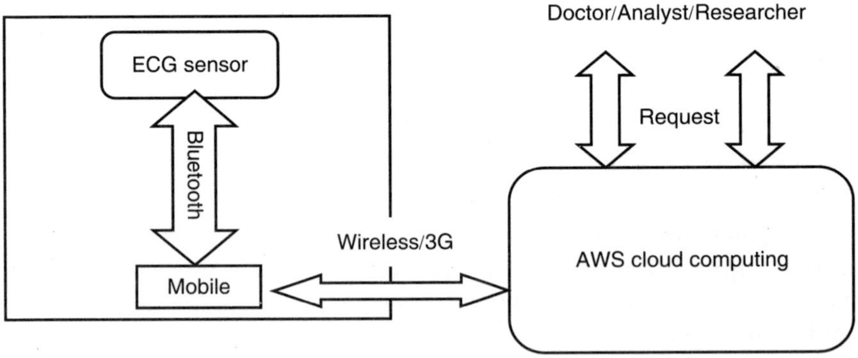

Figure 9.1 | ECG analysis in the cloud.

9.1.2 Protein Structure Prediction on Cloud

Biology- and medical research–related applications require high computing and extensive data-exhaustive operations; thereby, it is processed on a high-performance cluster machine or on supercomputer, but simpler capabilities can be leveraged using cloud computing services that offer on-demand computing and scalability, and are dynamic.

Protein structure prediction is a data-exhaustive application that infers the geometrical structure of a protein through a series of complex computations that require computing large numbers of gene sequences with multiple states.

9.1.2.1 Benefits of Using Cloud Computing

Following are the key benefits of leveraging cloud computing resources for protein structure prediction:

1. The computational power required for protein structure prediction can now be acquired on an on-demand basis without owning a set of clusters.
2. Computing capacity works on the pay-per-use model.
3. There is on-demand scalability.

Building a high-performance computing application requires multiple sets of clusters that perform high data processing in a cloud environment. These sets of cluster are built using the AWS EC2 services. Some unlimited on-demand storage capacity, such as that offered by AWS S3 (for Web-based http storage data) and AWS EBS (for storing persistent data), is also necessary.

Apart from this, other complementary services are required for end-to-end successful deployment completion such as Amazon Machine Image (AMI) and Identity and Access Management (IAM).

9.1.3 Gene Expression Data Analysis on Cloud

Gene expression profiling is another data-exhaustive medical application where expressions of more than thousand genes are measured simultaneously. This process helps identify the effect of medical treatment at a cellular level.

Gene expression is sometimes preferred as a complementary activity with protein structure analysis. To design accurate drugs for specific diseases, this is highly recommended. It is also very useful for cancer diagnosis and treatment.

The challenge with gene expression is data sampling into unique classes. Such a data-consuming and high-performance application can be built over a public cloud such as AWS by leveraging various on-demand resources. The same type of scenario can be used for building gene expression analysis as explained earlier about AWS deployment for protein structure prediction.

9.1.4 Satellite Image Processing on Cloud

One of the most efficient uses of cloud computing is to host data-exhaustive application over a cloud platform and achieve high-performance computing. Satellite image processing is an example of such an application without investing on high-performance hardware and systems. Gigabytes of raw images need to be processed on cloud platform instead on local storage.

A geo-imaging accelerator (GXL) is used for high-volume data processing at high speeds. A GXL system can be deployed easily over a cloud computing platform; for instance, using the public cloud AWS for hosting an end-to-end GXL system. PCI Geomatics has successfully deployed GXL system processing over AWS (Fig. 9.2). It did so with the help of the following AWS resources:

1. **EC2 instance:** AWS EC2 services are used to processing of GXL system is done over a set of clusters to build a virtual cluster.
2. **S3:** The Amazon Simple Storage Service is used for storing images and processing results.
3. **AMI:** The Amazon Machine Image is a pre-configured machine image used for creating new instances. Linux-based machine images are used for building a cluster.
4. **EBS:** Elastic Block Storage is used as a large storage hard disk for storing persistent data. EBS volumes are attached with instances.

PCI Geomatics used the Gluster File System (GlusterFS) and storage over EC2 instances because GlusterFS is open source, highly scalable and capable of serving petabytes of data.

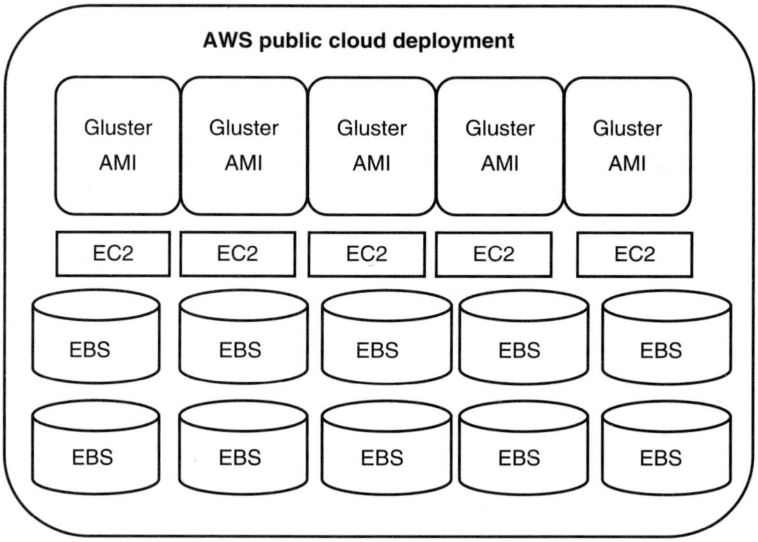

Figure 9.2 | GXL system deployment over cloud.

9.1.4.1 Key Benefits

PCI Geomatics observed the following key benefits after successful deployment of GXL processing over AWS cloud:

1. Easy setup.
2. Pay only for consumed resources.
3. On-demand processing.
4. Simple to scale up or down.

9.1.5 Social Networking on Cloud

In the era of social media, everybody is connected to various social media platforms. Social networking has become part of life, with everybody, including professionals and students spending several hours daily on social media. Some users are, however, active and some passive. We have already witnessed the huge impact of social media on our society and culture.

Social networking services can be developed with extension to service-oriented architecture (SOA) using cloud computing services. Most popular social services, such as Twitter, Facebook, LinkedIn and many others, have been using the cloud computing platform and are all on the cloud together. Imagine the following data in real time:

1. **Facebook:** As of the third quarter of 2014, Facebook had 1.35 billion monthly active users.
2. **Twitter:** As of the third quarter of 2014, Twitter had 284 million monthly active users.
3. **Skype:** Skype has last update on March 14, 2014, and had around 4.9 million users.
4. **LinkedIn:** LinkedIn has reached 300 million registered users at the beginning of 2015.

These sites leverage the power of virtual machines and cloud instances sources every day, otherwise on-demand scalability and continuous uptime would have not been possible to deliver.

9.2 Different Sharing and Collaborative Services in Cloud

This section discusses how some sharing and collaborative cloud software are used as services that covers both social and professional requirements of our daily life. The commonly used sharing and collaborative services are described as follows:

1. **Collaborating on to-do lists:** A to-do list is a traditional task management and monitoring process for assigning tasks to teams or individuals. There are plenty of great, free to-do list apps on the Web and many more on the iPhone, Android and Windows Phone. Following are some popular to-do list apps:
   - Google Keep (https://keep.google.com/)
   - Any.do (http://www.any.do/anydo)
   - Wunderlist (https://www.wunderlist.com/)
   - Sodalist (http://todoist.com/)
   - Habitrpg (https://habitrpg.com/static/front)
2. **Collaborating in task management:** Task management for professional services, such as team collaboration, team discussion, multiple tasks monitoring and module-wise monitoring in a distributed team environment, is more challenging than a to-do list. Task management is mostly preferred with combination of line groupware software and Web-conferencing tools.
3. **Collaborating on schedules and event management:** There are various distinct activities in our daily life such as attending a conference or seminar, participating in a cultural or technical function in universities or college, scheduling a football, volleyball or cricket match, scheduling an official team meeting or any other social gathering. With the help of online

collaborators and event management tools, all event management tasks and scheduling of an event can be done very easily in a collaborative manner. Following are some schedule and event management tools that are very popular:

- Cvent (www.cvent.com)
- Message Blocks (www.messageblocks.com)
- SocialTagg (www.socialtagg.com)
- YesEvents (www.yesevents.com)
- MeetMax (www.meetmax.com)
- Signup systems (www.signupsystems.com)

4. **Collaborating on event marketing:** Online event marketing is one of the fastest growin trends in digital marketing. When people create online events, they can expect more atten tion and can spread quick awareness about a product, service or event. Online surveys, emai marketing and customer feedback forms also fall into this category. Some examples of thes event marketing services are as follows:
   - Creating social event or page on Facebook
   - Google Docs (https://www.surveymonkey.com/)
   - Constant contact (http://www.constantcontact.com/)
   - SurveyMonkey (https://www.surveymonkey.com/)
   - Zoomerang (http://www.zoomerang.com/)
5. **Collaboration of budget:** To collaborate on budget and estimate costs for any marketing can paign, in-depth calculations are required in collaboration with teammates. Cloud-based Saa service Goggle Docs, which was discussed in detail in Chapter 3, could be very useful tool fo this purpose. Google Docs offers multiple sets of online services for various types of collabo ration including budget estimation and identifying common team opinions.

9.3 Outside the Cloud Services

This section covers those services that do not directly connect to core services and features cloud. Technically, it can fall in either the SaaS category or the Web services category. Howeve these services are much connected with daily activities and people have been using these servic from last decade. They are generally referred to as *online* services because these can be access anywhere, anytime over the Internet.

9.3.1 Centralizing Email Communications

Traditional email such as Microsoft Outlook or Outlook Express work on the post office protoc (POP), where the email client and server setup are done locally to send and receive messages. T system storage space is used for storing messages, whereas webmail services are like SaaS.

We have been using various SaaS-based email services where we do not need to host the em client or server, we can use it as simple login-based SaaS where the mail server and services a hosted by the provider. Another name of email services are HTTP or Web-based email service.

Since webmail services are based on the SaaS model, it can be accessed from any location, any machine through any Web browser and all emails are stored on the Web. It gives users flexibility; they just need an Internet connection to access their mail box anywhere, anytime.

9.3.2 Evaluating Webmail Services

Following are some prominent Web-based email service providers:

1. **Gmail:** It is one of the most commonly used Web-based email services provided by Google.
2. **Yahoo mail:** It is one of the oldest and most reputed Web-based email services offered by Yahoo. It allows offline access to messages via POP email clients.
3. **Windows Live Hotmail:** It is a pioneer Web-based email service offered by Microsoft. Earlier it was known as "Hotmail."

Apart from these three giants, there are several other Web-based email services such as

1. iCloud Mail (http://www.apple.com/icloud/)
2. AOL Mail (https://mail.aol.com)
3. Flashmail (www.flashmail.com)
4. GMX Mail (www.gmx.com)
5. Yandex Mail (https://mail.yandex.com/)
6. Inbox.com (www.inbox.com)
7. Mail.com (www.mail.com)
8. Zoho Mail (www.zoho.com/mail)

9.3.3 Evaluating Instant Messaging

Email is a traditional and formal way of communicating but using instant messaging services one can chat and communicate with friends and colleagues in real time without any message delay.

Instant message follows a different approach from the traditional one, in which a user sends a message to another user and the message goes directly to the other user's system without involving any other server or filtering. This approach is based on the peer-to-peer model where two systems make the peering connection and the message travels directly from one IP address to another. Following are some instant messaging giants:

1. Yahoo messenger
2. Google talk
3. Skype
4. Facebook chat instant messenger
5. Windows Live messenger

6. AOL Instant messenger
7. ICQ

Although nowadays people are more mobile and android platform–oriented, they prefer instant message, file and photo sharing apps such as WhatsApp, Viber WeChat, Hike, etc.

9.3.4 Evaluating Web Conference Tools

As seen in Sections 9.3.2 and 9.3.3, instant messaging and Web-based emails are very effective tools for one-on-one communication but are not effective for conferencing and group meetings. There exist many Web conferencing tools for video conferencing, team meetings and for knowledge transfer sessions between team members. Following are some popular Web conferencing tools:

1. **Cisco WebEx** (http://www.webex.co.in/): Cisco WebEx conferencing tool is simple to use, very effective and mostly preferred in all big industries and organizations (Fig. 9.3).
2. **Adobe Connect** (http://www.adobe.com/in/products/adobeconnect.html): Adobe Connect provides a collaborative platform for Webinars, learning sessions and Web meetings. It provides end-to-end full professional support and can be accessed using any device (Fig. 9.4).

Figure 9.3 | Cisco WebEx homepage. (Courtesy of Cisco Systems, Inc. Unauthorized use not permitted; From www.webex.co.in/products/index.html on December 15, 2014.)

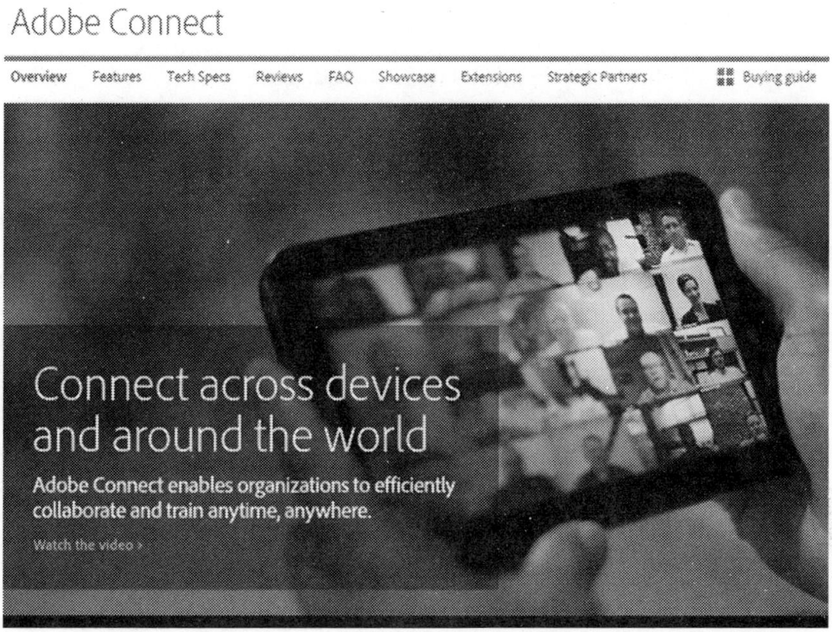

Figure 9.4 | Adobe Connect homepage. (Adobe product screenshot reprinted with permission from Adobe Systems Incorporated.)

3. **AnyMeeting** (http://www.anymeeting.com/): The AnyMeeting Web conferencing tool (Fig. 9.5) offers a variety of subscription plans for all types of users. It has some management facilities also with conferencing, such as creating custom registration forms, selling tickets to the Webinars and promoting meetings on Twitter and Facebook.

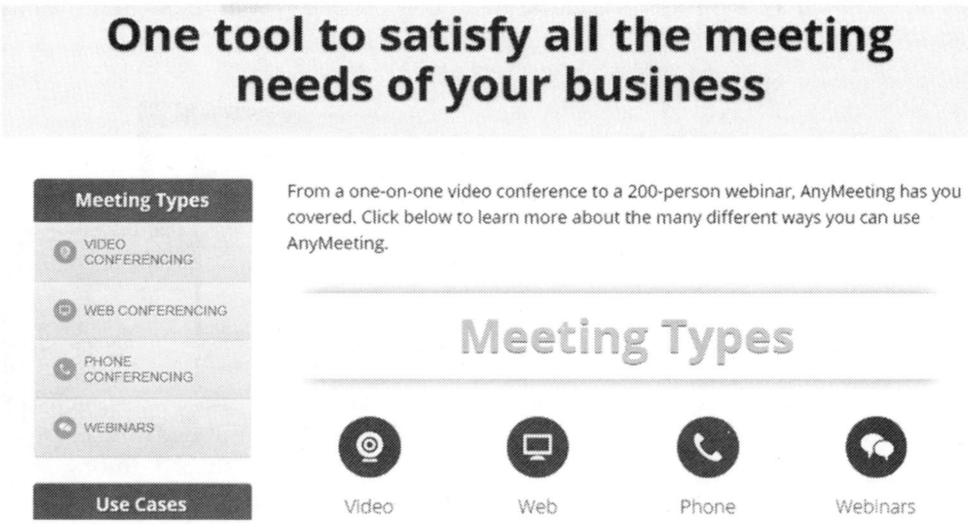

Figure 9.5 | AnyMeeting. (From www.anymeeting.com)

4. **ClickMeeting** (http://www.clickmeeting.com/): ClickMeeting is a very flexible and advanced Web conferencing tool. It provides full desktop sharing and control feature with Google translation of chat conversations in 52 languages.

9.3.5 Evaluating Online Groupware

The scope of social networking groups is specific to friends and family and cannot exactly be used effectively for businesses and managing collaborative project development. For effective group communication and collaboration within team members, a collection of tools or a single tool is required that can serve communication and collaboration needs in geographically distributed teams and through which project management tasks can be monitored and managed easily. Such a specific solution is known as *groupware*.

When this solution is used online, it falls under the SaaS category. It is also often called online groupware software. Some common features of online groupware software are as follows:

1. Task assignment
2. Task monitoring
3. Repository browsing and management
4. File and content sharing
5. Group discussion
6. Message board
7. Code or content synchronization
8. Instant messages or chat
9. Automated email notifications

Following are some online groupware cloud SaaS that are recently implemented in most of the organizations and businesses:

1. Github (https://github.com/)
2. Bitbucket (https://bitbucket.org/)
3. Slack (https://slack.com/)
4. Codebase (https://www.codebasehq.com/)
5. RhodeCode (https://rhodecode.com/)

9.3.6 Creating Groups on Social Networks

In the current scenario, everybody is quite aware of social media networking sites such as Facebook, MySpace, Google Plus and many others. Social media sites contain millions of user profiles; users maintain their profiles, post their views and comments, which are shared among their friends. Each user has enough personal information of his/her friends. A collection of common interests and activities of friends make a community of users where they share their views, post comments or promote any product, person or social cause.

Social networking sites facilitate users to create their topic-specific groups. Members of one common group communicate via discussion boards, share photos and videos, and even upload and download documents and other files. A social networking group is also very useful for huge businesses. Facebook has the following collaborative features that can be useful for many businesses:

1. Facebook group page
2. Recent news
3. Discussion board
4. Uploaded photos and videos
5. Posted Web pages
6. The Wall (a kind of group chat board)

Some businesses do not want user-typical social networking group features, they prefer other solutions that could be specific to corporate and business purposes only. Following are some other services that are also used for collaboration in business groups:

1. Yammer (https://www.yammer.com/)
2. MangoApps (http://www.mangoapps.com/)
3. Socialcast (http://www.socialcast.com/)
4. Chatter (https://www.salesforce.com/chatter/overview/)
5. IGLOO (http://www.igloosoftware.com/)
6. SocialText (http://www.socialtext.com/)

9.3.7 Collaborating via Blogs and Wikis

Group projects can be accomplished with continuous team collaboration and effective team communication among members. Some online groupware, Web conferencing and instant messages tools are mostly used in organizations. Apart from these, there are some other new trends for interacting with group members and sharing different views, collaborating, knowledge expansion and discussion.

9.3.7.1 Blogs

Blog is a term that evolved from "Web log" or "Weblog," which means an online journal or personal diary in which users write their views and comment on social, entertainment, technical, environmental, political, media or other issues. These users are called bloggers. Millions of users interact with each other and share their views via different blogs. Some of the most popular blogging sites are as follows:

1. Blogger (https://www.blogger.com)
2. WordPress (https://wordpress.org/)
3. Tumblr (https://www.tumblr.com/)

4. Quora (https://www.quora.com/)
5. Edublogs (http://edublogs.org/)

9.3.7.2 Wikis

Wikis provide a common platform where users develop, edit and modify Web content in a collaborative manner. In a blog, the author post cannot be modified by others, but Wiki has a shared authorship model where people can edit the contents and have access permissions. Some popular Wiki engines are as follows:

1. MediaWiki (http://www.mediawiki.org/wiki/MediaWiki)
2. TWiki (http://www.twiki.org/)
3. PmWiki (http://www.pmwiki.org/)
4. DokuWiki (http://www.splitbrain.org/projects/dokuwiki)
5. MoinMoinWiki (http://moinmo.in/)

9.4 Cloud Analytics

Cloud analytics is a kind of SaaS that is offered by cloud providers or any other service provider. Cloud analytics service is used for detailed data analysis and statics, including computing power, storage, data transfer, data models and data source analysis.

Cloud SaaS–based Website analytics, social media analytics and business intelligence (BI) applications are also part of cloud analytics. The pay-per-use model is generally prevalent, but some providers also offer monthly and yearly plans. Following is a list some popular cloud SaaS-based analytics tools:

1. Chart beat (https://chartbeat.com/)
2. Google Analytics (http://www.google.com/analytics/)
3. Kissmetrics (https://www.kissmetrics.com/)
4. Mixpanel (https://mixpanel.com/)
5. Bime analytics (http://www.bimeanalytics.com/)
6. Good Data (http://www.gooddata.com/)

9.5 Software Plus Services

Software Plus services is a combination of on-premises installed software and SaaS. This term was first introduced by Microsoft. Software Plus Services provide more flexibility to users so that they can use software services locally as well as over the Internet.

9.5.1 Benefits of Using Software Plus Services

Following are some key benefits of using Software Plus Services:

1. **Enhanced privacy:** Users have the flexibility of keeping organizationally sensitive data locally and not critical data on cloud. This facility is preferred by consumers and aligns with the traditional approach.
2. **Offline access:** Users can work offline and data is automatically synchronized with the cloud once a system is connected through the Internet. They do not need to worry about the availability and strength of the Internet connection.
3. **More flexibility:** More flexible enterprise architect to design innovative solutions by combining local and remote services because local devices could be more efficient and powerful for processing.

9.6 Cloud Content Delivery Network (CDN) Services

Traditionally, content of the websites is served from one main server or central server which is responsible for serving user requests all the time. If target users of any website are restricted to certain geographical regions, then traditional method works well. However if target users are distributed across different geographical regions, then this method is not relevant.

Content delivery network is a software service which solves distributed content delivery problems across all geographical regions; for example, AWS CloudFront is one of the popular content delivery service used by AWS business application users. Following are some other popular CDN services:

1. Akamai
2. EdgeCast
3. Level 3
4. Incapsula
5. Instart Logic
6. Aryaka Networks

9.6.1 Multi-CDN

If your business application needs are purely global and require multiple servers across the globe to give each user a faster website loading experience irrespective of their locations, then the concept of multi-CDN comes into picture.

There is a company, named MetaCDN (http://www.metacdn.com/), which provides multi-CDN service (Fig. 9.6). It combines existing CDN providers into one huge global network. It dynamically combines and optimizes all major cloud service providers and infrastructure providers to quickly and securely speed up the Web content to users irrespective of their physical location.

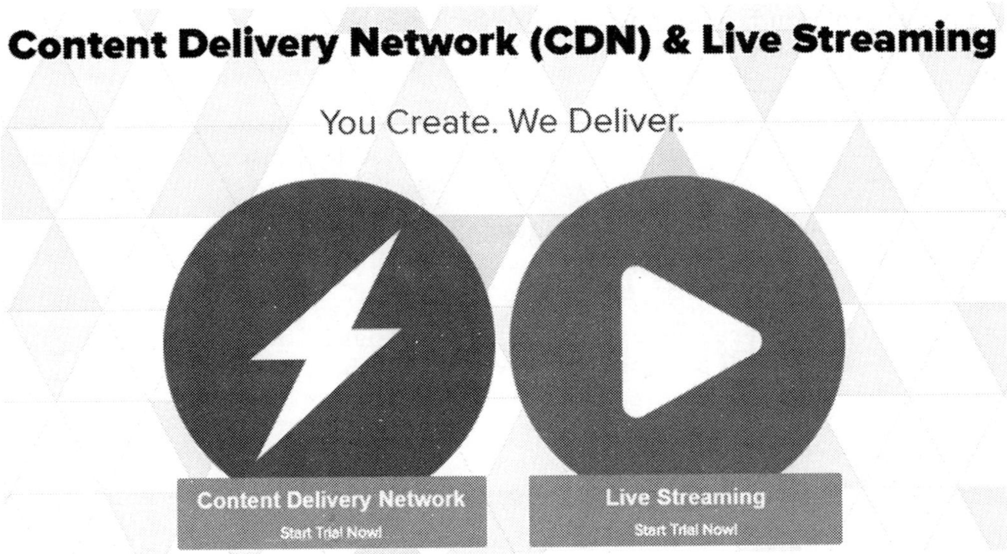

Figure 9.6 | MetaCDN. (From www.metacdn.com)

9.6.1.1 Features of MetaCDN

Following are the key features of MetaCDN:

1. **Global presence:** The business application of any user gets massive amount of CDN locations which is not possible with one single CDN provider.
2. **Fastest content delivery:** MetaCDN always selects the best optimal server for individual users. If there are multiple CDN providers in one region, users will always get the content from the fastest one within that region.
3. **Always uptime:** MetaCDN gives guarantee of 100% service uptime; because if one CDN network goes down, MetaCDN immediately routes the traffic through another provider.

9.7 Mobile Cloud Computing

Mobile cloud computing (MCC) is a concept related to cloud computing and it brings services such as on-demand access and no on-premise software. Mobile cloud computing uses network capabilities alone to deliver the desired service to customers and charges for their use. It could permit the user to reserve network bandwidth, thus confirming timely delivery of information.

MCC is a new paradigm for mobile applications where data processing and storage are moved from the mobile device to cloud. The mobile world is dependent on two factors: (a) network stability and (b) handset availability. Because mobile phones do not have adequate processing power or memory to support huge amounts of data, cloud computing seems to be the ideal solution for these mobile phone users. Cloud computing allows these mobile phone users to have the same amount of data access as "smart" phone users, and have their data stored onto the phone.

This extra advantage of cloud computing allows developers and mobile companies to start targeting a market larger than only "smart" phone users, which in turn gives cloud computing more thrust in the near future (Fig. 9.7).

Figure 9.7 | Mobile cloud computing vision.

9.7.1 *Why Mobile Cloud Computing?*

Following are some significant limitations with mobile devices, which can be overcome with cloud computing:

1. **Limited processing:** Mobile phones do not have adequate processing power or memory to support huge amounts of data.
2. **Loss of connection:** Due to the mobility of the clients and the wireless network setup, mobile clients can be removed temporarily from the previous connected network and may enter another network; therefore, service requests or responses may fail to be delivered to their destination.
3. **Bandwidth/Latency:** Cell networks have inadequate bandwidth and are often billed on the basis of the amount of data transferred.

9.8 InterCloud Issues: A Grid of Clouds

InterCloud is a global "cloud of clouds," which describes a service pattern and agreement among cloud providers to build interconnected cloud services for providing flexibility and enhanced experience to users. The situation when more cloud providers work and operate together is called a grid of clouds.

The key benefit of InterCloud is that it solves cloud interoperability issues. The vendor lock-in problem, where a user becomes dependent only on a single cloud service provider, can be solved with the help of InterCloud.

Cloud providers face some specific challenges when trying to implement InterCloud. InterCloud can be implemented successfully once the following challenges are solved.

1. **Lack of standards:** Because cloud computing standards are evolving, and research is ongoing on various developing standards, cloud resources such as virtual machine provisioning, object and block storage cannot be standardized for all cloud providers in InterCloud. Some common naming conventions, addressing, messaging and identity management are required to solve this.
2. **API translation:** There should be a common interface for all cloud providers that are part of InterCloud. This common interface should be responsible for API or other service request translations between two providers.
3. **Security:** Following are some possible security-related threats when InterCloud starts working:
   - Task and services migration form one cloud provider to another provider.
   - The question about who should monitor the common administration among all clouds.
   - Managing public key infrastructure of InterCloud.
   - Agreement on common encryption and decryption protocol for all cloud providers.

9.9 Sky Computing

The term *sky computing* was first published in IEE, September 2009. It is an emerging computing paradigm where the resources of multiple cloud providers can be shared and combined to create an extremely huge distributed virtual cluster. It is same as some popular grid projects OpenScience Grid and European Grid infrastructure.

The purpose of sky computing is to provide computational power environment for scientific and research applications and bring collaboration in distributed research teams. Currently, the most popular sky computing research project is the FutureGrid project, which is associated with Nimbus (an open source private cloud) with University of Florida, University of Chicago and INRIA.

9.10 Cloud Governance

Cloud governance is an industrial term that defines certain policies, controls and rules to enable cloud computing services into a specific organization or industry. The main purpose of cloud governance is to define a secure set of policies for remote data and application transfer.

Some people also define cloud governance as an extension of SOA governance, but it covers all the specific features of public cloud such as multi-tenancy and on-demand scalability. Cloud governance policies may, however, vary from organization to organization according to their business use case. Many organizations do not bother about cloud governance, but it is recommended to defined cloud governance before the implementation of cloud services for any organization as it is one of the best practices. Following are some common policies of cloud governance that could be applicable to any organization:

1. **Access controls:** Access control policies define the privilege of access to particular cloud resources. It just shows who can access what. It also controls the deployment access, quality assurance process, integration of LDAP directory with the user's cloud credentials.
2. **Financial controls:** There should be proper tracking of cloud resources and expenses, if a resource is being added then financial control policies should be able to track and limit the expenditure based on the organization's project requirement.
3. **Key management:** There should be continuous external and internal monitoring of key generation and key management system about who is keeping the main account login keys and who is sharing those credentials. Key encryption policies must evaluate and monitor this process under cloud governance.
4. **Integration policy:** Integration policies under cloud governance define and control the integration rules with REST-based APIs and any other integration with third-party tools and software.

Summary

In this chapter, we have learned about various mission-critical cloud-based applications and a variety of collaborative applications. All services are meant for some specific purposes and for solving existing IT challenges in simpler way. Of all these, SaaS services are the most connected to our daily life. Most of the Internet sites that users browse for using specific services are usually based on the SaaS model, such as different types of social and business collaboration services, Web conferencing, social networking and instant messaging, email services, online groupware, blogs, wikis and analytics services.

We have also learned about some new evolving computing paradigms in cloud computing such as Software Plus Services, Mobile Cloud Computing, Sky Computing and Cloud Governance. The next chapter discusses some successful cloud adoption case studies and the future of cloud computing.

Multiple Choice Questions

1. During ECG analysis in the cloud, how the numbers of workflow engines get controlled?
   (a) By AWS EC2
   (b) By AWS Elastic Load Balancer
   (c) By AWS EBS
   (d) By AWS CloudFront
2. Which type of cloud product is FutureGrid project?
   (a) Mobile cloud computing
   (b) Cloud CDN service
   (c) Sky computing
   (d) Cloud governance

3. Which one of the following options is the key challenge in InterCloud enablement?
   (a) API translation
   (b) SLA
   (c) Virtualization problem
   (d) Legal issues

4. Which limitation of mobile devices can be overcome using mobile cloud computing?
   (a) Limited APIs
   (b) Limited data
   (c) Limited battery power
   (d) Limited processing

5. Which one of the following options is the key feature of MetaCDN?
   (a) On line service
   (b) Fastest content delivery
   (c) First CDN service
   (d) Fast platform service

6. Which one of the following companies provide cloud CDN service?
   (a) AWS
   (b) Google
   (c) Microsoft
   (d) Akamai

7. Which type of service does Kissmetrics is an example of?
   (a) Web email services
   (b) Project management services
   (c) Cloud analytics
   (d) Online groupware

8. Which of the following things combine "Software plus service"?
   (a) SaaS and PaaS
   (b) On-premises installed software and SaaS
   (c) PaaS and IaaS
   (d) Hardware and storage devices

9. What is the purpose of Slack?
   (a) Online groupware-related activities
   (b) Email collaboration in groups
   (c) Instant messaging
   (d) Online video conferencing

10. What is the purpose of Adobe Connect tool?
   (a) Online video conferencing
   (b) Online calling
   (c) Instant messaging
   (d) Webinars and Web meetings

11. What is the purpose of SurveyMonkey service?
    (a) Providing budget estimation service
    (b) Providing event marketing service
    (c) Providing task management service
    (d) Providing to-do list apps

12. What is the purpose of Google Keep app?
    (a) Providing budget estimation service
    (b) Providing event marketing service
    (c) Providing task management service
    (d) Providing to-do list apps

13. What is the purpose of Cvent service?
    (a) Providing event management service
    (b) Providing event marketing service
    (c) Providing task management service
    (d) Providing to-do list apps

14. Which type of storing service is Amazon EBS?
    (a) Storing Temporary data storage
    (b) Storing Web session data
    (c) Storing persistent data
    (d) Storing static data

15. What is the role of integration policies in cloud governance?
    (a) Control the integration rules with SOAP-based APIs
    (b) Control the integration rules with REST-based APIs
    (c) Provide integration rules with cloud infrastructure services
    (d) Provide integration rules with cloud software services

Review Questions

1. Explain how ECG analysis can be done in the cloud.
2. Explain how satellite image processing system can be deployed over the public cloud AWS.
3. Explain the collaboration process in the team via instant messages and to-do lists.
4. How does collaboration happen through blogs and wikis? List out some product examples for both.
5. What do you mean by cloud analytics? Provide some product names of cloud analytics.
6. How are Web conferencing and line groupware software useful in effective team meeting and collaboration?
7. Explain the concept of mobile cloud computing. Why is mobile cloud computing necessary?
8. What do you understand by the "grid of clouds" and sky computing concepts?
9. What do you understand by cloud governance? Explain some common policies of cloud governance.

Answers to Multiple Choice Questions

1. (b), **2.** (c), **3.** (a), **4.** (d), **5.** (b), **6.** (d), **7.** (c), **8.** (b),
9. (a), **10.** (d), **11.** (b), **12.** (d), **13.** (a), **14.** (c), **15.** (b)

CHAPTER 10

Cloud Computing Consumer Case Studies

.earning Objectives

After reading this chapter, you will be able to:

- Understand cloud infrastructure adoption case study with detailed challenges, solution, approach, final outcome, success factors and lessons learned.
- Understand cloud platform adoption case study with detailed challenges, solution, approach, final outcome, success factors and lessons learned.
- Understand cloud software services adoption case study with detailed challenges, solution, approach, final outcome, success factors and lessons learned.
- Provide an overview of cloud simulation tools.
- Know the future trends of cloud computing.

0.1 Cloud Infrastructure Adoption Case Study

he first case study deals with Nutritious Food Inc., a company that had a $150 billion turnover 2014. Users can see details of the company's nutrition products on its Website and order these nline as well. Nutritious Food Inc. has reached in 19 countries across United States and Europe ith over 12 million online consumers and is today one of the leading consumer foods processors nd suppliers in Europe and US markets.

The case analyzes the IT infrastructure challenges Nutritious Food Inc. faced and how cloud frastructure solutions helped overcome those. It also studies the specific approach and strategy llowed by a giant cloud infrastructure as a service (IaaS) provider and the type of cloud infraructure services it offered to help Nutritious Food Inc. escalate their business at a faster rate at an -demand basis through the high availability of data.

0.1.1 *Challenges of the Nutritious Food Inc.*

utritious Food Inc. started as a dairy processing and packaging plant. Within a decade, it had unched over 130 plants and distribution centers all over North America and Europe.

Initially, to support their IT business and online services, they set up their own small on-premises tacenter to host all of their Web services and organizational database activities. They had to incur high upfront costs at the beginning in anticipation of their business growth but soon realized that there was urgent requirement for scalability within the existing IT infrastructure as well as the need of high speed all-time availability of services. They also realized the need for finances for the monitoring, administration and regular updating of services. In a nutshell Nutritious Food Inc. faced the following key challenges in their business:

1. Problems with proper utilization of IT resources.
2. Problems with instant scalability.
3. Problems regarding additional costs related to monitoring and regular updations.
4. Problems with high availability of data and services.

10.1.2 Solution

From among the various public cloud IaaS providers such as Amazon, Google, Rackspace an Microsoft, Nutritious Food Inc. chose Amazon public cloud to build their infrastructure or demand basis because of the attractive features of Amazon Web services (AWS), including their offe of numerous services to support end-to-end infrastructure, overall deployment procedure, mon toring and guaranteed high availability of data and services across the globe.

Nutritious Food Inc. adopted the AWS cloud infrastructure solution and architect the resource described in Fig. 10.1, which assisted them to emerge successfully from all online business cha lenges and succeeded in their business across the globe.

10.1.3 Cloud Infrastructure Service Approach

AWS offers multiple cloud infrastructure services but not all are applicable for all types of industr challenges. An architectural approach in accordance with the business requirements is necessar to choose the appropriate set of cloud infrastructure services. Following is the list of AWS-offere infrastructure services that matched Nutritious Food's business requirement and aligned wi their existing IT infrastructure architecture:

1. AWS EC2 (Elastic Compute Cloud) for building on-demand virtual servers.
2. AWS S3 (Simple Storage Service) for building unlimited, always-available storage.
3. AWS EBS (Elastic Block Storage) for persistent block storage.
4. AWS RDS (Relational Database Services) for database.
5. AWS CloudFront services for fast content delivery network.
6. AWS ELB (Elastic Load Balancing) for handling multiple load balancing requests.
7. AWS Route 53 for building highly available and scalable domain name system.
8. AWS Auto Scaling for quick scalability.
9. AWS CloudWatch for detailed monitoring of all the resources.

After adoption of AWS EC2, S3 and EBS services, no more on-premises servers and storage w required and everything was now on on-demand basis. The problem of instant scalability w resolved after using AWS's ELB and Auto Scaling features.

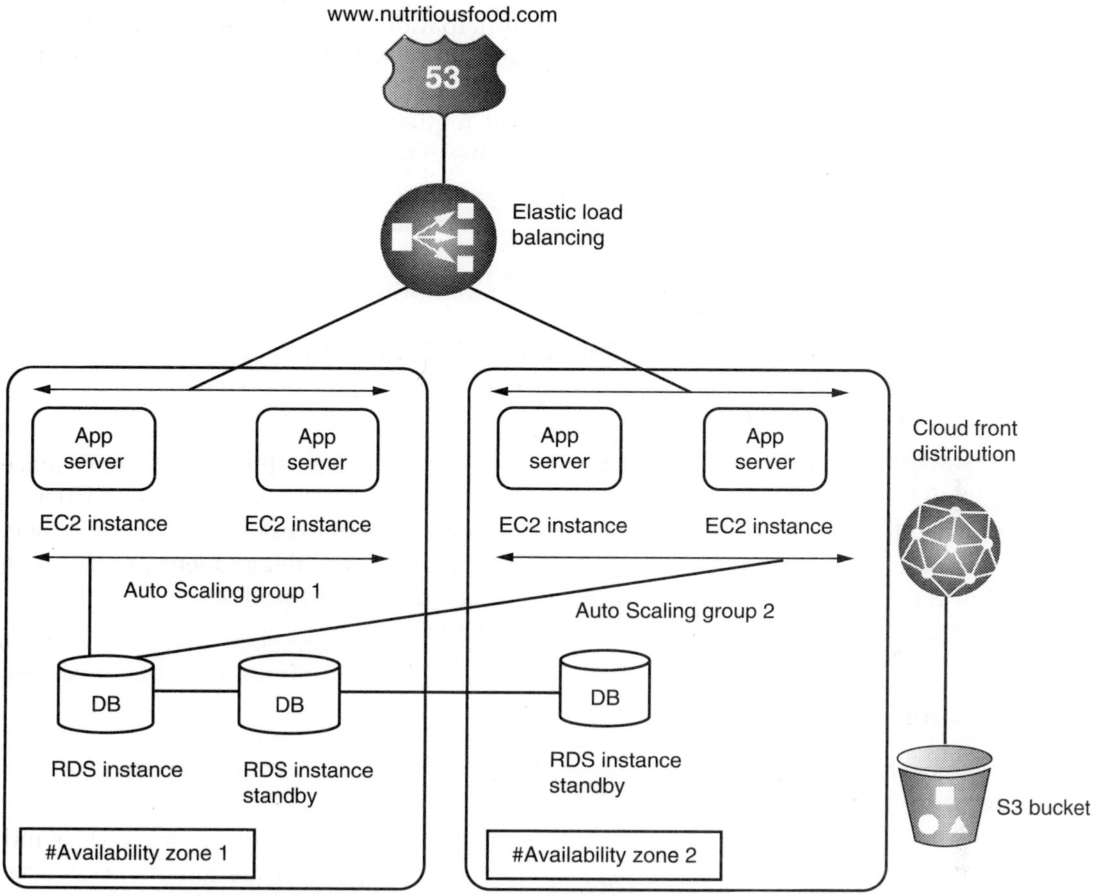

Figure 10.1 | AWS architectural solution for Nutritious Food Inc.

Specific additional cost and setup was no longer required for monitoring because AWS CloudWatch provides all resource monitoring details at a cheaper cost. AWS Route 53 and AWS CloudFront services can handle easily the problem of high availability and reliability of services.

10.1.4 Final Outcome

After successful adoption of the AWS cloud infrastructure and migration of the existing service onto the AWS cloud, Nutritious Food Inc. achieved the following key benefits:

1. Upfront cost no longer required.
2. Tangible saving of around 90% of operational cost.
3. Always-available services with anytime global access.
4. On-demand basis IT resources.
5. High availability of data with quick global access.

6. Strong disaster recovery backups migration plans.
7. Focus upon business innovation not on managing IT infrastructure.

10.1.5 Success Factors

Nutritious Food's success factors after adopting a smart architectural design and successfully deploying all the services in the AWS cloud environment are as follows:

1. **High fault tolerance infrastructure:** AWS have multiple regions and availability zones that ensure a high fault tolerance infrastructure.
2. **Optimized cloud infrastructure architecture:** AWS cloud monitoring service provides detailed monitoring of each and every service, which helped optimize cloud infrastructure architecture to reduce costs.
3. **Instant scalability:** AWS Auto Scaling and ELB ensure quick scalability as well as instant load balancing in virtual servers.
4. **Fast content delivery, persistent disk capacity and unlimited storage:** AWS EBS provides persistent disk drive capacity and AWS S3 provides always-available unlimited storage capacity and in combination with AWS CloudFront, the company was sure of fast content delivery across the globe because of AWS's multiple datacenters across the globe.

10.1.6 Lessons Learned

Now that we have a clear idea about Nutritious Food's infrastructure challenges, the AWS cloud solution they adopted and how their business became successful, we can summarize this case study as follows:

1. Amazon Public Cloud could be a very good option for handling such infrastructure challenges.
2. The IT infrastructure and business challenges must be identified properly before making a final decision on IaaS product selection.
3. Proper analyses of existing cloud service providers are also necessary before making a final decision.
4. Optimal architectural design and approach are essential after selecting a particular IaaS provider to reduce costs and enhance effective utilization of cloud resources.

10.2 Cloud Platform Adoption Case Study

This second case study analyzes Gamysoft Inc., a very popular online gaming company. The company has more than 15 million subscribers all over the world. This case specifically analyzes the IT challenges Gamysoft faced and how a cloud platform solution helped them overcome their infrastructure challenges.

It also studies the specific approach and strategy followed by a giant cloud platform as a service (PaaS) provider and how the cloud platform services helped Gamysoft escalate their business at a faster rate and at an on-demand basis through the high availability of data.

10.2.1 Challenges of Gamysoft

Gamysoft faced the following key challenges in their business:

1. Developing a Web-based online gaming solution where users did not need to download the game on their PC.
2. Providing an easy-to-use system where developers can easily build applications while focusing on user experience.
3. Scaling seamlessly to accommodate rapid increase in the number of online users.

10.2.2 Solution

Gamysoft used the following solution to address their development challenges:

1. Used Google's App Engine for developing gaming applications quickly and with less effort.
2. Leveraged App Engine features such as Datastore to save user gaming status and profile data.
3. Used Google Cloud Storage to securely store and serve gaming application data.

10.2.3 Cloud Platform Service Approach

Following is the list of Google App Engine services that matched Gamysoft's business requirement and addressed their development problems:

1. Google Chrome Native Client to enable the Chrome browser to run the programming languages used to develop video game consoles; fast, visually rich playing experience for users.
2. Python API for authenticating users via login credentials of Google; for registration and access to online games.
3. App Engine's Datastore for storing player current information to enable session continuity game resumption form previous state.
4. Administration console for monitoring game performance, response times, error logs and other data.
5. Google Cloud Storage for security and scalable storage of user's gaming data; high data transfer rate, quick storage, high consistency and availability of data.

10.2.4 Final Outcome

After the successful adoption of Google's App Engine, Gamysoft achieved the following key benefits:

1. Seamless scaling without human intervention to support unexpected user growth.
2. Elimination of hiring need for technical staff for server maintenance and technical support.
3. Consistency and high availability with Google Cloud Storage.

10.2.5 Success Factors

Following is a list of Gamysoft's success factors after utilizing Google's PaaS services in their online gaming business:

1. **Captivating user experience:** Google's services provided a captivating user experience that attracted widespread admiration and led to the company's success in the arena.
2. **Game on browser:** App Engine and Cloud Storage solved the most critical challenge of getting the game up and running on the Web browser. This was a significant achievement.
3. **All-time availability:** Using App Engine and Cloud Storage has ensured that the game remains available always, no matter how high the user demand. The platform was capable to handle spikes without any hitches.
4. **Saving the last-played gaming state of the user:** For a gamer, it is very important to have their last-played levels saved so that they do not have to start all over again. App Engine's Datastore enables session continuity if a user has left abruptly.

10.2.6 Lessons Learned

Now that we have a clear idea about Gamysoft's development challenges, the Google App Engine cloud solution they adopted and how their business become successful, we can summarize this case study as follows:

1. Google's App Engine proved optimal for the end-to-end development of the online gaming application that Gamysoft needed.
2. Google's PaaS can develop high performance and extremely scalable solutions for applications such as online gaming.
3. Developers can easily leverage all of Google's services for developing high-end on-demand solutions for users at a minimal cost.
4. There is no need to purchase licensed software, application development software and worry about regular patch updation, Google App Engine takes care of everything. Developers just need to focus on code development skills.

10.3 Cloud Software Services Adoption Case Study

The third case study analyzes the cloud software as a service (SaaS) adoption model in Andrew Sportswear, one of the world's leading textile companies. The previous financial year (2013–14), Andrew Sportswear had a turnover of \$180 billion. The annual report indicated a revenue of \$78 billion, which was a 60% sales volume increase since 2009. Andrew Sportswear has to manage different business process such as sales, distribution, procurement of sports and clothing products, HR and finance processes of their employees. This study shows how a leading cloud SaaS enterprise resource planning (ERP) solution provider helped Andrew Sportswear overcome its ERP challenges with minimum cost and effort.

10.3.1 Challenges of Traditional ERPs

Andrew Sportswear operates in 18 countries around the world, has nearly 15 million customers and a 27000 employee base, which means that their ERP system for managing the various processes for their employees is big. Following are the key challenges Andrew Sportswear faced when they applied traditional ERP in their global business.

1. Absence of data processing and communication with other systems because of client–server model architecture of traditional ERP applications.
2. Difficulty in upgrading and replacing existing processes.
3. Complicated integration with database such as SQL.
4. Expensive implementation and maintenance.

10.3.2 Solution

Andrew Sportswear had earlier used traditional ERP solutions (PeopleSoft's HRMS and FMS) for managing their employee details but soon the company realized that they would have to incur additional costs and maintenance charges if they persisted with the traditional ERP solution.

Of the multiple traditional options such as PeopleSoft, SAP, Banner and Oracle, Andrew Sportswear elected the cloud SaaS vendor Workday, which is an on-demand and pay-per-use human and capital management service provider and one of the pioneers in enabling human resource function as SaaS. Because it is one of the most in-demand SaaS ERP solutions in the world today, with over 500 fortune businesses having adopted it, Andrew Sportswear, too, decided on Workday.

10.3.3 Cloud Software Service Approach

Following are the unique ways in which Workday's features were in alignment with Andrew Sportswear's business requirements:

1. Total online ERP services; no need to purchase license, install and manage all things on premises.
2. Additions at the platform level, with custom field management tools for easy configuration and customization software by customers.
3. Detailed audit trails for all the transaction, workflow and approvals.
4. Complete tracking and documentation of all configuration changes.
5. Workday Integration Cloud Connect for third-party payroll for customized packaged integration and continuous support and maintenance to the selected integration process.

10.3.4 Final Outcome

After the successful adoption of Workday SaaS ERP, Andrew Sportswear achieved the following key benefits:

1. Elimination of purchase and management need of on-premises integration middleware or servers.
2. Extensively lower operating costs in administration, operations and maintenance.

3. Consolidation of disparate system and processes.
4. Development focus on current and future release.
5. Effective collaboration and simplification of entire ERP process.
6. One common platform to connect entire ecosystem.

10.3.5 Success Factors

Following is a list of Andrew Sportswear's success factors after turning to Workday SaaS ERP:

1. **Cost efficiency:** Andrew Sportswear managed to reduce huge amounts of capital investment involved in purchasing license maintenance, database administration and system administration.
2. **High security:** All customer data is encrypted and can be accessed only by the application server as Workday SaaS give priority to security.
3. **Granular-level analytics:** Workday SaaS solution enables more granular-level analytics of data.

10.3.6 Lessons Learned

Following are the key lessons learned from the ERP SaaS adoption at Andrew Sportswear:

1. Traditional ERP challenges can be eliminated after successful adoption of Workday's comprehensive standards-based Web services APIs.
2. Workday SaaS can offer a variety of packaged solutions and integration tools according to business requirements.
3. Workday ERP solution is easy to learn and implement.
4. Considerable saving in capital investment is possible through such a SaaS offering and organizations can focus on business innovation rather than on software upgradation and maintenance.

10.4 Cloud Simulation Tools

As we have studied about various open source private cloud computing platforms in Chapter 8, we can utilize any one of those private cloud platforms for learning, researching and testing purpose. Following is a list of some open source cloud simulation tools that can be used for cloud infrastructure resource modeling.

1. **CloudSim:** CloudSim was developed in the Cloud Computing and Distributed Systems (CLOUDS) Laboratory at the computer science and software engineering department of the University of Melbourne. CloudSim provides a test bed and simulation and modeling framework for experimenting cloud virtual resources and application services. With the help of CloudSim, researchers can investigate, design, test and create modeling for enhancing any existing feature of cloud infrastructure or implement any modification.

For complete installation and documentation of CloudSim, students can refer to the following Websites:

- http://cloudbus.org/cloudsim/
- http://www.cloudbus.org/cloudsim/doc/readme.txt
- http://www.cloudbus.org/cloudsim/doc/api/index.html

2. **GreenCloud simulator:** GreenCloud simulator is an easy-to-use energy-aware cloud datacentersimulator with detailed analysis and modeling of energy consumptions of datacenter services including all IT equipment, memory, storage, CPU and network switches. GreenCloud has an extension to the NS2 network simulator as well, which is very popular simulator. GreenCloud can be installed from the following link:
   - http://greencloud.gforge.uni.lu/install.html
3. **iCan cloud:** iCan is another cloud simulation framework developed by a research group of Carlos University, Spain. The main purpose of iCan cloud is to predict the cost and performance according to respective infrastructure resource configurations. iCan also supports a variety of users, including basic users (who use limited resources) and advanced users (who use huge infrastructure resources). iCan cloud can be installed from the following link:
   - http://www.arcos.inf.uc3m.es/~icancloud/downloads.html

These tools could be very beneficial for university research projects and for those who want to contribute to developing the standards of cloud computing.

Some other similar tools are as follows:

1. CloudAnalyst
2. MDCSim
3. NetworkCloudSim
4. VirtualCloud

10.5 Future of Cloud Computing

Cloud computing has been one of the fastest growing and most rapidly adopted trends in the IT industry. We have seen plenty of cloud-based services and success stories. In this final section, we will see which way future cloud computing trends and research direction are headed.

1. **More application availability on the cloud:** Cloud computing services are growing very rapidly and many new software services are evolving with some new infrastructure and platform providers as well. According to the 2013 Technology Industry Outlook Survey, there would be more than 48 million applications over cloud by 2016. In this situation, every big and small organization would be having application deployment over cloud. Thereby we can imagine the huge utilization of cloud resources in near future.

2. **Presence of Internet will boost its future:** Cloud computing has no meaning without the Internet. Cloud services are majorly dependent on high-quality and continuous Internet connection. Because cloud adoption is now widely prevalent across the globe and many software services have become essential to our daily activities, it is quite obvious that we need faster and continuous Internet to enable a synchronized and successful cloud adoption. For cloud adoption to succeed, more public Wi-Fi spots and Internet services through the help of satellite in the village areas are needed.
3. **Enforcing entrepreneurship:** Establishing any start-up infrastructure over the cloud requires just a few minutes. With this great evolution, the possibilities of new business and empowerment of entrepreneurship are endless because we do not need to think about IT infrastructure complexities and investment on initial cost.
4. **More innovation:** Because cloud computing facilitates data-exhaustive and high-computing operations, it is a trend among universities and research institutes to prefer cloud platforms for conducting various projects. We expect more research-based on various cloud-based applications in future.
5. **More hybrid cloud adoption:** Private cloud providers such as OpenStack, CloudStack, Eucalyptus, VCloud, OpenNebula are not just private clouds, they also offer public cloud vendor-specific APIs and plug-ins for transferring workload and services to the public cloud in case a cloudburst situation occurs, which means hybrid cloud solutions can be built using private cloud services. Although over the last few years, some vendors such as CloudSwitch, Nimbula and Citrix's DataBridge have been providing migration solutions and software from the private to the public cloud, these are still in the nascent stages of evolution and more research and integration is continuing. According to the Gartner Survey Report 2013, hybrid cloud adoption will be the most common trend in the industry from 2014 onward.
6. **More cloud interoperability:** As we have learned about cloud interoperability and evolving solutions in previous chapters, we now know that there is the possibility of more industry orientation and research directions and easy solutions toward cloud interoperability in future.
7. **Big Data on cloud platform:** Big Data is one of the popular terminologies in analytics and high-performance computing domain. With big data, terabytes of data and billions of rows can be analyzed within a couple of hours. Various commercial and open source software are available in this domain to leverage the benefits of big data capabilities. Although traditional SQL databases have certain limits with few millions of rows and are unable to process billions of records quickly and efficiently, big data technology solutions helps out enterprises worldwide in solving their data processing problems. Now the recent trends are going to transform big data applications and analytics process on cloud computing resources, and more industry successful case studies toward this direction can be witnessed in near future.

Summary

This final chapter has discussed a variety of case studies from different industries such as food, gaming, textile and their diverse cloud adoption solutions. In each case, we have observed the challenges, the solutions presented by the cloud services, the approach used by the cloud providers, the final outcome, the success factors that gave the companies good gains, and the lessons we learned from the cases. We have also briefly touched upon some open source tools for cloud simulation and looked into the future of cloud computing.

Multiple Choice Questions

1. What is the purpose of using AWS Route 53 in cloud infrastructure service approach?
   (a) For quick scalability
   (b) For highly available and scalable domain name system
   (c) For high speed content delivery network
   (d) For handling multiple load balancing requests
2. What is the purpose of using AWS Cloud Front in cloud infrastructure service approach?
   (a) For quick scalability
   (b) For highly available and scalable domain name system
   (c) For high speed content delivery network
   (d) For handling multiple load balancing requests
3. What is the purpose of using GAE Python API in cloud platform service approach?
   (a) To run the programming languages on Chrome browser
   (b) To monitor game performance
   (c) To authenticate users via login credentials of Google
   (d) To store player current information
4. What is the purpose of using GAE Datastore in cloud platform service approach?
   (a) To run the programming languages on Chrome browser
   (b) To monitor game performance
   (c) To authenticate users via login credentials of Google
   (d) To store player current information
5. Workday SaaS tool is same as:
   (a) On-premised ERP service
   (b) Online ERP services
   (c) Hosted ERP service
   (d) Cloud ERP service
6. What is the main purpose of GreenCloud cloud simulator?
   (a) Modeling of energy consumptions of data canter
   (b) Predicting the cost and performance
   (c) Modeling framework for cloud applications
   (d) Modeling framework for experimenting cloud virtual resources
7. What is the main purpose of iCan cloud simulator?
   (a) Modeling of energy consumptions of data canter
   (b) Predicting the cost and performance
   (c) Modeling framework for cloud applications
   (d) Modeling framework for experimenting cloud virtual resources

8. What could be the most prominent future trend of cloud computing?
   (a) Cloud security
   (b) Cloud-based application development
   (c) Big data on cloud platform
   (d) Testing of cloud service

Review Questions

1. Explain how AWS architectural solution for Nutritious Food Inc. solved their critical infrastructure challenges and what lessons did we learn from this case study.
2. Explain the approach of Google's App Engine and associated services for solving the development challenges of the online gaming company, Gamysoft.
3. Explain the challenges the textile industry faced with traditional ERP and how Workday SaaS resolved those issues.
4. What do you understand by cloud simulation? Explain with some open source cloud simulation examples.
5. Explain in detail the future trends of cloud computing.

Answers to Multiple Choice Questions

1. (b), **2.** (c), **3.** (c), **4.** (d), **5.** (b), **6.** (a), **7.** (b), **8.** (c)

Bibliography

Websites

1. Evolution of Cloud Computing, http://thoughtsoncloud.com/2014/03/a-brief-history-of-cloud-computing/
2. Cluster Computing, http://en.wikipedia.org/wiki/Computer_cluster
3. Grid Computing, http://en.wikipedia.org/wiki/Grid_computing
4. Parallel Computing, https://computing.llnl.gov/tutorials/parallel_comp/
5. Utility Computing, http://en.wikipedia.org/wiki/Utility_computing
6. Regions and Availability Zones, http://docs.aws.amazon.com/AWSEC2/latest/UserGuide/using-regions-availability-zones.html
7. Amazon VPC, http://aws.amazon.com/vpc/
8. Overcoming Cloudbursting Challenges, http://www.rightscale.com/blog/cloud-management-best-practices/overcoming-cloudbursting-challenges
9. Amazon EBS, http://aws.amazon.com/ebs/
10. Amazon s3, http://aws.amazon.com/s3/
11. AWS Elastic Load Balancing, http://aws.amazon.com/elasticloadbalancing/
12. Amazon Glacier, http://aws.amazon.com/glacier/
13. Rackspace Cloud, http://www.rackspace.com/cloud
14. AWS Cloud, http://aws.amazon.com/
15. Google Compute Engine, https://cloud.google.com/compute/
16. Microsoft Azure, http://azure.microsoft.com/en-in/
17. GoGrid, http://www.gogrid.com/
18. Google App Engine, https://cloud.google.com/appengine/
19. CloudFoundry, http://www.cloudfoundry.org/index.html
20. Salesforce, http://www.salesforce.com/
21. EngineYard, https://www.engineyard.com/

22. GoogleDocs, https://docs.google.com
23. Workday, http://www.workday.com/
24. EyeOS, http://www.eyeos.com/
25. iCloud, https://www.icloud.com/
26. VMware, http://www.vmware.com/products
27. Virtualization, http://www.vmware.com/in/virtualization
28. VMware, http://en.wikipedia.org/wiki/VMware
29. NetApp, http://www.netapp.com/in/
30. SCALR, http://www.scalr.com/
31. AppZero, https://www.appzero.com/
32. IBM SmartCloud, http://searchcloudapplications.techtarget.com/definition/IBM-SmartCloud
33. RightScale, http://www.rightscale.com/
34. Cloud Standards, http://cloud-standards.org/wiki/index.php?title=Main_Page
35. HDFS Architecture, http://hadoop.apache.org/docs/r1.2.1/hdfs_design.html
36. Google File System, http://en.wikipedia.org/wiki/Google_File_System
37. MapReduce, http://research.google.com/pubs/pub36249.html
38. AWS RDS, http://aws.amazon.com/rds/
39. AWS DynamoDB, http://aws.amazon.com/dynamodb/
40. Google Cloud SQL, https://cloud.google.com/sql/docs
41. Microsoft Azure SQL database, http://azure.microsoft.com/en-in/services/sql-database/
42. HP Cloud Relational Database, http://www.hpcloud.com/products-services/relational-database
43. Oracle Database Cloud Service, https://cloud.oracle.com/database
44. Rackspace Cloud Databases, http://www.rackspace.com/cloud/databases
45. MongoDB, http://www.mongodb.org/
46. Apache Cassandra, http://cassandra.apache.org/
47. Apache CouchDB, http://couchdb.apache.org/
48. Apache HBase, http://hbase.apache.org/
49. Neo4j, http://neo4j.com/
50. OSSEC, http://www.ossec.net/
51. Snort, https://www.snort.org/
52. Crypton, https://crypton.io/
53. Cloud Security & Control, https://www.brighttalk.com/webcast/288/33869
54. A Survey on the Security of Virtual Machines, http://www.cse.wustl.edu/~jain/cse571-09/ftp/vmsec/index.html

55. NetSkope, https://www.netskope.com/

56. Okta, https://www.okta.com/

57. Qualys, https://www.qualys.com/

58. Skyhigh, http://www.skyhighnetworks.com/

59. Vaultive, http://www.vaultive.com/

60. Cloud Computing Risks, http://www.jiscinfonet.ac.uk/infokits/cloud-computing/risks/

61. Quality, Issues in the Cloud, http://www.academia.edu/3001202/Understanding_Quality_Issues_in_the_Cloud

62. AWS Whitepapers, http://aws.amazon.com/whitepapers/

63. Best Practices for Enterprise Cloud Computing, http://www.itbusinessedge.com/slideshows/best-practices-for-enterprise-cloud-computing.html

64. Zenoss Cloud Monitoring, http://www.zenoss.com/solution/cloud-monitoring

65. RevealCloud, http://copperegg.com/tag/revealcloud/

66. Compuware APM, http://www.compuware.com/en_us/application-performance-management.html

67. Amazon CloudWatch, http://aws.amazon.com/cloudwatch/

68. Rackspace Cloud Monitoring, http://www.rackspace.com/cloud/monitoring

69. PlanForCloud, http://www.planforcloud.com/

70. Eucalyptus, https://www.eucalyptus.com/

71. OpenStack, http://www.openstack.org/software/

72. CloudStack, http://cloudstack.apache.org/

73. OpenNebula, http://opennebula.org/

74. Apache Virtual Computing Lab, https://vcl.apache.org/

75. Enomaly Elastic Computing Platform, http://wiki.libvirt.org/page/Enomaly_Elastic_Computing_Platform_(ECP)

76. Nimbus, http://www.nimbusproject.org/

77. Cloud Testing, http://en.wikipedia.org/wiki/Cloud_testing

78. SOASTA, http://www.soasta.com/

79. PushToTest, http://www.pushtotest.com/products-comparison

80. Cloud9, https://sites.google.com/site/dslabepfl/proj/cloud9

81. Software plus service, http://www.microsoft.eu/2010/01/20/cloud-computing-software-plus-services-explained/

82. Mobile cloud computing, http://thoughtsoncloud.com/2013/06/mobile-cloud-computing/

83. Mobile cloud computing, http://www.ibm.com/developerworks/cloud/library/cl-mobilecloudcomputing/

84. Cloud governance, http://www.cso.com.au/article/423088/cloud_governance_manage_cloud_challenge_/

85. Sky computing, http://ercim-news.ercim.eu/en83/special/large-scale-cloud-computing-research-sky-computing-on-futuregrid-and-grid5000

86. Inter cloud challenges, http://www.academia.edu/5794410/InterCloud_Trust_Model_Security_Issues_and_Challenges

87. http://www.Cloud-council.org/

88. http://Cloud-standards.org/wiki/index.php?title=Main_Page

89. http://www.comparetheCloud.net/6305/benchmarking-Cloud-server-performance-and-comparing-iaas-providers/

90. http://www.chorus.co/news/2013/october/10/iaas-performance-and-cost-Cloud-benchmarking.aspx

91. http://www.passmark.com/products/pt_advnet.htm

92. http://www.ncbi.nlm.nih.gov/pmc/articles/PMC3180542/

Papers

93. Steffen Haak, Michael Menzel. "Autonomic Benchmarking for Cloud Infrastructures – An Economic Optimization Model," Proceedings of the 1st IEEE/ACM Workshop on Autonomic Computing for Economics, Karlsruhe, June, 2011.

94. Senthil Nathan, Purushottam Kulkarni, Umesh Bellur. "Resource Availability Based Performance Benchmarking of Virtual Machine Migrations," ICPE'13 Proceedings of the 4th ACM/SPEC International Conference on Performance Engineering, Pages 387–398, ACM New York, NY, USA, 2013.

95. K Ye, Z Wu, B Zhou, X Jiang, C Wang, A Zomaya. "Virt-B: Towards Performance Benchmarking of Virtual Machine Systems," 2013, ieeexplore.ieee.org.

96. Brian F Cooper, Adam Silberstein, Erwin Tam, Raghu Ramakrishnan, Russell Sears. "Benchmarking Cloud Serving Systems with YCSB," SOCC'10 Proceedings of the 1st ACM Symposium on Cloud Computing, Pages 143–154, ACM New York, NY, USA, 2010.

Articles

97. "Enterprises Seek The Benefits Of Hybrid Cloud, And Work To Overcome The Challenges," A Custom Technology Adoption Profile Commissioned by Cisco Systems 2013.

98. "Fair Benchmarking for Cloud Computing Systems," University of Surrey, March 2012.

99. "State of the Cloud DNS Report," CloudHarmony, July 2012.

Index

A

accessibility, 3, 37–38
access transparency, 5
Adobe Connect, 182–183
advance cloud applications
  centralizing email communications, 180–181
  collaborating via blogs and wikis, 185–186
  ECG analysis and monitoring, 175–176
  gene expression profiling, 177
  instant messaging services, 181–182
  online groupware software, 184
  protein structure prediction, 176–177
  satellite image processing, 177–178
  sharing and collaborative services, 179–180
  social media networking, 184–185
  social networking services, 179
  Web-based email service, 181
  Web conferencing tools, 182–184
advanced SaaS products
  Google Docs, 84–85
  Microsoft Office 365, 85
  Salesforce CRM, 84
  Workday, 84
Amazon CloudFront, 151
Amazon CloudWatch, 152
Amazon DynamoDB, 116
Amazon Elastic Transcoder, 151
Amazon relational database service, 115
Amazon Web Services (AWS), 67–68
AnyMeeting Web conferencing tool, 183
Apache Cassandra, 116–117
Apache HBase, 117
Apache Virtual Computing Lab, 166
application portability, 99
application security, 35
application service virtualization, 99
application virtualization, 99–101
AppZero, 108
automatic billing system, 37
automation, 3
autonomic computing, 36
availability, 33–34
availability zones, 59

B

"bare metal" method, 90
best practices of cloud computing, 153–158
  for cloud capacity, 157–158
  for cost optimization, 156–157
  for data and migration services, 155–156
  for infrastructure setup, 153–155
bit-level parallelism, 9, 22
BOINC (Berkeley Open Infrastructure for Network Computing), 15
business continuity management, 62
business with cloud computing services, 40

C

capital expenditure of enterprises, 41–42
Chatter, 185
Cisco WebEx, 182
Citrix, 100–101
Citrix Xen server, 101
ClickMeeting, 184
cloud analytics, 186
cloud burst, 60
cloud computing, 4, 6. *see also* advance cloud applications; data migration and streaming in cloud
  accessibility and portability, 37–38
  architecture, 58
  automatic billing system, 37
  availability and reliability, 33–34
  benefits of, 39–44
  central ideas behind, 28–30
  challenges with, 60
  client-oriented requirements, 33
  cloud providers, 48
  control automation, 36
  definitions, 27–28
  deployment models, 55–58
  dynamic provisioning, 31–32
  enabling techniques of, 29
  for end users and individuals, 44–47
  future of, 203–204
  in IT, 18
  manageability and interoperability, 35–36
  for market and enterprises, 40–44
  in mathematical terms, 17–18
  multi-tenant design architecture, 32–33
  performance and optimization, 38–39
  properties and characteristics of, 30–33
  providers' perspective, 29
  resilient system, 34–35
  service models, 47–55
  system monitoring, 36
  system resilience, 34–35
  system security, 35
  unique features of, 16
  users' perspective, 28
  value drivers and effects, 18–19
  vs cluster computing, 21
  vs grid computing, 20
  vs parallel computing, 22
  vs utility computing, 21
Cloud Computing Interoperability Forum (CCIF), 106
cloud computing security architecture, 131–132
cloud computing services, management and administration of, 62–63
cloud content delivery network (CDN) services, 187–188

cloud databases
  non-relational or NoSQL (not only SQL), 116–117
  operation model for, 113–114
  relational database services (RDS), 114–115
cloud file system
  distributed file system (DFS), 117–118
  Google file system, 118–119
  Hadoop distributed file system (HDFS), 119–121
Cloud Foundry, 76–77
cloud governance, 190–191
cloud infrastructure service providers
  Amazon Web Services (AWS), 67–68
  benefits of selecting, 71–72
  comparisons between different, 72
  GoGrid, 70–71
  Google Compute Engine (GCE), 69–70
  identification of business requirement for choosing, 72–73
  Microsoft Azure, 70
  Rackspace Cloud, 68–69
  setup procedure, 73
cloud instances, 59
cloud interoperability standards, 106–110
cloud middleware, 145–147
cloud platform service providers
  benefits of, 79
  cloud application development with, 81
  comparison of, 79
  identification of business requirement for choosing, 80–81
  setup procedure, 81
cloud pricing model, 19
cloud programming model, 122–124
cloud risks, 127–128
  legal risk, 130–131
  natural disasters, 131
  policy and organizational risks, 128–129
  technical risk, 129–130
  theft, 131
  unauthorized access to premises, 131
cloud simulation tools
  CloudSim, 202–203
  GreenCloud simulator, 203
  iCan cloud, 203
cloud software service providers. *see also* Software as a Service (SaaS)
  Cloudo, 84
  comparison of, 86
  eyeOS, 83
  iCloud, 82
  Mint.com, 82–83
  Panda antivirus, 82
Cloud Standards Customer Council (CSCC), 106
cloud-supporting services
  backup and disaster-recovery services, 61–62
  database services, 61
  load-balancing services, 61
  storage services, 61
cloud testing, 170–172
cluster computing, 6
  advantages of, 7–8
  applications of, 8
  minimum requirements for, 7
  vs cloud computing, 21
clusters, 7–8
collaboration, cloud computing and, 4, 42–44
commodity computing, 7
community cloud, 57
complex instruction set computing (CISC), 9
computing
  benefits, 4
  definition of, 1
  distributed, 4–6
  fundamental differences between cluster, grid and cloud, 22–23
  paradigms, 3–4
  utility model, 2
computing paradigm, 6–7
  commodity computing, 7
  evolution, 15–16
computing power, 6, 13
Compuware, 152
concurency transparency, 5
consistent access, 37–38
Convex, 9
CouchDB, 117
CPU virtualization, 92–96

D

data backups, 35
database as a service, 114
data migration and streaming in cloud
  cloud provider, analysis of, 149
  key features of, 151
  process, 150–151
  working of, 151
data parallelism, 9, 22
data protection, 35
device and I/O virtualization, 97
disaster recovery, 35
distributed computing, 4–6
distributed file system, 5
distributed memory model, 11
distributed memory programming mode, 12
distributed program, 4
distributed system, characteristics of, 5
dynamic link library (DLL) programs, 99
dynamic provisioning, 31–32

E

Encore, 9
Engine Yard, 78
Eucalyptus, 161–163

F

Facebook, 184–185
failure transparency, 5
fault tolerance, 62
fault-tolerant system, 33–34
Floating Point Systems, 9
functional areas of control automation, 36

G

gaming applications, 6
GoGrid, 70–71
Google App Engine (GAE), 74–75
Google Chrome, 37
Google cloud SQL, 115
Google Compute Engine (GCE), 69–70
Google Plus, 184
GPS/Internet data, 6
grid computing, 4, 6, 13–15
  advantages of, 15
  architecture for, 13–14
  collaboration of resources in, 14
  examples of, 14–15
  grid applications, 15
  grid environment, 14
  rules of sharing, 14
  vs cloud computing, 20
guest operating system, 90

H

hardware-enabled virtualization, 95–96
hardware-level parallelism, 11
hardware parallelism, 22
Heroku Postgres, 115
horizontal scaling, 31
hosted virtualization, 90
HP cloud RDS, 115
hybrid cloud, 57–58
hybrid IT, 58
HyperSpace, 103–104
hypervisor, 90

I

IBM SmartCloud Orchestrator, 108
identity management system, 35
IGLOO, 185

Infrastructure as a Service (IaaS). *see also* cloud infrastructure service providers
- benefit of, 49
- billing models, 49
- component stack and scope of control, 51
- main service of, 50
- Nutritious Food Inc., cloud infrastructure adoption case study, 195–198
- providers and services, 49
- system architecture, 50
- traditional stack and virtualization stack, 50
- types of virtualized resources in, 51

Inmos, 9
instruction-level parallelism, 9, 22
integrated development environment (IDE), 74
Intel VT-x, 104
InterCloud, 189–190
Internet Cloud, 37
Internet Explorer, 37
interoperability, 4, 35–36
intranet, 57
IT and cloud services, 19, 41
IT budget model, 19
IT resource utilization, 43

J

JAVA RMI invocation method, 5
job scheduler, 39

K

Kendall Square Research, 9
kernel-based virtual machine (KVM), 102
knowing user's usage, methods of, 37

L

Large Hadron Collider (LHC) computing grid, 15
Linux, in a cloud environment, 170
load balancing, 20, 39
local computing power, 44–45
local storage systems, 45–46
location transparency, 5

M

machine images, 59
manageability, 35–36
MangoApps, 185
MapReduce programming model, 122–124
MasPar, 9
McCarthy, John, 2
memory virtualization, 96–97
message passing interface (MPI), 12
Microsoft Azure, 70, 75–76
Microsoft Azure SQL server databases, 115
Microsoft cluster service (MSCS), 7
Microsoft SoftGrid, 100
middleware, concept of, 145
migration transparency, 5
mobile cloud computing (MCC), 188–189
model view controller (MVC), 77
MongoDB, 116
Mozilla Firefox, 37
multiple instruction
- multiple data (MIMD) stream, 11
- single data (MISD) stream, 10

multi-tenant design architecture, 32–33
MySpace, 184

N

natural language processing, 6
Neo 4j, 117
NetApp, 109
network file system concept, 5
network virtualization, 98
Nimbus, 164–165
Non-Uniform Memory Access (NUMA), 22
n-stage pipelining, 9

O

on-demand computing utility model, 2
online groupware software, 184
OpenNebula, 163–164
open source solution products
- Crypton, 141
- CryptSync, 141
- OSSEC-HIDS (Open source security host-based intrusion detection system), 140
- SNORT, 140–141
- TrueCrypt, 141

Open Virtualization Format (OVF), 107–108
optimization, 38–39
Oracle cloud databases, 115
Oracle VM virtual box, 101–102
OS-level virtualization, 21, 97–98
overestimated system utilization, 32

P

parallel algorithms, 9
parallel computing, 6, 8–13, 38–39
- advantages of, 13
- applications of, 12–13
- architecture, 9–11
- *vs* cloud computing, 22

parallelism, methods of achieving, 38–39
paravirtualization, 21, 94–95
pay-per-use model, 37
peer-to-peer (P2P) computing, 3–4
performance monitoring tools in cloud
- Amazon CloudWatch, 152
- Compuware, 152
- Rackspace, 153
- RevealCloud, 152
- Zenoss, 152

performance transparency, 5
Platform as a Service (PaaS). *see also* cloud platform service providers
- component stack and scope of control, 52–53
- Gamysoft Inc., cloud platform adoption case study, 198–200
- main services of, 52
- providers and their environments, 51
- system architecture, 51–52

private cloud computing platforms, 56–57
- Apache Virtual Computing Lab, 166
- CloudStack, 169–170
- Elastic Computing Platform (ECP), 166–168
- Eucalyptus, 161–163
- Nimbus, 164–165
- OpenNebula, 163–164
- OpenStack, 168–169
- TPlatform, 165–166

programming integrated development environment (IDE), 52
public cloud, 56

Q

quality of service (QoS), 3, 147–149

R

Rackspace, 68–69, 115,153
reduced instruction set computing (RISC), 9
regions, 59
remote procedure calls (RPC), 5
replication transparency, 5
response time, 63
RevealCloud, 152
RightScale, 109
risk events, 34

S

Salesforce.com, 77–78
same program multiple data, 9
scaling transparency, 5
Scalr, 109

scheduling in a cloud, 39
Screensaver Lifesaver, 15
Search for Extra-Terrestrial Intelligence (SETI), 14–15
sensor data applications, 6
Sequent, 9
server cluster, 7
server virtualization, 98
service-level agreement (SLA), 4, 20, 30, 73
service-oriented architecture (SOA), 3, 30
SFDC (Salesforce.com) developer, 77
shared memory model, 11
single instruction
  multiple data (SIMD) stream, 10
  single data (SISD) stream, 9–10
Single Program with Multiple Data (SPMD), 12
sky computing, 190
Socialcast, 185
SocialText, 185
Software as a Service (SaaS). *see also* cloud software service providers
  Andrew Sportswear, cloud software services adoption case study, 200–202
  benefits of, 86
  classification based on services provided, 55
  component stack and scope of control, 55
  providers and their offerings, 53
  system architecture, 53–54
  Web portal using, 54–55
Software Plus services, 186–187
standalone computers, 3, 7
storage system, 44
super computing, 6
system control interface, 52
system monitoring, 36
system resilience, 34–35
system security, 35

T

Tandem, 9
task-level parallelism, 9–11, 22
thin client, 37–38
Thinking Machines, 9

U

underestimated system utilization, 32
Uniform Memory Access (UMA), 22
UNIX RPC, 5
utility computing, 2, 28
  service-level agreement (SLA), 30
  service-oriented architecture, 30
  utility service, 29
  vs cloud computing, 21

V

value drivers of cloud computing, 18–19
  lower IT operating and capital costs, 18–19
  pricing, 19
  rapid provisioning of services, 19
  user friendly, 19
vertical scaling, 31
virtual application appliances, 110
virtualization, 29, 50, 58, 132
  application, 99–101
  client or desktop, 98–99
  CPU, 92–96
  device and I/O, 97
  enterprise applications of, 99–100
  full, 94
  hardware-enabled, 95–96
  layer, 22
  local (client-hosted) desktop, 99
  memory, 96–97
  network, 98
  OS-enabled, 94–95
  OS-level, 97–98
  paravirtualization, 94–95
  products, 101–104
  remote (server-hosted) desktop, 98
  of resources, 21
  server, 98
  technology, 89–90
  types of, 92–101
  VMware resolved x86 hardware, 93
  x86, 90–91
virtual LAN, 104
virtual machine monitor (VMM), 90
virtual machine (VM), 51, 90
  security challenges, 132–135
virtual network, 51
virtual organizations (VOs), 4
virtual private cloud (VPC), 59
virtual storage, 51
virtual storage area network (VSAN), 104–105
VM consolidation and management, 106
VM image, 113
VM migration, 105–106
VMware ESX and ESXi, 101
VMware server, 102–103
vulnerable assessment tools for cloud
  Bitium, 140
  Boxcryptor, 140
  Certify, 140
  CipherCloud, 136–137
  HyTrust, 140
  Netskope, 135–136
  Okta, 137–138
  Prevoty, 140
  Qualys, 138–139
  SilverSky, 140
  Skyhigh networks, 137
  Vaultive, 139
  Zscaler, 140

W

Wang, Lizhe, 28
Web browser technique, 37
Windows Hyper-V server, 101
word size, 9

X

x86 virtualization, 90–91

Y

Yammer, 185

Z

Zenoss, 152